Citizens, Immigrants, and the Stateless

ASIAN AMERICA
A series edited by Gordon H. Chang

Citizens, Immigrants, and the Stateless
A Japanese American Diaspora in the Pacific

Michael R. Jin

STANFORD UNIVERSITY PRESS
STANFORD, CALIFORNIA

STANFORD UNIVERSITY PRESS
Stanford, California

© 2022 by the Board of Trustees of the Leland Stanford Junior University. All rights reserved.

No part of this book may be reproduced or transmitted in any form or by any means, electronic or mechanical, including photocopying and recording, or in any information storage or retrieval system without the prior written permission of Stanford University Press.

Printed in the United States of America on acid-free, archival-quality paper

Library of Congress Cataloging-in-Publication Data
Names: Jin, Michael R., author.
Title: Citizens, immigrants, and the stateless : a Japanese American diaspora in the Pacific / Michael R. Jin.
Other titles: Asian America.
Description: Stanford, California : Stanford University Press, [2022] | Series: Asian America | Includes bibliographical references and index. | Identifiers: LCCN 2021007891 (print) | LCCN 2021007892 (ebook) | ISBN 9781503614901 (cloth) | ISBN 9781503628311 (paperback) | ISBN 9781503628328 (ebook)
Subjects: LCSH: Japanese Americans—Japan—History—20th century. | Japanese Americans—West (U.S.)—History—20th century. | Citizenship—United States—History—20th century. | World War, 1939–1945—Japanese Americans. | Stateless persons—History—20th century. | Transnationalism—History—20th century. | Japan—Colonies—Asia—History—20th century.
Classification: LCC E184.J3 J56 2022 (print) | LCC E184.J3 (ebook) | DDC 973/.04956—dc23
LC record available at https://lccn.loc.gov/2021007891
LC ebook record available at https://lccn.loc.gov/2021007892

Cover design: Caitlin Sacks | Notch Design
Typeset by Motto Publishing Services in 11/14 Adobe Garamond Pro

For Neda

Contents

Acknowledgments ix
Note on Sources and Terminology xv

INTRODUCTION: The Making of
a Japanese American Diaspora in the Pacific   1

1 From Citizens to Emigrants: The Japanese American
   Transnational Generation in the U.S.-Japan Borderlands   14

2 From Citizens to the Stateless: Migration, Exclusion,
   and Nisei Citizenship   38

3 From Citizens to Enemy Aliens: The "Kibei Problem"
   and Japanese American Loyalty During World War II   56

4 Beyond Two Homelands: Kibei Transnationalism
   in the Making of a Japanese American Diaspora   84

5 Between Two Empires: Nisei Citizenship and Loyalty
   in the Pacific Theater   114

6 Buried Wounds of the Secret Sufferers: Memory, History,
   and the Japanese American Survivors in the Nuclear Pacific   135

   EPILOGUE   152

Notes 157
Selected Bibliography 195
Index 215

Acknowledgments

I embarked on the revision of this book in the midst of the COVID-19 pandemic and the nationwide wave of protests against systemic racism and police brutality in the wake of the senseless murders of George Floyd, Breanna Taylor, and countless other Black lives. At the same time, Donald J. Trump's repeated use of such racist terms as *kung flu* and *Chinese virus* to describe the epidemic crisis was fueling a rise in xenophobic harassment, discrimination, and hate crimes against Asians and Asian Americans across North America. As a historian writing a book about the lasting impact of institutional racism, state violence, and anti-Asian xenophobia, I found myself anxiously grappling with the cruel cycle of tragedies and injustices all too common in this nation's history. I am deeply thankful for the work of many organizers and protesters on the front line of the struggle to abolish the brutal regimes of police violence, mass incarceration, and immigrant detention and deportation; and for the rising global movement for Black lives and racial justice, often led by young people of color who are claiming the power to shape a more just future for themselves and others. Their courage, energy, sense of urgency, and creativity inspired and sustained me as I struggled to finish the manuscript during such deeply troubled times.

The life of this book began at the University of California, Santa Cruz, where I had the privilege of working with an excellent committee of mentors who were there for me every step of the way. Alice Yang, my adviser, introduced me to Asian American history and critical race and ethnic studies.

She guided my intellectual growth by letting me be who I am, stay true to my politics, and take charge of my own scholarly agenda and by providing critical intellectual, professional, and practical advice always at the right moment. Alan Christy helped me find a place for my project in the historiography of modern East Asia and also taught me the linguistic, cultural, and professional nuances indispensable for being a productive researcher in Japan. I am also indebted to Dana Frank for her inspiration and critical eye that pushed me to sharpen my analytical approach and to find an assertive voice to define my scholarship in my own way.

I could not have completed this book without generous support from numerous institutions. The Institute for the Humanities at the University of Illinois at Chicago provided a yearlong fellowship that allowed me time to prepare this manuscript. Over the years, funding for this project has been provided by the College of Liberal Arts and Sciences at the University of Illinois at Chicago; the Japan Foundation; the Humanities Department and the College of Liberal Arts at Texas A&M University—Corpus Christi; the Pacific Rim Research Program at the University of California; and the Institute for Humanities Research and the History Department at the University of California, Santa Cruz. The International Institute of Language and Culture Studies at Ritsumeikan University in Kyoto welcomed me as a visiting scholar and gave me institutional support during my research in Japan.

My sincere gratitude goes out to the librarians and archivists at institutions across the United States and Japan who offered their expertise and assistance necessary for the completion of my research. In particular, I want to thank the staff at the University of California, Los Angeles, Special Collections; the Bancroft Library and the C. V. Starr East Asian Library at the University of California, Berkeley; the Japanese American National Museum in Los Angeles; the Claremont Colleges Library; the National Archives and Records Administration facilities in Washington, D.C., College Park, Maryland, and San Bruno, California; the Diplomatic Archives (formerly the Diplomatic Record Office) of the Ministry of Foreign Affairs of Japan in Tokyo; the Ritsumeikan University Library in Kyoto; the Japanese Overseas Migration Museum in Yokohama; the Hiroshima Peace Memorial Museum; the Hiroshima Municipal Archives; the Yamaguchi Prefectural Archives; the Kajiki Folklore Museum in Kagoshima; and the Daley Library at the University of Illinois at Chicago.

At Stanford University Press, my editor, Margo Irvin, steadfastly advocated for my book project and ensured a rigorous and timely review process that strengthened my book. I am also grateful to Gordon H. Chang, the Asian America series editor, for believing in my book and offering helpful feedback. Many thanks to Cindy Lim, who patiently guided me through the publishing process. My production editor, Emily Smith, and the Press's Editorial, Design, and Production group ensured my manuscript's smooth transition into a book. The manuscript benefited from Mimi Braverman's excellent copyediting. David Luljak created an index. I thank Derek Thornton for designing the beautiful cover.

Various aspects of my project were presented at the conferences of the American Historical Association, the Association for Asian American Studies, the Organization for American Historians, the American Studies Association, the Association for Asian Studies, the American Studies Association of Korea, and the Western History Association. I also presented several portions of my research in invited lectures and symposiums hosted by various institutions: the Institute for the Humanities at the University of Illinois at Chicago; the Harpur College Dean's Speaker Series at Binghamton University; the USC–Kyoto University Symposium on Nikkei Studies at the University of Southern California; the Japanese American Museum of San Jose; the International Institute of Language and Culture Studies at Ritsumeikan University; the Migration Studies Society in Osaka, Japan; and the History Department at the University of Illinois at Chicago, among others. Part of this book expands on the research discussed in two of my previously published articles: "Americans in the Pacific: Rethinking Race, Gender, Citizenship, and Diaspora at the Crossroads of Asian and Asian American Studies," *Journal of Critical Ethnic Studies* 2, no. 1 (2016); and "The Japanese American Transnational Generation: Rethinking the Spatial and Conceptual Boundaries of Asian America," in *The Routledge Handbook of Asian American Studies*, ed. Cindy I-Fen Cheng (New York: Routledge, 2017).

It is impossible to list all the people whose support and intellectual generosity made this book possible. I wish to recognize the following scholars and friends on both sides of the Pacific who engaged with my research at various stages of this project through their feedback, offered invaluable advice and words of encouragement, and inspired me with their exemplary work: Eiichiro Azuma, Ana Maria Candela, Derek Chang, John Cheng, Stephen

Fugita, Arthur A. Hansen, Toshio Hayashi, Madeline Hsu, Masumi Izumi, Hiroshi Kadoike, Minoru Kanda, Norifumi Kawahara, Yuko Konno, Robert Ku, Teruko Kumei, Lon Kurashige, Chrissy Yee Lau, Soo Im Lee, Justin Leroy, Fuminori Minamikawa, Mariko Mizuno, Barbara Molony, Hiromi Monobe, Rika Nakamura, Meredith Oda, Manako Ogawa, A. Naomi Paik, Mitsuhiro Sakaguchi, Naoko Shibusawa, Kumiko Tsuchida, Naoko Wake, Tomie Watanabe, Yujin Yaguchi, Tomoko Yamaguchi, Jane Yamashiro, Hiroshi Yoneyama, Henry Yu, and Judy Yung. I also would like to express my heartfelt gratitude to the many individuals who shared with me their personal stories and life experiences, a number of which are included in this book.

My glorious colleagues at the University of Illinois at Chicago deserve to be recognized for making my institutional home an ideal place to work while I completed this book. My sincere thanks go out to Mark Chiang, Glenda Genio, Fredy Gonzalez, Adam Goodman, Anna Guevarra, Laura Hostetler, Robert Johnston, Nadine Naber, J. Lorenzo Perillo, Gayatri Reddy, Atef Said, Kevin Schultz, and Karen Su for always being there for me. I am also grateful to the following colleagues for their wonderful support: Sunil Agnani, Mahrad Almotahari, Jeffrey Alton, Catherine Becker, Cynthia Blair, Christopher Boyer, Jennifer Brier, Mark Canuel, Joaquin Chavez, Jonathan Daly, Gosia Fidelis, Leon Fink, Kirk Hoppe, Lynn Hudson, Lynette Jackson, Nicole Jordan, Ronak Kapadia, Young Richard Kim, Corinne Kodama, Anna Kozlowska, Mario LaMothe, Richard Levy, Mark Liechty, Carmen Lilley, Patrisia Macias-Rojas, Rama Mantena, Mark Martell, Ellen McClure, Radha Modi, Marina Mogilner, Mary Ann Mohanraj, Akemi Nishida, Pamela Popielarz, Junaid Quadri, Jeffrey Sklansky, Keely Stauter-Halsted, Elizabeth Todd-Breland, Linda Vavra, Javier Villa-Flores, Stephen Wiberley, and Xuehua Xiang.

At Texas A&M University—Corpus Christi, where I held my first full-time teaching position, I was fortunate to have the support of the following wonderful colleagues: David Blanke, Patrick Carroll, Eliza Martin, Peter Moore, Laura Munoz, Anthony Quiroz, Claudia Rueda, Sandrine Sanos, and Robert Wooster. Many special thanks to my friends, mentors, and colleagues at the University of California, Santa Cruz, for making graduate school such an edifying experience: Noriko Aso, Terry Burke, Ana Maria Candela, Shelly Chan, Stephanie Chan, Sarah Eunkyung Chee, Urmi Engineer, Sakae Fujita, Herman Gray, Gail Hershatter, Stephanie Hinkle,

Conal Ho, Fang Yu Hu, Minghui Hu, Catherine Jones, Wenqing Kang, Matthew Lasar, Haitao Ma, Yajun Mo, David Palter, Chrislaine Pamphile-Miller, Eric Porter, Martin Rizzo-Martinez, Jeffrey Sanceri, Amanda Shuman, Sara Smith, Noel Smyth, Xiaoping Sun, Jeremy Tai, Dana Takagi, Bruce Thompson, Colin Tyner, Tu Vu, Marilyn Westerkamp, J. Dustin Wright, and Karen Tei Yamashita.

I am indebted to the following people for generously taking the time to read different parts of my manuscript closely and offering their comments, critiques, and suggestions indispensable for completing this book: Mark Canuel, Adam Goodman, Anna Guevarra, Laura Hostetler, Robert Johnston, Helen Jun, Atef Said, Kevin Schultz, Xiaoping Sun, and Julia Vaingurt. I thank Jill Petty for being a source of inspiration that kept me writing and Summer McDonald for helping me develop my manuscript and get it ready for review. Many thanks to my students at Texas A&M University—Corpus Christi, and the University of Illinois at Chicago for making my job so much more rewarding than I could possibly imagine. My research assistant, Jesvin John, deserves thanks for helping keep this project together during its final stage.

As important as writing this book was to me, I am relieved that it was never a priority over my family and friends, especially during those challenging days of writing the manuscript during the pandemic. And I am deeply grateful for the overwhelming love and support that the members of my family gave me throughout the project. I thank my parents, Inok Lee Jin and Sung Cheul Jin, for embracing and respecting whatever I did with my life with the kind of trust and love that made me who I am today. My father did not live long enough to see this book come out, but I know he would have stayed up many a night to read it cover to cover, with an English-Korean dictionary by his side. I thank my parents-in-law, Mahin Mirzaei and Mehrdad Motallebi, who patiently sat out the COVID-19 quarantine with me, their daughter, and their grandson for over half a year. I am grateful for their enduring love and for their wonderful company during those difficult times.

I thank my son Aiden Suha Jin for always being the shining light—just like his name means in Persian—that gave me strength and hope while I struggled to multitask between homeschooling, writing this book, and simply trying to keep my shit together. He reminded me everyday what my priorities were; and I grew and learned with him as he finished preschool and started kindergarten at home during the pandemic. Last but not least, there is no way on earth I could have written this book without my wife, Neda Motallebi Jin, who graciously shared and endured my frustrations, pains, and joys over the years of working on this project. But most of all, I dedicate this book to her because she is the love of my life. *Mersi, eshghe man.*

Note on Sources and Terminology

Over the years, Japan-based scholars of emigration and ethnic studies, as well as those Japanese Americanists in the United States with expert reading knowledge of Japanese, have led the effort to excavate and compile Japanese-language sources that demonstrate the complexity and multiplicity inherent in Japanese American history. The decade of transnational research that culminated in this book contributes to this collective project of developing a growing body of primary sources in Japan and the United States that illuminate the variety of Nisei experiences on both sides of the Pacific. Among these sources are consular documents, intra-agency reports, and various other government records from the 1920s to the 1940s at the Diplomatic Archives of the Ministry of Foreign Affairs of Japan (formerly, the Diplomatic Record Office). These documents provide critical information about the Japanese government's perspectives on matters related to U.S.-born Nisei in Japan, their role in Japan's cosmopolitan empire, and the impact of their presence on U.S.-Japan diplomatic relations. In addition, many sporadic sources in Japan examined in this book offer valuable insights into the heavily understudied perspectives of Nisei migrants in the former Japanese Empire. They include material from the Japanese Overseas Migration Museum in Yokohama, the Kajiki Folklore Museum in Kagoshima Prefecture, and the Hiroshima Peace Memorial Museum.

In the United States a variety of archival sources related to Japanese American community organizations, immigration files, legal cases, and wartime records reveal the critical role that Nisei migrants and U.S.-born

Kibei played in shaping the politics and culture of the Japanese American community and U.S. policies on citizenship, naturalization, and the World War II incarceration. The Japanese American Research Project (Yuji Ichioka) Collection at the University of California, Los Angeles, was a major source of prewar and wartime documents in both Japanese and English for this book. The U.S. government documents examined in this book include the records of the Immigration and Naturalization Service, the War Relocation Authority (WRA), the Commission on Wartime Relocation and Internment of Civilians (CWRIC), the Department of the War, and the Department of State at the National Archives and Record Administration and the Claremont Colleges Special Collections. Also examined in this book are primary source documents at the Bancroft Library at the University of California, Berkeley, which illuminate the early-twentieth-century white nationalist campaign to exclude Nisei citizens in the American West.

Another critical aspect of my research involved tracing individuals in both countries to interview them and situate their experiences within Japanese and U.S. social, political, and cultural contexts from the early decades of the twentieth century to the post–World War II decades. I also used published memoirs, autobiographies, and a number of oral history collections in both countries, such as the Hibaku Taikenki (Atomic Bomb Memoir) Collection at the Hiroshima National Peace Memorial Hall for the Atomic Bomb Victims, the Nippon Hoso Kyokai (Japan Broadcasting Corporation) Senso Shogen (Wartime Testimony) Series, and the Japanese American National Museum's REgeneration Oral History Project. I also have examined many newspapers and magazines published in both countries from the 1910s to the 1980s. Thanks to the Hoover Institution's Hoji Shinbun Digital Collection, I was able to access a number of Japanese-language ethnic newspapers published in the United States during the first half of the twentieth century; these offered glimpses of Kibei's lives and perspectives often missing in the narratives of Japanese American history.

I follow the practice common among historians of Japanese America in using the terms *Issei* (first-generation Japanese immigrant), *Nisei* (second-generation Japanese American), and *Kibei* (Japanese American returnee from Japan) as both singular and plural. The names of Japanese individuals in Japan are listed as family names followed by given names, as is customary in Japan. The names of U.S.-born Japanese Americans and Japanese immigrants in the United States are written with given names followed by family names. Thus, at the risk of confusing some readers unfamiliar with how Japanese names are transliterated in different contexts, I have decided to render people's names the way that each individual used them at the time. All translations of Japanese-language sources are mine unless otherwise noted.

Citizens, Immigrants, and the Stateless

Introduction

The Making of a Japanese American Diaspora in the Pacific

THE TOKYO METRO SECTION of the Japanese national daily newspaper *Asahi Shimbun* on April 7, 1939, featured a story about a wedding held in the capital the previous evening. The report celebrated the international marriage between Tashima Yukiko, a gifted graduate of Keisen Girls' School and Oyu Academy in Tokyo, and Zheng Zihan, a resident scholar at Tokyo's Keio University. Zheng was a son of the then mayor of Mukden, the industrial center of Manchuria in northeast China. The groom's late grandfather, Zheng Xaoxu, had been the first prime minister of the Japanese puppet state Manchukuo when Manchuria had become an integral part of Japan's colonial empire in Asia in the early 1930s. The *Asahi Shimbun* depicted the matrimony as a symbol of "intra-Asian co-prosperity and friendship" and proclaimed Tokyo as the continent's reigning cosmopolitan center that allowed a modern Japanese woman and a young Manchurian aristocrat to pursue a romantic relationship across national borders.[1]

The celebratory article on Tashima's wedding was part of the efforts made by the Japanese press, under the watchful eye of the militarist government that had seized the country's political power by the late 1930s, to curtail the negative international publicity brought on by Japan's aggressive expansionist policy. Less than two years before Tashima and Zheng's wedding, the Japanese armed forces had launched a full-scale invasion of the Chinese subcontinent, marking the beginning of World War II in Asia. While the international community turned more and more critical of the brutal massacre committed by the Japanese Imperial Army in Nanjing in

1937 and the subsequent Japanese military campaigns elsewhere in the subcontinent, the Tashima wedding in Tokyo provided the domestic audience with a positive picture of Japan's cultural influence as a pan-Asian empire.²

The story of Tashima's marriage to Zheng illustrated another complex aspect of international relations in the broader transpacific world. A daughter of Japanese emigrants from Hiroshima Prefecture, Tashima had been born and raised in California's Central Valley. In 1933, six years before her wedding, she had relocated to Japan with her mother and three siblings amid the widespread anti-Japanese xenophobia in the United States and the Great Depression, which in tandem had worked to bankrupt their family farm. Born Yukiko Tashima and nicknamed Lucille, this bright modern Japanese woman was actually a young immigrant from the United States.³

There was much more to Tashima's transpacific life than the fairy tale wedding depicted in the *Asahi Shimbun*. A few months after their wedding ceremony in Tokyo, Tashima and Zheng moved to Mukden in Manchuria and then to Beijing, China, where the newlyweds started their family and sat out the Pacific War. There, Tashima went by her newly adopted Chinese name, Su Chung. After the Japanese defeat in World War II followed by the Chinese Civil War and the establishment of the People's Republic of China in 1949, the Zheng family became enemies of the communist state and were subject to political purge because of their service to the former Japanese puppet state in Manchuria. In 1950 Tashima used her American citizenship to leave China, but her husband and young daughter, both citizens of the new People's Republic, which had reclaimed sovereignty over Manchuria, remained stranded in Beijing. Within five years of her repatriation to Japan under the U.S. occupation, Tashima married an American navy officer named Kenneth F. Davis, with whom she resettled in her country of birth in February 1956. For the rest of her life, she would live with all three of her names—Yukiko Tashima, Su Chung, and Lucille Davis—which were products of her complex diasporic life.⁴

This book follows the transpacific journeys of U.S.-born Japanese Americans like Tashima who found themselves mired in a series of unpredictable, bizarre, and often tragic events at the crossroads of the U.S. and Japanese empires. However, this is not a book that simply uncovers these stories as though they were history's unintended accidents. Tashima was far from alone in her unique position as an American citizen living abroad before World War II. She was one of more than 50,000 second-generation

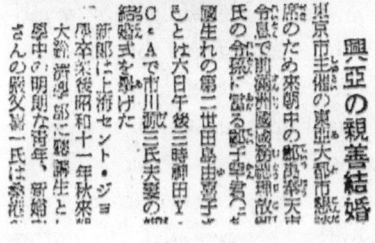

FIGURE 1 The announcement of Yukiko Tashima and Zheng Zihan's marriage in Tokyo, April 6, 1939.
Asahi Shimbun.

Japanese Americans (*Nisei*) who migrated to the rising Japanese colonial empire to escape anti-Asian racism throughout the U.S. West Coast.[5] As workers, students, travelers, and survivors of war and state violence between two empires, these transnational individuals have left traces of their journeys in archives and historical memories on both sides of the Pacific. By recuperating these scattered stories, *Citizens, Immigrants, and the Stateless* examines the deeply intertwined histories of Asian exclusion in the American West, Japanese colonialism in Asia, and volatile geopolitical changes in Asia-Pacific that converged in the lives of American migrants like Tashima.

All in all, at least one in four U.S.-born Nisei left the United States during the first half of the twentieth century.[6] Despite the transnational experiences that are remarkably common among Japanese Americans, scholars have written little about Nisei migrants' displacement across national and colonial borders in the Pacific—a set of global movements that does much to shatter the narrative of the United States as a country of immigrants. How, then, do we reconcile nation-centered narratives' silence about the Japanese American migrants who drew the American West with larger histories of nations and empires in the Pacific world? Instead of writing the history of Japanese Americans as a minoritized ethnic community that is geographically and socially rooted in the United States, I reconsider the emergence of Japanese America in the twentieth century as a highly mobile transpacific diaspora. Nisei migrants encountered multiple cultural and linguistic worlds, gender and racial ideologies, legal and social institutions, and geopolitical upheavals, and these encounters help us creatively push the conceptual and spatial boundaries of Asian and Asian American histories.

What does it mean to write a history of a Japanese American diaspora? First, such a project means rethinking the role of the United States as a national space and destabilizing the positionality of Japanese Americans as national subjects.[7] The displacement of U.S.-born Nisei emigrants in various corners of the former Japanese Empire in Asia disrupts the linear and predictable notions about "sending" and "receiving" nations prevalent in the U.S. immigration narrative. A re-placement of them within a larger diaspora also defies the subjectivities of Japanese Americans—as a race, as an ethnic group, and as citizens—predicated on the successful Americanization of the second-generation immigrants in the U.S.-centered ethnic studies model. Grounded in sources from both sides of the Pacific, the stories of human migration and racial formation in this book thus push the spatial and linguistic boundaries of the second-generation Asian American experience far beyond U.S. national borders.

Second, in *Citizens, Immigrants, and the Stateless* I use an interimperial approach to reconstruct a borderland space in which Japanese American migrants moved back and forth between North America and the former Japanese Empire in Asia. In so doing, I add to the emerging Pacific historical scholarship that has brought to the fore the experiences of marginalized peoples that national histories have long overlooked, such as emigrants from Asia in transnational and transoceanic diasporas, indigenous peoples of the Island world, and colonized subjects in the United States and other settler colonial empires in the Pacific. These perspectives illuminate the contradictions and theoretical limits of nationalist ideologies by exposing how gender and racial capitalism, state violence, war, and colonialism have operated in diverse transnational and imperial contexts.[8] In this book I offer a new perspective on these historical issues by illuminating how a distressingly understudied group of U.S.-born citizens, displaced in the transpacific borderlands, navigated the geopolitical, social, and ideological exigencies of the two empires.

Third, rewriting the history of Japanese Americans from the perspective of Nisei migrants challenges the dominant framework of loyalty and citizenship that has shaped both the academic and popular public narratives of the Japanese American experience. The legacies of the World War II mass incarceration of Japanese Americans in the United States and the question of Nisei's loyalty to their country of birth have driven the postwar Japanese American scholarship that has pushed the transnational experiences of Nisei migrants to the margins of history. There is no question that the wartime incarceration of Japanese Americans was a watershed moment in U.S. history that continues to dominate the Japanese American community's historical memory. However, the complex life experiences of Nisei who had migrated to Japan in large numbers to escape early-twentieth-century racism reveal that the promise of American citizenship for Japanese Americans had been denied well before the World War II internment. Also, as Tashima's experiences demonstrate, Nisei migrants and their families during and after the war found themselves in a fluctuating landscape of the colonial world that redefined their legal and cultural citizenship. Here, I center the fragility of Nisei's citizenship on both sides of the Pacific that forced Japanese American migrants to grapple with the shifting meanings of loyalty and nationalism at a variety of moments of diasporic upheaval.

Written against the predominant orientation of "diaspora" as fixated on diasporic subjects' belonging to a timeless, ethnicized, and often romanticized ancestral home (Japan), in this book I deploy a diasporic framework as a conceptual strategy to examine how Japanese American migrants redefined their relationship to both the United States and Japan on their own terms. Historically associated with forced dispersal of Jewish, African, and other globally displaced peoples, the term *diaspora* over the last few decades has been used much more liberally in many studies of human migration as a framework to examine meanings of home and belonging in contexts beyond parochial national narratives.[9] In Asian American studies, diaspora has emerged as an important framework for analyzing Asian immigrants' transnationalism and their enduring ties to their "homelands" vis-à-vis their systemic exclusion from U.S. citizenry. Critics of the diasporic turn have cautioned that diaspora's "essentialist" "global sweep" could diminish Asian Americans' shared historical struggle for agency in the United States by diverting scholars' focus away from the local structures of race, class, and gender oppression.[10] In contrast, I argue that an interimperial approach to the Japanese American diasporic experience exposes rather than obscures the critical transnational implications of those oppressions on the lives of U.S.-born Nisei migrants. Their history reminds us that the politics of exclusion and xenophobia was a powerful force that sustained the institutions of the United States, shaped the country's geopolitical exigencies, and altered individual lives, families, and communities inside and outside the nation's borders. American citizens of Japanese ancestry used transpacific migration as a powerful way to overcome what A. Naomi Paik has termed their rightlessness and exposed the contradictions inherent in America's celebrated identity as a liberty-loving country of immigrants.[11]

Because Japanese American history is rooted so strongly in U.S.-born Nisei's historical agency and belonging in the U.S. national context, it has been quite difficult to imagine Japanese America as a diasporic community driven by the frequent transnational mobility that shaped other Asian groups, such as Chinese Americans.[12] However, as demonstrated in the ensuing chapters, Japanese Americans' engagement with the Japanese Empire was a norm rather than the exception, as the movements of Japanese American migrants across the Pacific were common throughout the first half of the twentieth century. In fact, second-generation Japanese Americans were far more likely to have experienced transnational mobility than other U.S.-born Asian Americans. Ultimately, I offer a concept of Nisei's diasporic engagement with both the United States and Japan as a set of complex, varied, and historically grounded lived experiences rather than as a metaphorical reference to their Japanese heritage. To borrow Stuart Hall's assertion about the interdependence between diasporic identity and lived experience, a Japanese American diaspora emerged "out of very specific historical formations, out of very specific histories and cultural repertoires of enunciation."[13] Individuals like Tashima, who experienced transpacific migrations and spent various amounts of time in Japan and former Japanese colonies, are a group of second-generation Americans whose diasporic experiences were shaped by their physical presence on both sides of the Pacific. Their identities were both socially constructed and self-defined through their interactions with diverse groups of people in the U.S. and Japanese empires. Tracing their movements and experiences offers a unique analytical lens that sheds light on the embeddedness of Nisei's diasporic lives in multiple transnational sociopolitical fields, as they engaged in complex legal, political, and social transformations in both the United States and Japan that shaped their lives as migrants.

Japanese American migrants embarked on their transpacific journeys at a critical moment when the histories of Asia and Asian America intersected. The prewar U.S. West, where the vast majority of second-generation Japanese Americans lived, was intimately shaped by the history of Asian exclusion, dating from the anti-Chinese violence in the mid-nineteenth century.[14] By the 1920s, amid Japan's rise as a colonial power in Asia rivaling Western empires, the anti-immigrant campaign used the rhetoric of yellow peril to target the Japanese immigrant community in the United States as a cultural and socioeconomic threat to white America. The aggressive nativist movement led by anti-Japanese agitators throughout the United States had culminated in a series of legal and judicial enactments that excluded Japanese immigrants from American citizenry, such as restrictive alien land laws that had stripped Tashima's parents of the right to keep their farm. Exclusionary U.S. immigration and naturalization policies, such as the 1924 Immigration Act, which effectively blocked Asian immigrants, manifested the racialization of Asians as unassimilable aliens.[15] Moreover, U.S.-born Japanese Americans throughout the 1920s, 1930s, and 1940s routinely faced school segregation, job discrimination, anti-miscegenation laws, and other forms of legal discrimination and everyday racism that made them citizens in name only.[16]

If the regime of racial exclusion in the American West compelled many Nisei to look elsewhere to build their future and overcome their rightlessness, the rise of the modern Japanese state and its colonial empire in Asia facilitated their transpacific migration. By 1920 Japan had annexed Okinawa, Taiwan, Korea, and the former German Micronesia (*Nanyo*, or "the South Seas"), among other colonies; these colonies provided resources that expedited an unprecedented industrial boom that Japan had undergone since World War I. Although the global Great Depression slowed Japan's economic growth, the aggressive colonial expansion into northeast Asia and the Chinese subcontinent throughout the 1930s made Japan look like a formidable power in Asia.¹⁷ Many young Nisei children, such as Tashima, accompanied their Japanese immigrant parents (*Issei*) when they left the United States to resettle in Japan and Japan's colonial frontiers. Other Nisei young adults relocated to the Japanese Empire on their own to seek opportunities for employment or higher education unavailable to them in the United States because of systematic racial discrimination. Also, many Issei parents sent their U.S.-born children to Japan so that they could receive a Japanese education and acquire business or farming skills, with the goal of one day returning to the United States to help sustain their immigrant families.

Born as citizens of the United States but treated like unwelcome aliens in their putative homeland, these Japanese Americans came of age as immigrants in their parents' homeland. Many of these young migrants spent their formative years studying in public schools and institutes of higher learning throughout Japan. Some worked in industrial centers such as Tokyo, Osaka, and Kyoto, joining the workforce from all across the Japanese archipelago and Japan's Asian colonies. Others tended potato farms and rice fields in their parents' hometowns in agricultural regions such as rural Hiroshima, the prefecture that had sent the largest number of Japanese emigrants to North America since the 1880s. Some Nisei migrants even became agents of brutal Japanese imperialism, as they found employment in Japanese firms, agricultural settlements, government agencies, and media outlets in Japan's colonial outposts in Asia throughout the 1930s up to the eve of the Pacific War.

Yet this book is more than a linear immigrant narrative about Japanese Americans' exodus from the United States in search of better lives on the other side of the Pacific. Nisei migrants found themselves mired in the rapidly deteriorating diplomatic relations in the Pacific world that forced them to negotiate shifting ideologies of race, gender, and citizenship. Many Nisei in various corners of the transpacific world continued to navigate myriad new social and legal constraints that further destabilized their status as citizens, immigrants, and the stateless. For instance, the anti-Japanese movement and restrictive U.S. nationality and immigration laws designed to exclude Asian immigrants from American citizenry from the 1920s to the 1940s wielded unexpected power to take Nisei migrants' citizenship away and separate them permanently from their families in the United States. This development had an especially devastating impact on many

Nisei women in Japan, as their marriages to Japanese men cost them their U.S. citizenship because of the U.S. government's discriminatory policy that forced American women who married noncitizen Asian men to forfeit their U.S. citizenship. Once they were stripped of their U.S. citizenship and rendered stateless, these Nisei women were prohibited from setting foot on U.S. soil again when the Immigration Act of 1924 permanently blocked legal entry of immigrants from Asia.[18] Japanese American migrants' extended stay away from home in this volatile moment of tension thus threatened the integrity of their legal citizenship, as the politics of exclusion that sustained the United States as a gatekeeping nation caught up even with Japanese Americans living abroad.

Moreover, the social realities that U.S.-born Japanese Americans faced in the Japanese Empire often defied their hopeful imagination about their ancestral home. Many Nisei migrants who relocated to their parents' homeland with a romantic idea that the Japanese would welcome them with open arms would soon realize that, despite their purported diasporic identity as Japanese, they were, after all, immigrants from the United States living in an unfamiliar and frequently unwelcoming territory. Although those with means and abilities indeed capitalized on the opportunities abroad, the kind of upward social mobility envisioned by many Nisei in the Japanese Empire proved to be as difficult as getting ahead in America. In addition to language and cultural barriers, they faced myriad challenges of living in a liminal space as migrants who had moved from one metropole to another. Furthermore, those Nisei who relocated to Japan to escape racism in the United States found themselves in a world with its own complex racial ideology and hierarchy. Many Nisei in Japan witnessed firsthand the vicious social discrimination endured by colonial subjects from Korea, Taiwan, and elsewhere in the Japanese Empire who were forced to work in factories and mines throughout the archipelago. Those Nisei who journeyed through Japan's colonial frontiers in Asia saw how the settler colonial regimes exploited those territories. The "Greater East Asia Co-Prosperity Sphere," the euphemistic moniker for Japan's colonial empire in Asia, proved to be far from the sanctuary that many Nisei had envisioned. Even though most of the Nisei who migrated to Japan remained there through the Pacific War, those disillusioned by less than ideal socioeconomic realities in Japan joined the well over 10,000 returnees who resettled in the United States before the outbreak of the Pacific War in 1941.[19] These Japanese American migrants

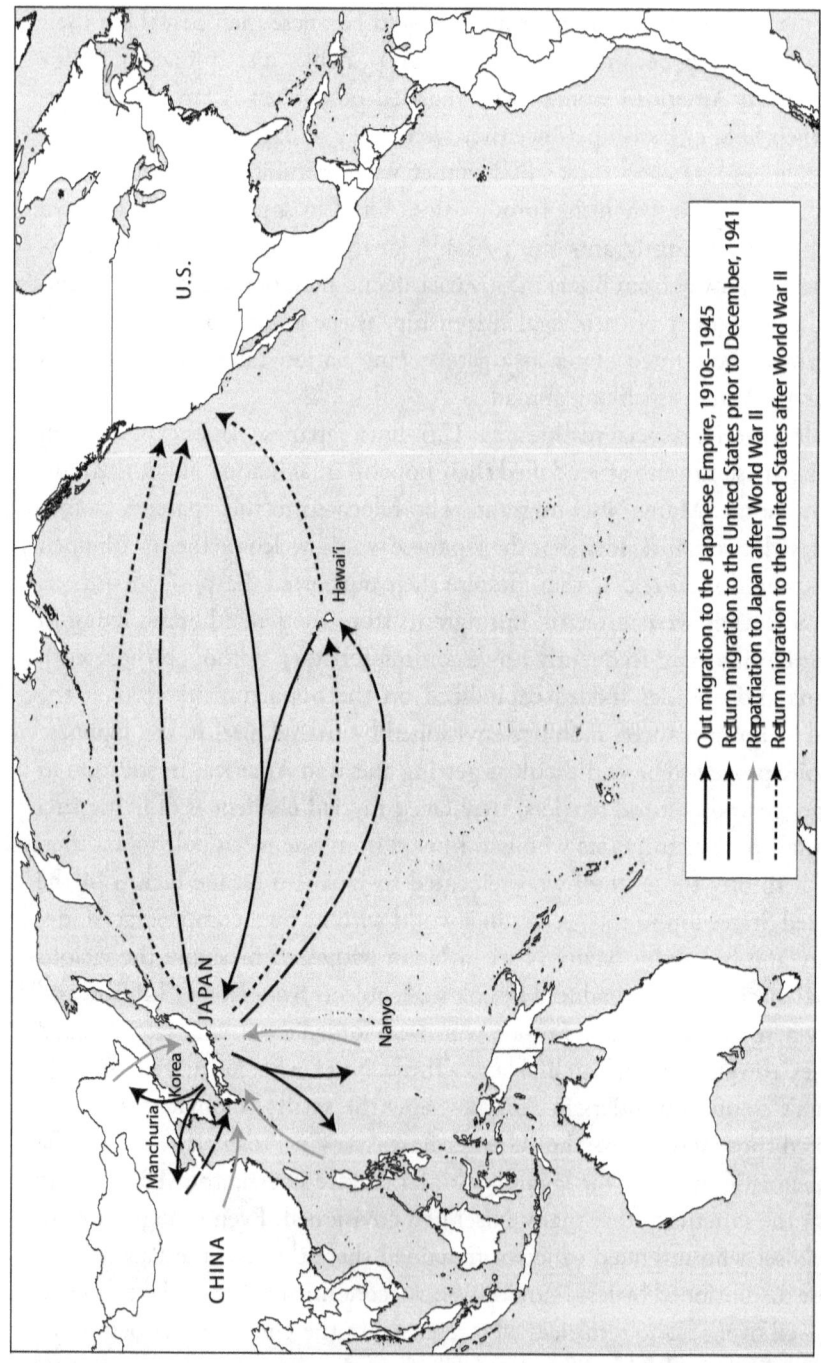

MAP 1 Transpacific migrations of U.S.-born Japanese Americans. Map by Bill Nelson.

brought with them diverse perspectives of the Japanese Empire that added to the linguistic and cultural dynamics of the Japanese American community in the United States on the eve of the war.

The stories of former Nisei migrants who returned to the United States before World War II after spending their formative years in Japan help us rethink the meanings of loyalty, nationalism, and identity central to Japanese American history. The existence of these Nisei returnees in the United States—known as *Kibei* (one who returned to America)—shaped U.S. policy on the incarceration of Japanese Americans from 1942 to 1946.[20] After the Japanese attack on Pearl Harbor in December 1941, the U.S. Department of War justified its "military necessity" for mass incarceration of Japanese Americans based on the existing white nationalist argument that the U.S.-born Nisei were essentially Japanese and indistinguishable from their foreign-born parents. Lieutenant General John L. DeWitt of the U.S. Army's Western Defense Command, who spearheaded the mass removal of Japanese Americans from the U.S. West Coast in 1942, infamously stated, "It makes no difference whether [a Nisei] is an American citizen; he is still a Japanese."[21]

The wholesale characterization of U.S.-born Nisei as Japanese aliens engendered a profound social burden for Japanese Americans to prove their loyalty and Americanization, even as they endured mass incarceration. Throughout the war U.S. government authorities suspected Kibei of being pro-Japan elements and treated them like a dangerous fifth column among Japanese Americans. Japanese American community leaders identified and policed the Kibei as a group that could damage the image of loyal Japanese Americans, because their education and upbringing in Japan made them stand out as potential Japan sympathizers. As a result, the Kibei became ostracized throughout the internment years. Their voices were then continuously silenced after the war, as Japanese American community leaders actively promoted the image of patriotic, Americanized Nisei to gain public support for an official government apology and reparations, often citing the wartime heroism of Japanese American servicemen who had joined the U.S. Armed Forces out of internment camps to fight the Axis powers.

Such polarizing notions about the "Americanized" Nisei and the "Japanized" Kibei during the war have compounded the marginalization of Nisei migrants in Japanese American scholarship. Few postwar scholars have been willing to come to grips with the transnational experiences of

Japanese Americans because of the negative public perception that saw Kibei as predominantly Japanese in their cultural and political orientation, contradicting the image of "Nisei as Americans first."[22] As Eiichiro Azuma has noted, the war between the United States and Japan from 1941 to 1945 "culminated in a complete polarization between things Japanese and things American." For the Japanese American community in the United States, it became no longer possible "to openly fancy" Nisei's "mediating roles in the Pacific."[23] Postwar scholars have understandably grappled with the need to challenge and complicate the meanings and implications of history centered on Nisei Americanism, predominantly in the context of the World War II internment.[24] Today we must also reimagine the conceptual and political boundaries of Japanese American history beyond the wartime mass incarceration and its dominant domestic framework. This book makes such a contribution.

Citizens, Immigrants, and the Stateless offers an alternative history of the Japanese American experience before, during, and after World War II on both sides of the Pacific as a series of diasporic ruptures. Japanese American migrants in the Japanese Empire were forced to negotiate ways to survive the war in unfamiliar territories, from the firebombed city of Tokyo to the battlefronts of the Pacific. Also, many U.S.-born Nisei in Japan during the Pacific War found themselves caught between the two empires, as they came under enormous social pressure to sever their ties to America and fulfill their loyalty to the country of their ancestors by serving Japanese war efforts against the United States. Thousands of Nisei male dual citizens were conscripted into the Japanese military and took arms, generally under duress, against their country of birth. After the war the U.S. government punished these men for their service to the Japanese emperor by enforcing the Nationality Act to strip their American citizenship. The war also rendered many Nisei men and women victims and survivors of atrocities throughout the Pacific Theater, including the atomic bomb that devastated Hiroshima, a city with a heavy concentration of U.S.-born Japanese American residents. Unrecognized by both the U.S. and Japanese governments, the Nisei atomic bomb survivors became essentially stateless in the postwar regime of redress and reparations. The U.S.-centered liberation narrative of "the Good War" further silenced these A-bomb victims and other Americans of Japanese ancestry who survived the conflict. In this book I reclaim these Nisei survivors' place in the postwar debates about wartime violence, compensatory justice, and the Japanese American politics of redress.

The chapters that follow move between the spaces and times in Nisei's transpacific world in the U.S.-Japan borderlands. I have no illusions that what this book delivers is a definitive reconstruction of Japanese American transpacific history in its entirety. Instead, I work closely with case studies—for example, that of Yukiko Tashima—that best represent Japanese Americans' diasporic engagement long overlooked by dominant national narratives on both sides of the Pacific.[25] This book breaks the long silence imposed on the voices of those who negotiated the legacies of brutal Japanese colonialism, xenophobia in the United States, and the politics of race, citizenship, and historical memory at the crossroads of Asian and Asian American studies. *Citizens, Immigrants, and the Stateless* reclaims these shattered yet deeply connected histories in the making of a Japanese American diaspora.

CHAPTER 1

From Citizens to Emigrants

*The Japanese American Transnational
Generation in the U.S.-Japan Borderlands*

We were seeking better lives for ourselves.¹

CHIBA KOH'S CREDENTIALS as director of the Japanese Foreign Ministry's European and American Affairs Bureau looked impeccable when he arrived in Washington, D.C., in late 1957 as an envoy on Prime Minister Kishi Nobusuke's official visit.² A graduate of the prestigious Tokyo Imperial University in 1932, Chiba was a career diplomat with an exemplary bureaucratic record, and he spoke English with a flawless American accent. However, few outside his immediate professional circle knew about his closer ties to the United States. Born David Koh Chiba in Berkeley, California, to Japanese immigrants in 1910, he was once an American citizen who migrated to northeast Asia with his parents to escape the ferocious Japanese exclusion movement that threatened his family's survival in the American West.³

Chiba's family left the United States in 1921 to settle in Manchuria, the prized future possession in Japan's expanding settler colonial empire, less than a year after California's voters passed the Alien Land Law of 1920. The law bolstered the Webb-Haney Act of 1913, the state's original alien land law, to permanently strip Japanese immigrants' right to own or lease agricultural properties. Other Western states, such as Washington and Oregon, were on the verge of legislating their own alien land bills, modeled after California's, as the fierce anti-Japanese political campaigns were spreading rapidly throughout the region. David Chiba's immigrant father, Toyoji Chiba, a Miyagi Prefecture native who moved to San Francisco in 1906, served as managing director of the Central California Japanese Agricultural Association. For years, he led the organization's bitter struggle against the powerful statewide movement to drive out the Japanese. The new alien land law dealt a crushing defeat to Toyoji and many Japanese immigrant families whose future depended on their access to land. Having put up with the system of white supremacy for nearly two decades, Toyoji Chiba declared the American dream unachievable and immediately began preparations for the family's return migration across the Pacific.[4]

Although he was only 10 years old, young David Koh Chiba had a grim premonition of his own about his future in the United States as a child of Japanese immigrants. "It became quite clear that there was no hope," he reflected on the dire implications of the mounting anti-Japanese racial hostility for the U.S.-born Nisei's abilities to claim their place in American society.[5] Dependent on their immigrant parents and too young to muster a political voice of their own, the Nisei in America found themselves victims of the same racial hostility and politics of exclusion that immigrants from Japan had faced for decades. Exclusionary legal measures, such as the new alien land law, only served as a reminder that the American public was bent on expelling all Japanese, both foreign- and native-born, so much so that three-fourths of California's voters helped enact such a restrictive bill, which threatened the survival of entire Japanese American families.[6] Moreover, concerted efforts by anti-Japanese agitators, such as the Asiatic Exclusion League in California, aimed to strip Nisei's citizenship rights through school segregation and other forms of legal restrictions throughout the first two decades of the twentieth century.[7] Their U.S. citizenship by birth far from protected Chiba and other second-generation Japanese Americans from anti-Asian xenophobia in the United States.

When Chiba's parents picked Manchuria as their next destination in search of land and opportunity, the young Nisei saw an alternative future abroad for himself. He offered little resistance to the family's relocation from their home in California to an unfamiliar colonial frontier in northeast China, where they joined some 150,000 agricultural settlers transplanted from the Japanese archipelago. Chiba did well for himself there, making the most of the new opportunity provided by Japanese settler colonialism in Asia. He finished middle school in Manchuria and moved to the metropole on his own to study at Tokyo Imperial University, the most selective training ground for the Japanese elite.[8]

Chiba's journey from a humble immigrant family in California to the exclusive professional and social circle at the center of the Japanese Empire was complete by the early 1930s. After graduating from the university with a law degree, he pursued a career as a diplomat, for which he could take advantage of his bilingual and bicultural background. In 1932 he passed an advanced civil service examination and started his post at the Ministry of Foreign Affairs of Japan. Soon thereafter he broke into the empire's high society through his marriage to Ishibashi Utako, the eldest daughter of renowned journalist, politician, and future prime minister Ishibashi Tanzan.[9] After surviving World War II in the firebombed city of Tokyo, Chiba went on to become the highest ranking foreign-born employee of the Japanese government in modern history, a career that would include ambassadorships to Mexico, Brazil, Iran, and Australia.[10] The trip to Washington, D.C., in 1957 marked one of his several homecomings to his country of birth since he left California in 1921 to live the rest of his life as Chiba Koh, a Japanese citizen.[11]

Chiba's rise from a child of Japanese immigrants in California to an elite public official in Japan was a rare achievement, but far from unique was his transpacific life as an American-born Nisei in the former Japanese Empire. In this chapter I examine the making of a Japanese American diaspora as a process that redefined U.S.-born Nisei's identity as American migrants in the U.S.-Japan borderlands during the first half of the twentieth century. The exclusion movement in the United States that targeted Japanese immigrants during the interwar period had the most consequential impact on the disruption of the Japanese American community; more than 50,000 young Nisei were compelled to leave their country of birth. However, as suffocating as the racial capitalism of the American West was in shaping many Nisei's dismal social outlook, it was the rise of Japan's colonial empire in Asia that played a decisive role in facilitating their transpacific exodus. Expanding Japanese settler colonialism allowed U.S.-born Nisei to claim a distinct diasporic role as migrants in their parents' homeland, as well as in what Eiichiro Azuma has termed Japan's borderless empire throughout Asia-Pacific.[12] Nisei migrants found themselves at a variety of volatile historical moments that defined U.S.-Japan relations before World War II.

The perspectives of U.S.-born Nisei like Chiba on the exclusion movement's broader generational implications illuminate the critical missing link between the histories of Asian exclusion in the United States and the Japanese Empire. As a conceptual and methodological strategy, a diasporic history of Japanese Americans offers an alternative, interimperial paradigm for Nisei's transpacific engagement with both the United States and Japan.¹³ U.S.-born Nisei's diasporic mobility was a critical aspect of the Japanese American experience during the interwar period. Not only did Japanese Americans live, work, and study throughout the Japanese archipelago, but they also moved through frontier societies settled by Japanese emigrants.

Japanese American migrants found themselves entangled in sociopolitical developments on both sides of the Pacific during this volatile period before the Pacific War. Recuperating the stories of these Nisei as *emigrants* who moved from their country of birth to the country of their parents reveals the complex interconnections between the social, political, and cultural histories of the two Pacific empires that altered their lives. Many Nisei's encounters with a Japanese society shaped by fluctuating U.S.-Japan relations and the geopolitics of Asia-Pacific also informed how they negotiated and understood their liminal position between two homelands.

Asian Exclusion in the American West and Nisei Transnational Migration

By the time Chiba's family left California in the early 1920s, anti-Asian xenophobia had intimately shaped the operational regime of racial exclusion in the American West. The dominant anti-Asian rhetoric from the mid-1800s until the turn of the twentieth century had focused on portraying Chinese immigrants as undesirable "cheap coolie labor" that threatened the socioeconomic interests of the white working class. In 1877 the California State Senate's committee on immigration urged the U.S. Congress to stop the influx of all Chinese, on the basis of its claim that the immigrants from China represented the "lowest orders of the Chinese people" who were "incapable of adaptation" to American institutions.¹⁴ The anti-Asian rhetoric served to justify the racial violence aimed at complete physical expulsion of Chinese immigrants from cities and towns throughout the western United States.¹⁵

Simultaneously, the Asian exclusion movement had established the nation's first regime of immigration policy, which made the entry of Chinese permanently illegal, when the U.S. Congress passed the Chinese Exclusion

Act in 1882 and continued to extend it. Even after the passage of this law, the call to expel the Chinese population in the United States further fueled the blatantly violent manifestation of xenophobia in race riots and lynching that routinely terrorized Chinese immigrant communities. One of the most prominent exclusionists who thrived on anti-Asian policies, San Francisco mayor James Phelan, in 1901 described the Chinese as the most inferior and intolerable aliens who were the antithesis of the "dignified" white working class.[16] Such wholesale dehumanization of the Chinese was emblematic of the anti-Asianism that would continue to fortify the legal and ideological architecture of exclusionist politics well into the twentieth century.

During the first two decades of the twentieth century, Phelan and other leading anti-immigrant activists in the region organized themselves across class and ideological lines into a powerful political base that targeted the Japanese and their U.S.-born children as the new "immigrant menace." Although the characterization of Japanese immigrants as an unassimilable Asian alien group and a threat to the white working class persisted, the anti-Japanese rhetoric also featured much more complex class elements that reflected the broader Western hostility toward the emerging Japanese Empire. After Japan's victory in the Russo-Japanese War in 1905, the Japanese Empire's position as a dominant military and economic power in East Asia contributed to the new yellow peril rhetoric targeting the Japanese in America.[17]

Leading U.S. social theorists of the time interpreted this new brand of anti-Asian xenophobia as a sign of white America's reckoning of Japan as a source of immigrants who posed a much more formidable socioeconomic threat than the "coolie" laborers of the past. University of Chicago economist Harry A. Millis argued in 1922 that Japan's position as a global competitor to U.S. geopolitical interests fueled the fierce anti-Japanese sentiment in the United States. "Without question," Millis contemplated, "there is much more fear that the Japanese government stands for power very much as Germany did before the [First World War]."[18] Noted Chicago sociologist Robert E. Park compared the anti-Japanese agitation in America to anti-Semitism, depicting the Japanese as "a racial group which is small in numbers, intimate, compact, and well organized as is the case of the Jew." "In the long run," Park argued, the industriousness of Japanese immigrants would exacerbate the existing "racial prejudices" against Asians.[19]

In California, the state with the largest Japanese population in the contiguous United States, the voices of Japanese exclusion included prominent leaders in politics, industry, and the media, such as newspaper mogul William Randolph Hearst. Mayor Phelan continued to thrive on his yellow peril rhetoric to gain a seat in the U.S. Senate in 1914. Phelan's reelection campaign in 1920 to "Save Our State from Oriental Aggression" featured the infamous slogan, "Keep California White."[20] However, it was the broad grassroots coalition of white labor, agricultural community, and nativist groups in California that sustained these leading anti-Japanese agitators' campaign for exclusionary legislation.[21] In 1920 the Japanese Exclusion League of California was formed with a goal to enact the strictest anti-immigration laws that would block further entry of Japanese and permanently exclude the Japanese immigrant community from American citizenry. The League's officers included representatives from the American Legion, the California State Federation of Labor, the California State Federation of Women's Clubs, the Native Sons and Daughters of California, the California Farm Bureau, the Loyal Order of Moose, and the California State Grange.[22]

Although Phelan was unseated from his Senate position amid a landslide Republican sweep in the 1920 elections, the "Keep California White" movement nevertheless had helped anti-Japanese sentiment gain broader nationwide momentum.[23] In addition to alien land laws throughout the western states, the exclusion movement's aggressive lobbying effort throughout the first three decades of the twentieth century culminated in a series of legal and judicial enactments at both the state and federal levels. These exclusionary measures manifested the Japanese as unassimilable permanent foreigners.[24] In 1922 the U.S. Supreme Court case *Takao Ozawa v. United States* denied the naturalization rights to Japanese nationals and stamped their permanent status as "aliens ineligible to citizenship."[25] Then, pandering to the relentless political pressures from such groups as the Japanese Exclusion League of California, the U.S. Congress enacted the Johnson-Reed Act, or the Immigration Act of 1924. Designed to keep America permanently white, the law effectively halted Asian immigration by denying "aliens ineligible to citizenship" entry to the United States as legal immigrants.[26]

The widespread anti-Japanese sentiment and resulting exclusionary laws in the early decades of the twentieth century had a devastating socioeconomic impact on many Japanese immigrant families in the United States.

Within a decade after the Chiba family's departure from California in 1921, young David Koh Chiba and his father's premonitions about the exclusion movement's damning consequences on the lives of the Japanese in America became tragic realities. Yukiko "Lucille" Tashima saw her family's American dream shattered by the anti-Japanese movement, which culminated in California's alien land laws. Her father, Takayuki Tashima, had left his hometown in Hiroshima Prefecture in 1905 to pursue a new life in the American West. Like many Japanese emigrants from Hiroshima's rural towns, he was a versatile farmworker well suited for the labor market in California's Central Valley, which was on its way to becoming the nation's most prosperous agricultural community. Tashima proved to be not only a skilled farmhand but also a savvy entrepreneur. Within fifteen years after his arrival in California, he established himself as the number one lettuce producer in San Benito County. By the end of 1920 he ran a highly profitable transcontinental produce distribution business. In the spring of that year he commissioned as many as fifteen refrigerated railcars to move his lettuce to Chicago and New York.[27] In 1925 he packed more than 200 carloads of lettuce and expected to double his shipment the following year.[28] By then, local California newspapers had named him the "lettuce king" of the Central Valley.[29]

However, Takayuki Tashima's success did not outlast the mounting anti-Japanese sentiment that shaped the political economy of the American West. He was able to survive California's first comprehensive alien land law in 1913 that had banned Japanese landownership by strategically leasing lettuce farms throughout San Benito County. Seven years later, he was far less successful in withstanding the devastating consequences of the revised alien land law, the most restrictive one in the country, which made it impossible for "aliens ineligible to citizenship" to lease agricultural land.[30] Although his shipping business allowed him to sustain his fortune throughout the 1920s, the new alien land law, the organized price fixing by white farmers of San Benito County, and the Great Depression eventually drove him out of business. By 1931 Takayuki Tashima was no longer the lettuce king of the Central Valley. His "vast holdings dwindled to nothing"; he attempted to rebuild his lettuce kingdom in Napa Valley in northern California, to no avail.[31] Yukiko Tashima had turned 16 when her father drank pesticide to end his life in September 1933, leaving his wife and four children behind in Napa Valley.[32] Two months after her father's suicide,

TABLE 1 Japanese American Population, 1920–1940

Year	Contiguous United States			Hawaii		
	Foreign-Born	Native-Born	Total	Foreign-Born	Native-Born	Total
1920	81,383	29,672	111,055	60,688	48,586	109,274
1930	70,477	68,357	138,834	48,446	91,185	139,631
1940	47,305	79,642	126,947	37,353	120,552	157,905

SOURCES: U.S. Department of Commerce, Bureau of the Census, *Fourteenth Census of the United States Taken in the Year 1920* (Washington, DC: U.S. Government Printing Office, 1922); U.S. Department of Commerce, Bureau of the Census, *Fifteenth Census of the United States: 1930* (Washington, DC: U.S. Government Printing Office, 1932); U.S. Department of Commerce, Bureau of the Census, *Sixteenth Census of the United States: 1940* (Washington, DC: U.S. Government Printing Office, 1943).

Tashima was in Tokyo with her dejected mother and siblings, as they began a new life in Japan on a small sum from the insurance payment.[33]

David Chiba's premonition about the far-reaching generational impact of the exclusion movement thus came true in Yukiko Tashima's life. Like Chiba, Tashima offered little objection to her mother's decision to move the family to Japan, as the young Nisei saw no future for herself and her siblings in the United States. Throughout the 1920s widespread Japanophobia and the exclusionary movement not only denied Japanese immigrants' access to American citizenry but also gave rise to a fierce organized movement to strip U.S.-born Nisei of their citizenship rights. Leading anti-immigrant activists during this period increasingly targeted Nisei citizens in their all-out attack on the Japanese community in America. Influential California publisher and anti-immigrant activist V. S. McClatchy argued in 1919 that U.S.-born Japanese Americans were a dangerous foreign element that needed to be expelled from America along with their Japanese parents. "It is a dangerous experiment," wrote McClatchy, "to attempt to make good American citizens of such material!"[34] At an appearance before the Honolulu Rotary Club two years later, he added that Nisei's "racial characteristics" and "heredity" made them "absolutely unassimilable."[35] Soon after California's voters passed the nation's most restrictive alien land law in 1920, McClatchy publicly advocated for adding further restrictions that would ban Nisei's right to landownership, claiming that they should be treated as Japanese aliens despite their U.S. citizenship.[36] The newest attack on their birthright citizenship rendered the young second-generation Japanese Americans the most vulnerable target of xenophobia and institutional racism in the American West.³⁷ The specter of yellow peril that had fueled anti-Asian hysteria in the United States since the nineteenth century blurred the line between citizens and aliens for people of Japanese ancestry.

The discrimination against Japanese Americans directly contributed to the dismal socioeconomic outlook for many Nisei in the United States, as indicated by numerous studies from the mid-1920s to the late 1930s in the Japanese American community. The doors to vocational opportunities outside the ethnic community were closed to most young Nisei in the United States, including those with college educations and professional aspirations. In 1929 Japanese immigrant scholar Junichi Takeda lamented the problem of Nisei employment in the United States as resulting from "racial prejudice" against Japanese Americans.³⁸ Many Nisei themselves echoed this sentiment that their U.S. citizenship far from guaranteed their acceptance into American society, as they were frustrated by the limited prospect for social mobility. Isamu Nodera's master's thesis in 1936 found that seven of ten Nisei young adults in Los Angeles worked for Japanese immigrant-run retail or wholesale businesses, whereas others toiled away as gardeners and farmhands and in other types of blue-collar jobs in the Japanese American community.³⁹ According to the Los Angeles based Japanese American newspaper *Rafu Shimpo* in 1937, the jobs most desired by these Nisei included engineering, teaching, architecture, and nursing, precisely the kinds of work from which they were shut out.⁴⁰

"We were seeking better lives for ourselves," Southern California native Kay Tateishi said, speaking on behalf of other Nisei migrants almost forty years after he had left his home to pursue a career in Japan.⁴¹ In 1939 Tateishi was an 18-year-old son of struggling Japanese strawberry farmers just outside Los Angeles. An aspiring journalist, he saw no prospect of being hired by the mainstream news outlets on the West Coast, which were owned by anti-immigrant publishers like William Randolph Hearst and the McClatchy family. Tateishi felt rejected by American society despite his U.S. citizenship by birth, and like thousands of other Nisei migrants, he used transpacific migration as a way to achieve social mobility outside the Japanese American ethnic enclave: "We didn't want to toil the earth, work in fruit and vegetable stalls and gasoline stands, handle dirty clothing and laundries, sling hash in cheap restaurants and cafeterias, or slave away as gardeners and domestics."⁴²

Tateishi's sentiment defied the ideal of the American dream in the dominant immigrant narrative of U.S. history—the ideal that he himself once cherished as a child of immigrants. In 1934, five years before his migration to Japan, Tateishi had visited Tokyo on a short-term study tour program (*kengakudan*) sponsored by the Young Buddhist Association in Southern California. After Tokyo, Tateishi toured various cities and towns throughout the Japanese archipelago, as well as Japan's colonial frontiers in Korea and Manchukuo. Although Japanese culture and customs did not impress Tateishi much, he was struck by Japanese city folks' access to modern amenities and the kinds of professional opportunities denied to the "humble" Japanese immigrants and their American children in California.[43] For many Nisei young adults and teenagers like Tateishi, relocation to Japan and its expanding empire to pursue careers in business, public service, and other professional fields seemed like a logical alternative for socioeconomic advancement outside the Japanese American community in the United States.[44]

In addition to the young children of Japanese return migrants and those Nisei who migrated to Japan on their own, a significant number of U.S.-born Nisei children in Japan had been sent to Japan to live with their relatives while their immigrant parents remained in the United States. For many Japanese immigrant parents in the United States, this was a sensible economic option during hard times. When both the Issei mother and father needed to work, sending at least one child to their relatives in Japan alleviated the cost and labor associated with child care.[45] Also, many immigrant parents pulled resources together to send at least one of their children to Japan to be educated and return to America one day with practical skills in agriculture and management that would help sustain their family businesses. The increasing Japanese economic and political might in Asia-Pacific during the 1920s and 1930s compelled other Issei parents to send their children to Japan to jump-start their Japanese education and seek opportunities in the potentially lucrative field of international commerce between the United States and Japan.[46]

Japanese American migrants such as David Koh Chiba, Yukiko Tashima, and Kay Tateishi embarked on their transpacific journeys during these conjunctural times in which the history of Asian exclusion in the United States and the history of Japanese colonialism in Asia intersected. Since the turn of the twentieth century, the political economy of xenophobia in the American West manifested power to strip U.S.-born Nisei's opportunities to build their future. As a consequence, thousands of young Japanese American citizens left home to seek new lives in an unfamiliar territory in the Japanese Empire. That escape from racial oppression shaped Nisei migrants' shifting identity from citizens to emigrants as they embarked on their transpacific journey. Migration became a powerful way for these rightless people to claim their agency.[47]

At the Crossroads: Living as Americans in the Japanese Empire

The diverse life experiences of Chiba, Tashima, Tateishi, and other Nisei migrants expose how nation-centered narratives have largely overlooked the critical role of U.S.-born Japanese Americans as cultural brokers on both sides of the Pacific. These young Japanese Americans found themselves negotiating complex sociopolitical conditions in the Japanese Empire that help us rethink the conceptual boundaries of Asian history and American history. One of the earliest examples of Nisei migrants whose lives were actively shaped by the transpacific convergences of historical developments in the U.S. and Japanese empires was Glendale, California, native Goso Yoneda. In 1913 the 7-year-old son of struggling immigrant farmers joined his family's return migration to his ailing father's hometown of Yasuno in Hiroshima Prefecture. Yoneda spent his formative years in this poverty-stricken rural town, where rice was hard to come by and he never saw "any meat, milk, or eggs." The childhood spent in a poor rural household in California and Hiroshima shaped Yoneda's social consciousness and intellectual development at the critical moment in Japanese history when a radical revolutionary intellectual movement began to flourish. He immersed himself in the writings of influential Marxist and anarchist intellectuals, such as Nagatsuka Takashi, whose work focused on exposing the wretched conditions of rural Japanese towns like Yasuno.[48]

Yoneda's decade-long odyssey in the Japanese Empire demonstrates how the migration of U.S.-born Nisei across borders contributed to the movement of ideas across the Pacific. Driven by his insatiable intellectual appetite, Yoneda traveled through Japan's colonial empire at the age of 16 to meet his favorite anarchist writer, Vasili Yakovlevich Eroshenko, a Russian Esperantist whose work had influenced many leftist intellectuals in Japan.

Eroshenko resided in Japan for two years, working with the Japanese Socialist Party before being deported in May 1921 for allegedly spreading anarchism among the Japanese youth.[49] Upon learning that Eroshenko had gone to China to teach at Beijing University, Yoneda skipped school to work as a longshoreman to buy a ferry ticket from Shimonoseki to the port of Busan in the then Japanese colony of Korea. Yoneda's itinerary to Beijing was typical of many Japanese travelers' in their journey from Busan, the southeastern terminus of Eurasian railways, through the Korean Peninsula and Mukden in Manchuria. Yoneda worked for Eroshenko for two months in Beijing, transcribing the blind Russian anarchist's fairy tales, before returning to Japan to become a labor organizer.[50]

The expansion of the Japanese Empire through the continent and the presence of Japanese emigrants in Korea and Manchuria enabled Yoneda to complete his journey through Japan's colonial frontiers in northeast Asia. By the time Yoneda traveled through Busan and Mukden in 1922, the number of Japanese emigrants to Korea and Manchuria had been steadily rising. According to a conservative figure, Korea, which was Japan's most prized colony at the time, had 350,000 Japanese settlers. Although Manchuria was not yet a Japanese colony, nearly 150,000 emigrants, including David Koh Chiba's family from California, had settled there. Hiroshima Prefecture, which had been known since the late nineteenth century as a "prefecture of emigrants" for having sent the largest number of migrants to Hawaii and North America, was one of the top ten prefectures that produced agricultural settlers in Manchuria.[51] Thus, as daring and adventurous as Yoneda's trip to China was, he traveled through territories that were familiar to people from his own prefecture and from other corners of the Japanese diaspora. He certainly did not have to learn new languages and customs to survive in places that were well settled by Japanese emigrants.

During the four years after his return from China, Yoneda further exposed himself to anti-imperialist and pro-labor activism when he participated in strikes in major Japanese cities. In 1926, having no desire to serve the expansionist ambitions of Japan's colonial empire, 20-year-old Yoneda left Japan to escape conscription into the armed forces and resettled in California. Known as Karl Yoneda throughout the rest of his life, he would establish himself as one of the state's most influential labor organizers and a vocal critic of Japanese militarism throughout the 1930s and during World War II thanks to his experience as a longshoreman and labor activist in

Japan. Yoneda's exposure to the social realities of both the U.S. and Japanese empires and to the radical intellectual development in Japan was indispensable for his emergence as a household name in the history of the Asian American labor movement in the United States.[52]

By the time Yukiko Tashima and her siblings arrived in Japan in 1933, Japan's position as a formidable colonial power in Asia-Pacific lured a significant number of Nisei from the United States. Besides the migrants and students from Japan's Asian colonies, the Nisei from the United States became the largest community of foreign-born residents in Japan. According to the Japanese Home Ministry in 1933, almost 20,000 Japanese American residents from North America had settled in various parts of the archipelago.[53] Soen Yamashita, a Hiroshima-born journalist who had emigrated to Hawaii, wrote extensively about the U.S.-born Nisei in Japan in the 1930s. Yamashita claimed that by the mid-1930s, some 40,000 Nisei had arrived in Japan as young migrants, with half of them living in Hiroshima and Yamaguchi, two prefectures that had sent the largest numbers of emigrants to the United States since the second half of the nineteenth century.[54]

For most young Nisei in Japan, the issue of where to settle was determined rather easily, at least at the beginning of their lives in that country. Once they arrived in Yokohama, many Nisei were usually taken in by their relatives, who lived in or near their parents' hometowns. Naturally, many Japanese American children settled in regions in Japan that had sent large numbers of emigrants to North America. As noted by Yamashita, Hiroshima and Yamaguchi Prefectures, in the southwestern part of the main island of Honshu, had the heaviest concentration of young Nisei migrants. Other regions with significant Nisei populations included Kagoshima, Kumamoto, and Fukuoka Prefectures on the island of Kyushu and the area around Tokyo (commonly known as the Kanto region). In 1931 Issei community historian and influential Los Angeles businessman Tsunegoro "Paul" Hirohata reported that nearly one-third of the 6,000 U.S.-born Nisei children of immigrants from Fukuoka Prefecture had traveled across the Pacific to live with relatives in their parents' hometowns.[55]

As the center of Japanese economy, politics, and culture, Tokyo attracted a growing number of young Japanese Americans in pursuit of education. According to Yamashita, 1,700 Nisei arrived in the Tokyo area by 1935 exclusively to seek educational opportunities unavailable to them in the United States.[56] Efforts began in Japan to accommodate the growing number of Japanese American students in Japan. In 1932 the Japanese Ministry of Foreign Affairs established the Kaigai Kyoiku Kyokai (Institute of International Education) to prepare Japanese American students for college. Within three years the institute opened the state-run Mizuho Gakuen, a school designed specifically to offer bilingual education to Japanese Americans.[57] Soon a number of private institutions and prep schools emerged, such as Aoyama School and the YMCA's Nichigo Bunka School; these schools attracted Nisei students who wanted to get acclimated to Japanese language and culture before enrolling in public schools or universities.[58] In 1936 a "Hawaii Home" Planning Committee was formed in Tokyo to build a new twenty-room dormitory for Nisei students from Hawaii. Funded by Japanese American families in Hawaii and their relatives in Japan, the facility accommodated up to eighty residents at a time and also served as a guesthouse for nonstudent visitors and vacationers from Hawaii.[59]

The presence of young U.S.-born Nisei students in major cities served Japan's effort to promote its metropoles as cosmopolitan intellectual and cultural centers. By the mid-1930s many Nisei were enrolled in major Japanese universities in the Tokyo, Kyoto, and Osaka metropolitan areas. A number of universities in Japan during the 1930s opened "international programs" with curricula to accommodate foreign-born students, especially Nisei from the United States, who began to outnumber international students from Japan's Asian neighbors. In 1935 the prestigious Waseda University in Tokyo opened its International Institute, which offered Japanese-language immersion programs as well as opportunities to audit regular classes at the university. The Waseda International Institute attracted students with long-term interests in pursuing careers in Japan. The school produced graduates who went on to work for Japanese government agencies, newspapers, and leading corporations.[60]

Among the students who benefited from Waseda's international program was Yukiko Tashima's future husband from Manchukuo, Zheng Zihan, who moved to Tokyo in 1936 to pursue a university degree. Thanks to his family's wealth and prestige, Zheng had already spent many years of his youth attending international schools in China, most recently at Saint John's University in Shanghai, an Anglican school founded by American missionaries. A proficient English speaker, Zheng joined the circle of international students from Waseda and other schools in Tokyo led by young

Nisei from America. One of Zheng's Nisei associates during his Waseda years was Yukiko Tashima's younger brother Yutaka, who introduced the young Manchu aristocrat to his sister.[61] The relationship between Zheng and Tashima that blossomed into a celebrated marriage in 1939 was thus a product of Japan's emergence as an expanding empire that had brought not only workers and students from East Asia but also tens of thousands of Nisei who had transplanted themselves from the American West in search of opportunities in their parents' homeland.

The Nisei in the Japanese Empire did not sever their connection to the United States and the Japanese American community. Instead, many Nisei migrants in the Japanese metropole found themselves in a unique position to cultivate their American identity and deploy their cultural capital. Although Yukiko Tashima moved to Japan to live the rest of her life as a Japanese, she attributed her own diasporic identity to her enduring connection to America. She was one of the many young Nisei women in Japan who studied at girls' schools founded by Japanese social reformers educated in the United States. After her arrival in Tokyo in 1936, Tashima attended Keisen Jogakuen (Keisen Girls' School), one of the most well-known academies for young women in Japan. The founder and principal of Keisen Girls' School was Kawai Michiko, a Bryn Mawr College graduate and former national director of the Japanese YWCA. One of the most influential women educators in Japan, Kawai used her American education and Quaker background to shape Keisen's academic culture. Kawai opened a new international studies program at Keisen in 1935 and infused her internationalist and progressive Christian values into the classes catering to U.S.-born Nisei. She encouraged her students to embrace their bicultural identity and encouraged them to express in their writings opinions critical of Japanese imperialism in Asia.[62]

The centrality of international ideology and de-emphasis on Japanese nationalism in Keisen's curriculum also influenced Yukiko Tashima's self-identity as a U.S.-born Japanese. Despite the interest she developed in Japanese life and culture during her years in Tokyo, the Keisen curriculum helped Tashima embrace her American heritage.[63] Los Angeles native Haruko Kawai, who taught English at Keisen when the international program for the Nisei started, was also impressed by the school's emphasis on internationalism. Ironically, Japan's militaristic expansion into Asia allowed the Keisen students to enjoy this early version of multicultural education. According to Kawai, activities at Keisen included numerous excursions to historical heritage sites throughout Japan, Korea, Manchuria, and even China.[64]

Tashima's assertion of her American identity, despite her permanent displacement from the United States, demonstrates the complexity inherent in Nisei migrants' diasporic consciousness. To many young Nisei migrants who felt rejected by U.S. society and were denied the right to pursue the promise of their American citizenship, Japan served as an alternative place to reclaim their American identity and cultural capital. Like Kawai Michiko of Keisen Girls' School, Japanese educators with higher degrees from the United States were instrumental in establishing programs that offered Nisei students in Japan opportunities to experience American-style higher education. In addition to Waseda University, several Japanese institutes of higher learning offered international programs that attracted young Nisei men and women privileged enough to pursue advanced degrees. These Nisei were well represented at elite Japanese universities, such as Waseda, Meiji, Rikkyo, Keio, Toyo, Doshisha, and Ryukoku.[65] Some Nisei even studied at Japanese colleges and universities in the parts of Asia under Japanese occupation, such as Toa Dobun Shoin, a special institution in Shanghai that trained future Japanese diplomats and administrators.[66]

Meiji University in Tokyo in particular proved to be among the most Nisei-friendly universities in Japan. Professor Matsumoto Takizo, better known among Japanese Americans as Frank Matsumoto, played a major role in mentoring Nisei students at Meiji. Born in Hiroshima in 1901, Matsumoto moved to Fresno, California, as a toddler with his mother and grew up speaking English. He excelled in sports at Fresno High School, lettering in baseball and football. After high school Matsumoto went to his native prefecture of Hiroshima to study Japanese, with a plan to return to the United States to pursue a higher degree. After finishing middle school in Hiroshima, he moved to Tokyo to study at Meiji University. By 1933 he had finished college and graduate studies at Meiji and joined the school's English faculty. His bilingual and bicultural background and his love of American sports drew him to Nisei students and their interests. Meiji University had enough Nisei students in 1933 to form one of the first American football teams in Japan under Matsumoto's guidance. The inaugural football team at Meiji University consisted of members of the school's all-Nisei fraternity, Sigma Nu Kappa.[67] The young Nisei boys who could not

FIGURE 2 Sigma Nu Kappa, the all-Nisei fraternity at Meiji University in Tokyo, ca. 1934.
Meiji University.

have dreamed of being accepted into high school football teams back in the United States finally got to play this quintessential American sport at a major Japanese university.

Sports, especially American football, was one of the cultural institutions transplanted from the United States that allowed young Nisei men and women in Japan to deploy their American cultural capital as a way to gain socioeconomic traction. The presence of Japanese American student-athletes in Japan in the 1930s played a crucial role in the creation of Japan's intercollegiate athletic leagues, which were modeled after the American system. Matsumoto's mentor, Paul Rusch, a native Kentuckian Episcopalian missionary who taught English at Rikkyo University, was widely known to have introduced American football to Japan. In 1933 Rusch enlisted California Nisei Jiro "Jimmy" Ota to form athletic clubs at Rikkyo University, including the first American football team in Japan. Other schools with Japanese American student-athletes, such as Waseda and Keio Universities, soon followed suit. Japanese American athletes excelled in baseball and hockey, but football drew the most enthusiastic participation from Nisei student-athletes. On December 26, 1933, the *Yomiuri Shimbun* reported on the result of the first American football match in Japan, held at the Rikkyo University field and refereed by Matsumoto and Rikkyo's head football coach, George Marshall. Meiji University's Sigma Nu Kappa defeated a club consisting of Hawaiian Nisei in Tokyo to claim the first ever victory in an American football game on Japanese soil.[68] The following year, Nisei students and their American coaches arranged the first intercollegiate football games among Meiji, Waseda, and Rikkyo Universities, all captained by Japanese American student-athletes. These founders of the intercollegiate league were also instrumental in establishing the Japan American Football Association, the sport's governing body in Japan that continues to oversee the country's top-level semiprofessional league today. In 1935 Meiji University's American football team hosted the first international game at Koshien Stadium outside Kobe, losing to the visiting University of Southern California Trojans.[69]

College football was far from the only American cultural institution to which U.S.-born Japanese Americans found access upon their migration to Japan. A number of young Japanese American performers found opportunities in the pre–World War II Japanese world of entertainment. The pioneering, and by far the most famous, Japanese American artist in Japan was jazz singer and dancer Alice Fumiko Kawabata. Born in Hawaii in 1916, Kawabata was a dance phenomenon who started her professional career in Los Angeles at the age of 12, before graduating from middle school.[70] Contracted by the Los Angeles Orpheum Theatre circuit, she made her Broadway debut in late 1929 to rave reviews from leading New York theater reviewers. The Palace Theater in New York billed her vaudeville act as "one of the most sensational dance hits of the current New

FIGURE 3 Honolulu's *Nippu Jiji* announcing Alice Fumiko Kawabata's return to Hawaii as "Japan's foremost dancer."
Nippu Jiji, November 23, 1938.

York theatrical season."[71] By 1932 the aspiring young vaudevillian had performed in more than forty theaters in New York, Los Angeles, and other major cities throughout the United States before taking a break that winter to visit her relatives in Japan. During the few weeks of vacationing, she discovered opportunities for stardom in Japan's burgeoning pop culture scene that she could not have dreamed of back home. Despite her talent and aspiration for fame, racial barriers in the U.S. entertainment industry limited her chances for success outside the grueling dance circuits. Already an experienced performer at 17 years of age, she attracted major record labels in Japan that recognized her potential as a recording star and stage performer. In 1933 she signed with Columbia Records Japan and became the country's leading jazz vocalist. Kawabata "skyrocketed to fame like a red-headed comet on a rampage" before turning 20 years old.[72]

Kawabata's success prompted other Nisei artists to seek fame in the burgeoning Japanese pop culture scene. In 1935 Betty Inada from Sacramento built her career as a rising jazz star in Japan, joining Seattle natives Rickey Miyagawa and his sister Mine in dazzling Tokyo's jazz fans with "authentic" American singing styles. According to *Taihoku Nippo*, many Japanese audiences found these Nisei's exotic "American accent" in their broken Japanese particularly attractive. Inada would soon rise to national stardom in Japan as a dancer and actor, rivaling Kawabata's popularity.[73] The Japanese entertainment industry's embracement of the unique Japanese American flavor served Kawabata and other talented Nisei artists a way out of their ethnic enclaves in the United States.

What made the diasporic identity of many Japanese American migrants unique was that the life in Japan—their purported diasporic homeland—was an extension of their American experience. Their American citizenship, upbringing, and ties to their families back home actively shaped their experiences in Japan. Moreover, many young Nisei in Japan deployed their American identity, as well as their linguistic and cultural capital, to fulfill the social mobility unachievable in the United States.

Encounter with Japanese Colonialism

Facing increasing negative international publicity because of its aggressive China policy, in 1939 the Japanese government took part in bringing

U.S.-born Nisei to Japan. The Japanese Foreign Ministry tapped young Japanese Americans from the United States as cultural brokers who could promote positive images of the Japanese Empire. The man behind the project was Kawai Tatsuo, who became the director of the Foreign Ministry's Intelligence Bureau in 1937. Having served as a consul in Canada and first minister in the United States, Kawai conceived of recruiting talented young Nisei and training them to become spokespersons for the ideal of the Greater East Asia Co-Prosperity Sphere. Upon approval from the Minister of Foreign Affairs, Kawai named the training program Heishikan and led the recruitment effort in early 1939. He carefully devised a plan to place the graduates of Heishikan in positions in public relations at major companies, such as the South Manchurian Railway Company on Japan's colonial frontier. Also, the two-year education at Heishikan would offer Nisei graduates employment as English correspondents at the Tokyo-based *Japan Times* and the state-run Domei News Agency. The opportunities to work for prominent companies and press outlets attracted applications from many Nisei in the United States, once the Japanese consulates general in the U.S. Pacific states and Hawaii sent out a call for applications through local Japanese American newspapers. Successful candidates would receive scholarships and stipends for two years.[74]

Kay Tateishi, who had dropped out of college in 1936 because of financial difficulties, seized the opportunity to compete for a two-year scholarship. Tateishi saw the education at Heishikan as a way to escape his family's strawberry farm and fulfill his dream of becoming a journalist. Sam Masuda, another Southern California Nisei from Garden Grove, also fit the profile of a talented Japanese American stuck on his family farm. Masuda was a gifted debater who won the national speech contest sponsored by the Japanese American Citizens League. He was forced to drop out of high school in 1935, when his father died of an illness, to run his struggling family farm and later worked at a fruit and vegetable stand. On learning of Masuda's struggle, Sei Fujii, publisher of the Los Angeles–based Japanese American newspaper *Kashu Mainichi*, praised the young man as a model Nisei youth who sacrificed his own education to support his family. Masuda nevertheless pushed himself to continue his education at Santa Ana Junior College and, after graduation, applied for the Heishikan scholarship in 1939.[75]

In the summer and fall of 1939, the Japanese consulates general selected candidates from a large pool of applicants. In Los Angeles, consuls interviewed twenty or so students in August out of more than fifty applicants; in October they picked four students, including Tateishi and Masuda, to join the first class at Heishikan.[76] Heishikan opened on December 1, 1939, and the first class included sixteen students (fourteen men and two women) from the U.S. West Coast, Hawaii, and Canada.[77]

The curriculum at Heishikan reflected the program's focus on offering optimal courses that would train students as journalists. The students at Heishikan took classes on the Japanese constitution, Japanese language, economics, history, geography, stenography, and writing. In addition, they learned to read Chinese characters and Japanese newspapers. Also included in the curriculum was an excursion program that offered students the opportunity to tour various historical and cultural sites throughout Japan. In October 1939 students visited the ancient Japanese capitals Nara, Kyoto, and Osaka as well as Ise Shrine, a Shinto shrine dedicated to the mythical sun goddess who is said to be the direct ancestor of all Japanese emperors.[78]

These cultural excursion tours became a significant part of the Nisei students' education at Heishikan. School officials devoted a great deal of time and resources to sending students to different parts of the archipelago in hopes that the Nisei would cultivate positive impressions of their ancestral land. In return, the students devoted most of the pages in *Heishikan News*, the school's official newsletter in Japanese, to accounts of their encounters with the splendors of the Japanese countryside and cultural heritage. To Yuichi Doiguchi from San Francisco, exploring the historical and cultural sites in the ancient capitals was an indispensable form of education that helped him develop a greater appreciation for Japan's culture and the country's role in "building a new East Asia."[79]

Heishikan students had varied reactions to Hokkaido and Sakhalin Island, the northernmost frontiers of Japan's colonial empire. Hokkaido had become a Japanese territory in 1886 and was the country's second largest island, where the indigenous Ainu people had once outnumbered Japanese settlers. The vast frontier province presented the students a dramatic contrast to the crowded cities on the main island of Honshu. To California native George Kyotow and other students in the group, Hokkaido's spectacular hills and lakes could easily rival the most splendid national parks in

North America. In Hokkaido students also visited an Ainu village. This encounter with an indigenous people in a colonized land reminded Hawaii-born Kokuro Nakata of his home, as he was moved by the "simplicity" and "innocence" of Hokkaido's natives.[80]

On the other hand, Sakhalin, then known as Karafuto Prefecture, did not impress the students as much. Tamaye Tsutsumida's excitement about the opportunity to tour this colonial territory turned into mild disappointment when she encountered the bleak and "desolate" landscape of Sakhalin. The itinerary on Sakhalin included Shinto shrines, museums, and agricultural settlements that had been established when the southern half of the island became a Japanese territory in 1905 as a result of Japan's victory over Russia in the Russo-Japanese War. The highlights of the tour included a visit to a fox farm, which supplied fur to Japan and Japanese military posts in Asia. Although most students were anxious to return to Tokyo, Kaoru Furuya from Los Angeles thought the trip was worthwhile. The short visit to the frontier had intrigued him about Sakhalin's future development, and he could not wait for a chance to revisit the prefecture one day.[81]

Most of these students had little trouble securing employment as press attachés at various colonial posts in Asia once they graduated from Heishikan. Within two years after his relocation from Los Angeles to Tokyo in 1939, Kay Tateishi was hired by the Japanese state-run Domei News Agency and became an English-language correspondent in Japanese colonies. Bill Ishikawa, a Hawaiian Nisei, started his post at the Japanese Consulate General in Nanjing, China, a city ravaged by the brutal massacre at the hands of Japanese invaders not long before. Another Heishikan graduate, Kazumaro Uyeno, departed for northeast China to work for the Central Broadcasting Station in Changchun, the capital of the Japanese puppet state Manchukuo.[82] The expansion of the Japanese Empire indeed offered these Nisei ideal career opportunities, as they found themselves working as agents of Japanese colonialism.

Mobility, Movement, and the Nisei Transnational Generation

From Goso Yoneda's participation in the radical social movement to Nisei college students' embrace of the cosmopolitan metropole to the Heishikan graduates' work in Japanese colonies, Nisei's encounter with various aspects of colonialism actively shaped their lives as Americans in the Japanese Empire. Once transplanted to the Japanese colonial world, many young Japanese Americans found opportunities to deploy American cultural capital for their socioeconomic gains in ways they could not in their country of birth. This mobility was key to the making of a Japanese American diaspora. Despite their legal citizenship by birth, Nisei's social mobility and movement in the American West had been incredibly limited because of widespread xenophobia and systemic discrimination. In contrast, many Nisei found in Japan a creative space to reclaim and experiment with their American citizenship to attain an alternative version of the American dream, represented by their educational pursuits and socioeconomic ascendance. Although not all Nisei in the Japanese Empire were able to accomplish this goal, their relocation to Japan gave Japanese American migrants a chance to build new lives. However, as I show in the next chapter, many Japanese American migrants also discovered how complex legal, political, and diplomatic developments in the United States and Japan made their citizenship fragile and vulnerable. Whether by choice, circumstance, or coincidence, Japanese Americans in diaspora found themselves in a world that was intimately shaped by the volatile relationship between the United States and Japan.

CHAPTER 2

From Citizens to the Stateless

Migration, Exclusion, and Nisei Citizenship

IN EARLY SEPTEMBER 1928, 20-year-old Toshiko Inaba and her 18-year-old brother Akira arrived at the Port of San Francisco from Japan on the transpacific vessel *Taiyo Maru*. Natives of Walnut Grove in California's Sacramento Delta, they had gone to Japan as toddlers to be raised by their uncle's family in Kumamoto Prefecture. After spending more than fifteen years of their lives in Japan, they decided to return to the United States with the intention of resettling permanently in their hometown in northern California, where their parents ran a grocery store.[1] Although both of the Inaba siblings carried birth certificates verifying their U.S. citizenship, the U.S. Bureau of Immigration authorities at San Francisco's Angel Island Immigration Station granted admission only to Akira.[2] They declared Toshiko Inaba a "person of a race ineligible to citizenship, not excepted by any of the provisions of the Immigration Law" and denied her entry to the United States. Deemed permanently ineligible to set foot on American soil, she found herself detained on Angel Island awaiting a deportation order, whereas her brother was allowed to return to their home in Walnut Grove.[3]

Toshiko Inaba, like her brother Akira, was not a Japanese immigrant but an American citizen by birth with proper paperwork who wanted to reunite with her family in the United States. What, then, prompted the U.S. immigration authorities to claim that she was a noncitizen and forbidden from returning to her country of birth? Inaba's fate reveals one of the most bizarre consequences of the early-twentieth-century Asian exclusion movement, which culminated in restrictive U.S. immigration and naturalization laws. During her entry interview on Angel Island, the immigration officials inspecting Inaba's papers discovered that she had married and divorced a Japanese national named Yamamoto Torao in Kumamoto in 1927.[4] These officials then invoked two federal laws that the U.S. Congress had passed while Inaba was in Japan to strip the young Nisei's U.S. citizenship, reject her entry application, and banish her from her country of birth.[5]

The first law they enforced was the Married Women's Independent Nationality Act, better known as the Cable Act of 1922. This law repealed the Expatriation Act of 1907, which had forced any American woman marrying a foreign national to forfeit her U.S. citizenship and assume the citizenship of her husband.[6] The Cable Act purported to protect an American woman's birthright citizenship regardless of her husband's national origin. However, the law made a critical exception to this women's right by continuing to strip U.S. citizenship from American women like Inaba who married "aliens ineligible to citizenship," namely, Asian men.[7] Such a glaring loophole in the Cable Act allowed the U.S. Bureau of Immigration to declare that Inaba had given up her American citizenship by virtue of her "marriage to an Oriental."[8]

If the Cable Act's unambiguously discriminatory clause against women marrying Japanese men made Toshiko Inaba stateless, the Immigration Act of 1924 served as the legal measure that denied her the right to return to the United States. In addition to imposing restrictive "national origins" quotas to limit the number of immigrants from non-Western European countries, the most exclusionary immigration law in U.S. history barred the admission of "aliens ineligible to citizenship" altogether, effectively shutting America's gates on Asian immigrants.[9] After revoking Inaba's U.S. citizenship, the officials at Angel Island reclassified her status as an alien from Japan who was ineligible for citizenship and thus permanently inadmissible to the United States. All in all, it took the U.S. Bureau of Immigration less than two weeks after Inaba's arrival to transform her legal status from a U.S. citizen by birth to a stateless individual and then to an illegal immigrant from Japan.[10] This sudden change of Inaba's identity was not by her choice but by the mandate of the exclusionary U.S. laws that had recast her legal and racial status as Japanese while she was away from home.[11]

Inaba refused to accept her permanent exclusion from the United States and immediately appealed her deportation case. However, a series of hearings conducted by the U.S. Bureau of Immigration Board of Special Inquiries in the weeks that followed did nothing to restore her right to reunite with her family. She persevered by filing a petition in the U.S. District Court for her entry to the United States as a natural-born American citizen. As her case dragged on, Inaba remained imprisoned on Angel Island for well over a year before the federal court's final rejection of her petition in December 1929. She was deported a month later, on January 15, 1930. The sixteen-month confinement that Inaba endured at the Angel Island Immigration Station was the longest immigration detention ever served by a person of Japanese ancestry in U.S. history.[12]

Inaba's case sheds light on the far-reaching transnational and generational implications of anti-Asian immigration and citizenship policies on the lives of Nisei migrants. The fierce nativist movement in the United States that resulted in exclusionary laws throughout this period manifested the racialization of Asian immigrants in America as inassimilable foreigners.[13] However, it was the young U.S.-born Nisei citizens living abroad, especially women like Toshiko Inaba, who became the most vulnerable victims of these unprecedented exclusionary U.S. policies. Even after the aggressive Asian exclusion movement had pushed tens of thousands of young Japanese American citizens to relocate to the Japanese Empire, the U.S. regime of exclusion demonstrated extraterritorial power to strip Nisei migrants of their American citizenship. As Inaba's case demonstrates, those Nisei migrants who became denaturalized found themselves permanently separated from their families in the United States as a result of the exclusionary immigration law that made their entry to American soil illegal.

Yet there was much more to this story. In this chapter I argue that what Toshiko Inaba went through during her sixteen-month detention on Angel Island was far from an unexpected or unintended by-product of the exclusionary laws targeting Japanese immigrants. The involuntary expatriation of Inaba was, in fact, a direct consequence of the U.S. white nationalist movement's efforts since the nineteenth century to strip Asian Americans' birthright citizenship. This much overlooked aspect of the Asian exclusion movement represents the most dramatic legal ramification of American xenophobia that justified the U.S. government's ability to revoke birthright citizenship based on one's racial background.

Such a devastating effect of the exclusionary regime of U.S. citizenship exposed the limits of Nisei migrants' mobility in the liminal space between the United States and Japan. It was women like Inaba who challenged this fundamentally gendered exclusionary institution by asserting their independent American citizenship. In this chapter I also examine how the exclusion movement and racist immigration laws designed to exclude Japanese immigrants in the American West created an inevitable long-term crisis for the Japanese American diaspora. Many Nisei migrants who had left the United States found themselves unable to escape the transnational impact of the exclusion movement, despite their relocation to Japan. Throughout the 1930s, as the souring U.S.-Japan relations fueled the intensified anti-Japanese movement in the United States, Nisei migrants lived with varying degrees of fear that they would lose their U.S. citizenship and become permanently stranded in the Japanese Empire. In this way, Japanese Americans' diasporic experience in Japan became a critical extension of their American lives as rightless citizens, as they continued to grapple with the impact of the exclusion movement in the American West.

From Citizens to the Stateless: Race and Birthright Citizenship

As bizarre as Inaba's case was, it reveals that the systemic assault on Asian American birthright citizenship was a powerful feature of the regime of racial oppression in the United States throughout the early decades of the twentieth century. Leading anti-immigration lobbyists such as V. S. McClatchy argued that Nisei's American citizenship made them an even greater long-term threat to white America than Japanese nationals, who were permanently ineligible for naturalization and subject to immigration restrictions. In 1919 McClatchy alleged that Nisei were "non-assimilable" and "always Japanese," who "claimed the right to hold land" and other benefits of their U.S. citizenship. In McClatchy's view, any legal effort to exclude Japanese would not be complete until the growing number of U.S.-born Nisei were made "aliens ineligible for citizenship," just like their parents.[14] Although Japanese Americans constituted less than 1% of the population of California, the state with the largest Japanese population in the contiguous United States, the anti-Japanese rhetoric had turned these young Nisei into the most dangerous threat to white America.[15] In an article published in his family-owned *Sacramento Bee*, McClatchy joined other anti-Japanese agitators to declare that the U.S.-born children of Japanese aliens should be made permanently ineligible for the Fourteenth Amendment's guarantee of birthright citizenship.[16]

U.S.-born Asian Americans remain more or less absent in the broad discussions of how Jim Crow laws enforced the apparatus of citizenship that hinged on racial hierarchy. This is symptomatic of the liminal and ambivalent place that Asian Americans have occupied in the general U.S. discourse on race, in which people of Asian ancestry appear historically as immigrant communities in the periphery of the dominant Black-white race relations. However, the call for the removal of Asian Americans' birthright citizenship had actively shaped the politics of xenophobia and the Asian exclusion movement since the nineteenth century and played a delicate role in the Jim Crow–era legal institution.

As Leslie Bow has argued, Jim Crow laws manifested power to "accommodate a third race" based on the construction of Asians as permanent foreigners.[17] The Fourteenth Amendment to the U.S. Constitution in 1868 had invalidated *Dred Scott*, the 1857 U.S. Supreme Court case that had excluded Blacks from American citizenry, and restored Black citizenship rights. African Americans' legal citizenship became "indisputable even if the Jim Crow segregation had demoted them to 'second-class' citizens." Since then, as noted by Mae M. Ngai, the formal exclusion of Asians as "aliens ineligible" for American citizenship represented the "most complete race-based legal exclusion from citizenship" in the United States.[18]

However, as discussed in Chapter 1, Asians—both foreign- and U.S.-born—constituted much more than a "third race" in the American West, as anti-Asian xenophobia and legal exclusion directly shaped the operational regime of race relations in California and other western states. As early as 1854, the Supreme Court of California determined that individuals of Chinese ancestry should be subject to the state's statute that prohibited Blacks from testifying against whites.[19] California's miscegenation statutes throughout the late nineteenth century and early twentieth century made it illegal for white individuals to marry a "Negro, mulatto, or Mongolian." In 1909 the Japanese specifically were added to this list of prohibited races in California's anti-miscegenation laws.[20]

The exclusion of Asians in the United States, based on the powerful idea of their perpetual foreignness, shaped the core of the U.S. politics of xenophobia and helped to sustain the apparatus of race-based citizenship enforced by the Jim Crow regime. Even the language of civil rights in the late nineteenth and early twentieth centuries that purported to dismantle racial segregation in the American South relied on the deployment of anti-Asian rhetoric. In his famous dissent in *Plessy v. Ferguson*, Supreme Court justice John Marshall Harlan exemplified how the representation of Asians as perpetual foreigners was crucial to restoring Black citizenship. As the sole objector who would go down in history as a champion of civil rights, Harlan eloquently defended African Americans' citizenship rights, but he also justified his position by effectively endorsing the permanent exclusion of Asians from American citizenry. In his dissenting opinion, Harlan described the Chinese as "a race so different from our own that we do not permit those belonging to it to become citizens of the United States." He then lamented what he saw as an appalling injustice in the South: "A Chinaman can ride in the same passenger coach with white citizens of the United States, while citizens of the black race . . . are yet declared to be criminals if they ride in a public coach occupied by citizens of the white race."[21]

Less than two years later, in another Supreme Court case, *United States v. Wong Kim Ark*, Harlan confirmed his position in favor of permanent race-based exclusion of Asians when he joined Chief Justice Melville Fuller as the only dissenters who refused to recognize San Francisco native and Chinese American Wong Kim Ark's Fourteenth Amendment right of birthright citizenship. In August 1895 the collector of customs at the Port of San Francisco invoked the Chinese Exclusion Act to deny Wong Kim Ark permission to enter the United States upon his return from a temporary visit to China. Wong spent the next five months in detention while he challenged the U.S. government's decision to treat him as a subject of China despite his U.S. citizenship by birth. In the landmark decision the Supreme Court held that Wong's citizenship "has not been lost or taken away by anything happening since his birth," upholding the Fourteenth Amendment's birthright citizenship clause regardless of Wong's race or parentage. In language similar to the dissenting opinion in *Plessy v. Ferguson*, however, Harlan and Fuller contended that the constitutional protection of birthright citizenship did not apply to the children of Chinese immigrants, whose "belief, traditions," and "filial piety" allegedly made them perpetually loyal to China. The dissenting justices argued that the U.S. government has "the power, notwithstanding the Fourteenth Amendment," to withhold citizenship from all individuals—native or foreign born—of the Chinese "race."²²

Despite their failure to strip Wong Kim Ark's birthright citizenship, Harlan and Fuller's articulation of Asian Americans' perpetual foreignness would nevertheless remain a popular sentiment that shaped the culture and politics of xenophobia in the twentieth century. Throughout the early decades of the twentieth century, anti-Japanese lobbyists called for removing birthright citizenship of American children born to Japanese immigrants and even eliminating the birthright citizenship clause from the Fourteenth Amendment altogether.²³ In 1921 McClatchy claimed that granting U.S.-born Nisei "all the rights and privileges of American citizenship" was "a striking exemplification of the suicidal policy."²⁴ That year, the California legislature endorsed the resolution of the Japanese Exclusion League of California calling for "absolute exclusion" of Japanese immigration and measures to effect federal laws that would take away U.S. citizenship from "races of yellow color."²⁵

Thirty years after *Wong Kim Ark*, the exclusion movement's campaign to strip the birthright citizenship of Asian Americans came to fruition when the Cable Act of 1922 and the Immigration Act of 1924 worked in tandem to deny Toshiko Inaba the right to return to the United States. The fragility of Nisei migrants' American citizenship during this period exposed the extraterritorial power of the U.S. nation-state that excluded Asian Americans from the foundational institution of birthright citizenship (*jus soli*). So long as the "races of yellow color" remained perpetual foreigners, the culture and politics of American xenophobia granted the U.S. government power to reinterpret the principle of *jus soli* based on the dominant racial ideology.

The Fallacy of Independent Nationality and Nisei Women's Diasporic Citizenship

On the heels of the Nineteenth Amendment's guarantee of women's right to vote in 1920, the push for women's civil rights continued to gain momentum when the Cable Act of 1922 granted most American women the right to keep their citizenship independent of their husbands' nationality. However, the law's protection of women's independent citizenship did not extend to those who married Asian men.²⁶ The Inaba case reveals how Japanese American women who shared her plight had to negotiate both the Japanese and the American legal and cultural institutions to articulate, reassert, and reclaim their citizenship, lest they face permanent separation from their families and communities back home.

Inaba chose to fight her way home by filing a series of court appeals, and as a result, she endured an extended incarceration on Angel Island. In her appeals Toshiko Inaba argued that her marriage to Yamamoto in Japan should have been null and void in the first place because the marriage had not been in accordance with Japanese law. According to her testimony, she found out about her alleged marriage to Yamamoto in September 1927, four months after her uncle's family had registered her marriage "without her own knowledge and without the consent of her parents."²⁷ Japan's Family Registry Law (*kosekiho*) granted a woman the right to file for release from such a marriage "contracted without consent."²⁸ Inaba asserted that, upon discovering that her uncle had married her off to Yamamoto, she promptly resorted to what she viewed as something any good, independent young American woman would do: She "caused her family record to be changed so that she would no longer be a member of Yamamoto's family, but a member of her own family." This act, according to Japanese law, constituted Inaba's "complete and absolute" release from the alleged marriage.²⁹

Inaba's strategy was thus twofold. First, she emphasized the illegitimacy of her marriage to Yamamoto in Japan on the grounds that the Japanese civil code considered a marriage "owing to coercion" to be unlawful.³⁰ Second, she emphasized her cultural citizenship as an independent American woman who had kept her identity and values intact, despite her upbringing in her uncle's Japanese household. She and her lawyers hoped that this approach would convince the U.S. government to honor and restore her birthright citizenship.

However, Inaba's bold claim to her independent American citizenship moved neither the immigration officials nor the U.S. federal court judges. The Bureau of Immigration flatly rejected Inaba's assertion that her proactive measures to release herself from Yamamoto's family registry had annulled her marriage in the eyes of existing Japanese family law. The bureau's acting commissioner, Edward Haff, demanded that Inaba produce a Japanese legal document equivalent to a U.S. court-ordered annulment paper.

Without such a document by a judicial decree—essentially nonexistent in the system of Japanese family registry law—his agency refused to accept Inaba's claim that her marriage to Yamamoto had been invalidated.[31]

Although Inaba hoped that her appeals in the U.S. judicial system would reverse the Immigration Bureau's decision, the opinion of the presiding American judge was hardly sympathetic to her plight. Judge Franklin H. Rudkin of the U.S. Ninth Circuit Court of Appeals firmly sided with Haff's determination that Inaba's marriage to a Japanese national was irreversible. The judge insisted that Inaba's marriage to Yamamoto, arranged by her uncle or not, provided the Bureau of Immigration with enough legal grounds to enforce the Cable Act. Moreover, Rudkin also deployed his own racial prejudice to dismiss Inaba's claim to her independent American citizenship. As to Inaba's argument that the marriage had taken place without her knowledge, Rudkin responded that the "only evidence of coercion was the fact that her husband was selected for her by her relatives, according to Japanese custom." "If such coercion will invalidate a marriage between Orientals," Rudkin added, "it is a matter of common knowledge that few, if any, of such marriage [sic], will result, or can result, in expatriation."[32] Rudkin's opinion was thus based primarily on racialized perceptions of Asian "culture" and his insistence that arranged marriages without women's consent were common in Asia. Inaba's appeal to her American citizenship, both legal and cultural, proved to be of no avail in the American court, which effectively upheld racially coded U.S. citizenship and immigration laws of the 1920s.

Inaba's case earned little sympathy from the American press. The *Sacramento Bee* described Inaba as a "Japanese woman . . . claiming Sacramento as her first home."[33] Instead of critiquing the fallacy of the U.S. court's interpretation of the Japanese family registry law, the *El Paso Times* echoed Rudkin's sentiment that "an old Japanese custom" of "parental marriage arrangement" was to blame for her deportation.[34] Inaba's case went nearly unnoticed even by the Japanese American ethnic newspapers, except for a brief report of her deportation in January 1930 as a cautionary tale that a Nisei woman marrying a "Japanese alien" was barred from returning to the United States.[35] Inaba's experience revealed that, so long as these exclusionary legal institutions existed, Nisei women living in Japan constantly faced the possibility that they would not be allowed to return to their homes in the United States upon their marriage to Japanese men.

Inaba was not the first Japanese American woman who waged a legal challenge in the American courts to reclaim her U.S. citizenship that had been stripped away by the Cable Act. Since the enactment of this law in 1922, Japanese diplomats in the United States had paid attention to its impact on Nisei women who married Japanese immigrant men.[36] In 1927, two years before Inaba's appeals in the U.S. federal court, the Japanese consuls in Hawaii reported on the case of Hawaii-born Nisei Yoshiko Hoshino, who had lost her U.S. citizenship as a result of her marriage to a Japanese citizen in Hawaii soon after the enactment of the Cable Act. In 1925 Hoshino divorced her Japanese husband and applied for naturalization to regain her citizenship. As a result of the 1922 Supreme Court ruling in *Ozawa v. United States*, which permanently stamped Japanese nationals' ineligibility for American citizenship, the U.S. Attorney rejected her application based on the U.S. legal system's "racial limitation of naturalization," which rendered Asians ineligible. Hoshino refused to give up her quest to reclaim her American citizenship and filed a petition in the U.S. District Court for the Territory of Hawaii for permission to become a naturalized citizen.[37]

Unlike Toshiko Inaba, who had lost her U.S. citizenship while in Japan, Hoshino benefited from the fact that she had never left the United States. Although she had lost her U.S. citizenship and become a Japanese national, she was a "legal alien" so long as she remained on U.S. soil. In addition, even though Inaba's appeals were met with hostility from the court, which effectively sided with immigration officials, Hoshino's case had benefited from a federal judge who exhibited remarkable sympathy for her plight. Even more important, the presiding judge on her case did not face the burden of defending a deportation order issued by the Bureau of Immigration. U.S. District Court judge De Bolt was willing to forgo citing the *Ozawa* case in granting Hoshino an opportunity to reapply for naturalization. De Bolt declared that while the Cable Act of 1922 had deprived Hoshino of U.S. citizenship as a result of her marriage to a Japanese national, she was nevertheless a law-abiding legal resident whose naturalization case should be treated in a manner that is "fair and equitable, and accords with reason and justice."[38]

On the contrary, Toshiko Inaba's case demonstrates that the Japanese American women who had lost their U.S. citizenship while in Japan were in double jeopardy, because the Immigration Act of 1924 permanently banned their entry to the United States. Their inability to return to the United States not only prevented them from regaining their citizenship through naturalization but also forced them to remain permanently separated from their families back home. They were a group of American citizens who had become a direct target of the immigration and deportation regime that kept Asians on the outside of the immigration gate to the United States. Their experiences serve as powerful proof of the contradiction inherent in the United States's celebrated identity as a nation of immigrants: that immigration was a fundamentally restrictive and exclusionary arm of the state that maintained its racial hierarchy.

Anti-Japanese Sentiment and the Crisis of Nisei Citizenship

Before the Inaba case illuminated the impact of the Cable Act on Nisei women's American citizenship, the bureaucrats at the Japanese Foreign Ministry already had foreseen that the increase in U.S. exclusionary legal measures against Japanese immigrants would potentially affect the citizenship status of their U.S.-born children living abroad. As U.S.-Japan relations began to sour in the 1920s and especially in the 1930s with Japan's military aggression in China, the presence of American citizens of Japanese ancestry in Japan became a diplomatic issue that neither of the two governments had dealt with before. Japan's high diplomats became increasingly mindful of the presence of American citizens of Japanese ancestry in Japan. They understood that these laws not only affected the lives of Japanese nationals in the United States but also might require the Japanese government to reevaluate the administration of a significant population of American citizens who could lose their citizenship and settle permanently in Japan and Japanese colonies in Asia.[39]

However, it was not until Inaba's arrival in San Francisco in 1928 and the ensuing court cases that Japanese diplomats and American legal experts grasped the complex gendered impact of exclusionary American laws on the lives of Nisei women in Japan. In 1926 Vice Consul K. Tsurumi in Los Angeles consulted the Japanese Consulate General's legal adviser Ray E. Nimmo about the citizenship problem of Japanese Americans residing in Japan. In a letter, Tsurumi asked Nimmo whether Japanese Americans in Japan would face the danger of losing their U.S. citizenship as a result of their extended stay abroad.⁴⁰ Nimmo's legal opinion, based on his research on U.S. citizenship cases, was that for Nisei in the Japanese Empire to lose their American citizenship, they would have to voluntarily forswear their allegiance to the United States. Based on Nimmo's explanation, the only realistic cause for Nisei migrants to lose U.S. citizenship would be their service in the Japanese armed forces, as it would require them to swear allegiance to the Japanese emperor.⁴¹

The Japanese Foreign Ministry's concern at this time focused mainly on Nisei men's citizenship in Japan, as their potential military records in Japan and its colonies in Asia seemed to be the only viable evidence of their voluntary expatriation.⁴² In reality, however, the number of adult Nisei in Japan in the 1920s was insignificant.⁴³ Nisei military service in Japan would become a more realistic problem once Japan entered a full-fledged war against the Allied powers during World War II and conscripted Japanese American men living in Japan, as Chapter 5 demonstrates. Many Nisei men in Japan would reach military age by then and indeed lose their U.S. citizenship as a result of their service in Japan's war against the United States.⁴⁴

It was not until the Japanese diplomats in the United States learned of Toshiko Inaba's detention on Angel Island, her appeals cases, and her eventual deportation to Japan that they finally realized that Nisei women were more likely to face the possibility of losing their U.S. citizenship and being permanently stranded in the Japanese Empire.⁴⁵ They paid close attention to the Inaba case and reported to their superiors in Tokyo on the proceedings of her appeals in U.S. District Court. At the same time, the Japanese Foreign Ministry and Home Ministry began an effort to find out more about the whereabouts of Nisei residents in Japan. In 1929 the Japanese Ministry of Foreign Affairs estimated that the number of Nisei from the contiguous United States and Hawaii in Japan had reached 30,000. This report claimed that these Nisei were present in Japan mainly for "educational purposes."⁴⁶ The Ministry of Foreign Affairs and the Home Ministry made an attempt to gather more comprehensive data in 1932. Official census reports on the number of Nisei arrived from prefectural offices based on family registries, local school enrollment records, and the estimates prepared by "overseas associations" (*kaigai kyokai*). These reports determined that the number of U.S.-born Nisei in the Japanese archipelago remained consistently between 20,000 and 30,000 in any given year since 1929.⁴⁷

What concerned the Ministry of Foreign Affairs officials more than the census data was the impact of the Nisei presence in Japan on growing anti-Japanese sentiment in the United States. In the 1930s, reports from the consuls general in California particularly alarmed the ministry officials, because leading anti-Japan and anti-immigration activists in the United States, who actively penned criticism of Japan's colonial expansion, began to make specific reference to the Nisei in Japan.[48] For instance, long after Toshiko Inaba's deportation in 1930, McClatchy thought that the Immigration Act of 1924 was not restrictive enough to stop the influx of all individuals of Japanese race.[49] McClatchy began to pay close attention to the existence of Nisei migrants in Japan and incessantly warned the American public of what he alleged was Japan's plan to dispatch "fifty thousand" Kibei—Nisei returnees from Japan—to the U.S. West Coast and Hawaii as spies. "To all intents and purposes when they return here," the Kibei were "alien Japanese immigrants who have the privileges of American citizenship," McClatchy wrote in June 1936.[50] In a widely circulated article in 1937, McClatchy claimed that the Japanese government had harbored these Nisei in Japan and indoctrinated them with the "duties and loyalty of Japanese citizenship." He argued that these Nisei would then be sent back to North America to lead Japan's effort to invade the United States by "forc[ing] entrance for her emigration." McClatchy also claimed that those Kibei already in California freely infiltrated into the Japanese American Citizens League (JACL), an emerging Nisei community and civil rights organization on the U.S. West Coast, and thus had added logistical and organizational prowess to their operation as Japanese agents.[51] In his effort to disseminate his message of warning against the alleged Kibei espionage in the United States, McClatchy effectively used his personal connections with anti-immigration groups in California as well as leading newspapers, such as the Hearst-owned *San Francisco Examiner* and his family's *Sacramento Bee*.[52]

Anti-Japanese sentiment and the negative public perception of Japanese Americans educated in Japan before World War II had far-reaching transnational consequences. McClatchy's commentaries caught the attention of not only Japanese American community newspapers in the United States but also the Japanese state-run Domei News Agency, which fed translations of McClatchy articles to local newspapers in Japan.[53] In the first half of 1937, these stories of McClatchy's anti-Kibei messages were often accompanied by a report that the U.S. government had an immediate plan to ban the return of all Japanese Americans residing in Japan. The report warned that the U.S. Congress planned to enact a bill that would require all Japanese Americans residing in Japan to register with U.S. diplomatic missions. The failure to do so would cost the Nisei in Japan the right to return to their homeland.[54] According to the San Francisco–based *Nichibei Shimbun*, Wisconsin's Democratic congressman Raymond Cannon sponsored the alleged bill "to prevent the return to the United States of thousands of American-born Japanese." Cannon's initiative had the enthusiastic "public blessings of" McClatchy, who touted the bill for offering a legal mechanism that would force Nisei migrants in Japan to "forfeit citizenship." Togo Tanaka, a noted Nisei journalist and leader of the JACL, criticized the "Cannon bill" for making "the unwarranted assumption" that Nisei in the Japanese Empire had become indoctrinated by their Japanese education.[55]

In May 1937 the Hiroshima Overseas Association reported to the director of the Japanese Foreign Ministry's American Affairs Bureau that McClatchy had written his support for such a bill. This bill would force U.S. citizens who had spent more than two years overseas without registering with the U.S. consulate to lose their citizenship.[56] This kind of report was so widely circulated by the Japanese press that the Ministry of Foreign Affairs in Tokyo soon received a number of requests for confirmation of the news, as well as for instructions to Japanese Americans living in Japan on the proper course of action. In a letter to the minister of foreign affairs on June 28, 1937, the governor of Wakayama Prefecture demanded clarification of an account in an *Osaka Mainichi Shimbun* report earlier that month on the alleged U.S. bill banning the return of Kibei to their country of birth. The paper reported that the United States had launched a legislative campaign to block the return of Japanese Americans from Japan as a response to the ongoing return migration of Kibei to the U.S. West Coast in the 1930s. The paper claimed that the Cannon bill would go into effect as early as July of that year and admonished local Nisei residents in western Japan to report to the U.S. Consulate General in Osaka to register their American citizenship and denounce any intention to seek permanent residence in Japan.[57] In Kobe, in western Japan, an emigration brokerage agency ran an advertisement offering to file registration paperwork on behalf of Nisei residents in Japan. The ad quoted a Domei News Agency

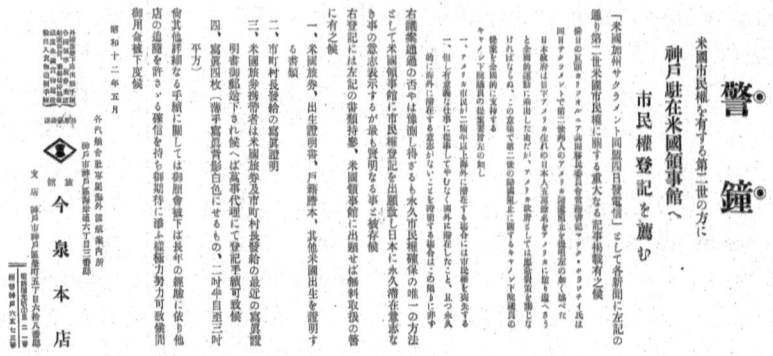

FIGURE 4 An advertisement, titled "Warning Bell," encouraging Japanese Americans in Japan to register with the U.S. consular office, May 1937.
Nikkei gaijin kankei zakken, K.1.1.0.9.3, Diplomatic Archives of the Ministry of Foreign Affairs of Japan.

report on the alleged anti-Nisei/Kibei bill and urged the Nisei in Japan to begin the process of registration with the local U.S. Consulate General.[58]

In the end, it turned out that the reports on the U.S. banning of overseas Nisei had actually started out as a rumor that spread rather quickly. A report from the Japanese consul general in Los Angeles later that year clarified the matter; no evidence was found of any immediate activism to enact such an exclusionary law.[59] However, the effect of this rumor in Japan proved significant, as it revealed the centrality of the issue of citizenship among the Nisei in Japan. The potential loss of their U.S. citizenship and the consequent expatriation of thousands of American-born Nisei would become a critical diplomatic issue at a time of growing tension between the United States and Japan. This incident also demonstrates that Japanese American residents in Japan had experiences that were deeply embedded in legal and political institutions in the United States and Japan and in the ever present anti-Japanese sentiment in the United States.

The clarification by the Japanese consul general in Los Angeles about the Cannon bill controversy, and even the repeal of the Cable Act in 1936, far from ended Nisei migrants' fear of the potential loss of their U.S. citizenship. In early 1939 about 150 Nisei residents in Japan from nine organizations under the flagship of the League of Young Japanese Americans convened in Tokyo for a special meeting. According to a Tokyo metropolitan police report, the league had organized the gathering to provide a one-day information session on Nisei citizenship. The meeting's purpose was to help ease the anxiety within the Japanese American community in Japan about the possible loss of their U.S. citizenship while residing overseas.[60]

The keynote speaker at this meeting was Tetsuichi Kurashige, a Nisei journalist who had worked in Japan for ten years. A graduate of the University of Oregon School of Law, Kurashige had written articles for the Tokyo-based *Japan Times Weekly* on the issue of Nisei migrants' citizenship. A self-proclaimed legal expert in citizenship laws, Kurashige fielded heated questions from the audience about the matter of Nisei citizenship and marriage. The speaker offered textbook answers: First, Japan's 1924 Nationality Law allowed the Nisei to choose between U.S. and Japanese citizenship; and, second, one could lose his or her U.S. citizenship by becoming a naturalized citizen of another country or by formally pledging allegiance to the government of another country. He also assured the audience by explaining that a Nisei woman would not lose her U.S. citizenship by marrying a Japanese man, because the Cable Act had long been repealed.[61]

Hardly more informative than what the Nationality Law had already stipulated, this meeting in Tokyo nevertheless showed that many Nisei in Japan had to live with varying degrees of fear that the life choices they made while living overseas might strip them of their citizenship. Almost a decade after Toshiko Inaba's deportation from San Francisco, legal measures designed to exclude Japanese immigrants still had equally significant implications on the lives of American citizens of Japanese ancestry living abroad. Furthermore, anti-Japanese activists in the United States were targeting them as the enemy. Their transpacific exodus from home far from guaranteed their complete escape from the exclusion movement in the American West.

Nisei Return Migration and Anti-Kibei Sentiment in the United States

When Nisei labor activist Goso Yoneda arrived in San Francisco on the *Shunyo Maru* in December 1926, he was "shocked and disheartened" to find himself detained on Angel Island for immigration inspection. The Glendale, California, native dreaded the possibility of being denied entry to the United States after spending thirteen years in Japan. A dual citizen at birth, he had left Japan in time to avoid being inducted into the Japanese military. As Toshiko Inaba's case demonstrated, Nisei returnees upon arrival immediately confronted the immigration gatekeepers, who closely scrutinized the integrity of their birthright citizenship. Yoneda was lucky to have escaped conscription in Japan and carried a copy of his birth certificate. In less than a month, he was free to return to his hometown.[62]

Yoneda was one of the earliest Nisei returnees from Japan, but by the eve of the Pacific War in 1941, various political and socioeconomic circumstances compelled well over 10,000 Japanese American migrants to return to the United States. Like Yoneda, some of these returnees had become fed up with Japanese imperialism in Asia and with what they viewed as increasing signs of fascism in Japan. San Francisco native Karl Ichiro Akiya, who had been a labor activist in Japan, grew resentful of Japanese militarism, so much so that he decided to return to the United States and face the system of racial oppression instead. A lifelong activist and leftist intellectual, Akiya later reflected on the impact of Japanese imperialism on his political consciousness in an interview during World War II: "It was through my experience in Japan that I dedicated my life to the emancipation of all peoples . . . and especially the common people of Japan . . . [because in Japan, I] learned the meaning of fascism and learned to fight against its oppressive measures."[63]

Moreover, numerous signs during the global economic depression throughout the 1930s indicated that the opportunities for the Nisei in the Japanese Empire were dwindling. The Tokyo-based *Japan Times Weekly* in late 1939 warned young Japanese Americans not to be fooled by the false notion that they could automatically find better jobs in Japan. "Stay west, young men," the paper admonished, because the competition for jobs in Japan for the Nisei was as fierce as it was in the United States.[64] In the summer of 1939 the students at the Keisen Girls' School found through their research project on "Nisei life" in Japan that the situation for Japanese Americans in Japan was indeed far from favorable. The school's summer class that year conducted a survey of more than 400 Japanese Americans living in Tokyo and Yokohama and produced a summary of census data in a pamphlet titled *The Nisei: A Survey of Their Educational, Vocational, and Social Problems*. The authors of the study found that, because of the language barriers and the lack of understanding in the nuances of Japanese customs, the Nisei in Japan had difficulty establishing viable careers. The study made a conclusion quite similar to the *Japan Times Weekly* assessment: that the Japanese Americans "who had been unable to find jobs elsewhere seemed to think that in Japan they would be able to find something." However, *The Nisei* writers found that most of the working Nisei who responded to the survey had "continued in the same type of work the Nisei were in" in the Japanese American community in the United States before they relocated to Japan, such as retail and farming.[65]

The Japanese American community in the United States also led an effort to bring back Nisei migrants from Japan. Mindful of the socioeconomic challenges faced by the Nisei migrants abroad and the fragility of their citizenship status, many Japanese immigrant parents in the United States urged their children to return to the United States.[66] In 1935 the Japanese Association of North America sent representatives to Japan to facilitate the effort to bring back Nisei migrants to their families back home.[67]

Those Nisei migrants who returned to the United States on the eve of the Pacific War would find themselves continuing to confront the social, political, and legal limits of their diasporic citizenship. Having dealt with the transpacific impact of V. S. McClatchy's anti-Kibei rhetoric and the Cannon bill controversy, many Nisei returnees were well aware of the racial hostility that awaited them back home. Few among them could expect the near complete ostracization of the Kibei by the U.S. government and the leaders of the Japanese American community immediately after the attack on Pearl Harbor in December 1941. As the next chapter illuminates, Kibei's transnational experiences would cast them as the most dangerous enemy aliens among Japanese Americans during World War II.

CHAPTER 3

From Citizens to Enemy Aliens

The "Kibei Problem" and Japanese American Loyalty During World War II

WHEN THE U.S. GOVERNMENT published in 1943 its official explanation for the decision to intern Americans of Japanese ancestry, few among the press and American public problematized its racist rhetoric. Titled *The Final Report: Japanese Evacuation from the West Coast, 1942* and formally authored by the U.S. Army's Western Defense commander John L. DeWitt, the document consisted of DeWitt's 1942 "Final Recommendation" to Secretary of War Henry Stimson. In the "Final Recommendation" DeWitt claimed that "the racial strains" of Japanese, including U.S.-born Nisei, were "undiluted," and he insisted that both U.S. citizens and noncitizens of Japanese ancestry were a threat to the defense of the Pacific Coast.[1]

The *Final Report* attempted to mask the recommendation's blatantly racist language by highlighting the military logic of the mass evacuation. In so doing, DeWitt used the existence of the Kibei, Nisei migrants who had returned from their sojourn to the Japanese Empire, on the West Coast to justify his view that racial strains could indeed pose a realistic problem to military objectives. Much like V. S. McClatchy's anti-Japanese writings in the 1930s, DeWitt found in the Kibei convenient scapegoats and used their education in Japan as evidence of their alleged pro-Japan attitudes. DeWitt claimed that the Kibei, despite their U.S. citizenship by birth, were a "homogeneous, unassimilated element" who possessed unbreakable "ties of . . . custom and indoctrination of the enemy" as a result of their education in Japan. He argued that Kibei's ideological contamination of the entire Japanese American community could not be overlooked.[2]

DeWitt's warning was that the significant number of militant Kibei in the Japanese community in the United States would only expedite the process of turning the rest of Japanese Americans into an army of saboteurs. This assumption of the Kibei's cultural homogeneity and imperialist indoctrination helped weave the racial and military reasoning behind the decision to intern Japanese Americans.

The presence of Kibei thus served DeWitt and other proponents of internment in the U.S. government as a justification for the "military necessity" of removing all Nisei from the West Coast without due process of law. The policymakers had to be mindful of the fact that most of the 120,000 West Coast residents of Japanese descent were U.S. citizens by birth. The government could use the alien status of the Issei as the legal basis for mass wartime incarceration. However, forced removal of American citizens, including infants and children, posed a critical question of future legal ramifications. In their debate on the means and necessity of mass evacuation of citizens, military and federal authorities had to find a way to avoid the high court's potential ruling of the internment as unconstitutional. The *Final Report*'s depiction of Kibei as de facto Japanese nationals and dangerous enemies offered the military wing of the government a rationale to advance its "military necessity" argument for the mass incarceration of U.S. citizens. Because there was no hard evidence of Nisei's potential role as Japanese saboteurs, labeling the Kibei as a dangerous pro-Japan element would allow the proponents of internment to argue that all American citizens of Japanese ancestry could be a national security threat.

Such extreme distrust of the Kibei would shape the debate on Japanese American loyalty to the U.S. government and, ultimately, U.S. policies on internment throughout the war. Both as a subset of the Nisei and as a separate identity, the Kibei became scapegoats as a disloyal element and a symbol of anti-American sentiment in the internment camps. When the War Relocation Authority's civilian administrators, headed by Dillon S. Myer, took over the management of the internment camps in the summer of 1942, they devoted considerable effort to policing and rehabilitating the Kibei in the camps.

What Myer described as the "Kibei problem" also shaped the politics in the Japanese American community throughout the war. The Nisei leaders of the Japanese American Citizens League (JACL), who emerged as the most prominent voice representing the Japanese American community during the war by actively cooperating with the War Relocation Authority (WRA), also targeted the Kibei as scapegoats. The mass incarceration exacerbated the ostracization of Kibei in the Japanese American community. Since the attack on Pearl Harbor in December 1941, some JACL leaders, such as Mike M. Masaoka, Ken Matsumoto, and Fred Tayama, had worked vigorously to police the thoughts and behaviors of the Kibei within the community in their effort to promote the image of the rest of the Nisei as loyal Americans. Even after this effort failed to prevent the mass incarceration of Japanese Americans, many JACL members continued to use the image of disloyal and troublemaking Kibei as the antithesis of Americanized Nisei in order to shape the image of most of the Japanese Americans in the camps as patriotic citizens.

This representation of Kibei as outsiders among the Americanized Nisei would continue to ostracize them for decades after the war. Both postwar scholarship and public discourse on the wartime incarceration of Japanese Americans have grappled with the issue of locating the proper place of the Japanese American internment and various notions of Nisei Americanism. From the sociological studies of the camps by researchers hired by the U.S. government to JACL accounts of Nisei patriotism to scholar-activists' analyses of Nisei resistance in the camps, historians of the Japanese American incarceration have produced some of the most thoroughly researched and debated scholarship in Asian American studies.[3] Remarkably, despite numerous commentaries related to the Kibei in both U.S. government and JACL documents throughout the war, the voices of individual Kibei remain a relatively untouched subject in the scholarship. The national historical narrative that claims the loyalty of Japanese Americans to the U.S. government has had little room for the perspectives of transnational individuals like the Kibei during World War II.

The prevailing image of Nisei as loyal Americans and patriotic victims of racism has shaped the dominant historical memory of the Japanese American internment. However, what buttressed that loyalty is the description of the Kibei as a "problem" during the war. The war between the United States and Japan exacerbated Kibei's struggle for acceptance by their country of birth and by their own community. However, just as the Kibei are not a culturally and economically homogeneous group, their wartime experiences also varied significantly. To say that all Kibei went through the same internment experience would betray the diversity inherent in their transnational experiences.

In this chapter I explore the wartime mass incarceration of Japanese Americans in the United States as a critical extension of a Japanese American diaspora. The history of Kibei internment experiences is as complex as the history of the World War II Japanese American incarceration as a whole. Many Kibei internees actively cooperated with the JACL and the WRA's campaign to promote the loyal Nisei image. For various political and personal reasons, some Kibei even volunteered to serve as informants for camp authorities and intelligence agencies. The exemplary service of Kibei volunteers and draftees in the U.S. Army between 1943 and 1945 defied the previously unchallenged notion of their Japanese nationalism and further complicated the WRA and JACL's dealings with the question of Kibei loyalty. By analyzing the perspectives of the parties involved in the debate on that key aspect of Nisei loyalty—government authorities and social scientists, JACL leaders, and many individual Kibei themselves—I examine how the Kibei emerged as a political and cultural construct that transformed the issue of wartime loyalty from a "Japanese problem" to a "Kibei problem."

From the "Japanese Problem" to the "Kibei Problem"

In 1942 the general consensus among the U.S. intelligence community was that DeWitt more or less based his intelligence work on public hysteria and political pressure to remove individuals of Japanese ancestry from the West Coast. On February 1, 1942, FBI director J. Edgar Hoover told Attorney General Francis Biddle that the Western Defense Command's intelligence activities were "disorganized" and "incapable" and were swayed largely by wartime racial hysteria and "lack of judgment."[4] Hoover's report to Biddle two days later again discredited DeWitt's proposed mass incarceration as a solution to the "Japanese problem." Hoover argued that California state and local officials' demand for removal of Japanese and Japanese Americans put immense pressure on the movement for an executive order. Moreover, Hoover noted that fierce anti-Japanese sentiments expressed by media commentators also played an equal role in putting pressure on the military's involvement in devising a plan to evacuate all Japanese Americans from the West Coast.[5] Even some senior-ranking army generals later criticized DeWitt's intelligence unit (the G-2) for relying on political pressure instead of factual data. Major General Joseph W. Stillwell viewed DeWitt's

G-2 as "just another amateur, like all the rest of the staff [of the Western Defense Command]."[6]

Public pressure in favor of the mass evacuation of Japanese Americans was indeed mounting in early 1942. Anti-immigrant organizations in California seized the post–Pearl Harbor hysteria as an opportune moment to fulfill their decades-long effort to expel the Japanese from the West Coast. The California Farm Bureau Federation and local chapters of the Native Sons and Daughters of the Golden West swiftly passed resolutions in support of mass incarceration as a way to remove "the ethnic Japanese from the coast." Politicians also took active measures to aid the mass removal of Japanese Americans. In February 1942 Los Angeles City and County offices fired all Japanese American public employees and called for removal of all Japanese from the West Coast. Prominent West Coast political leaders, including California attorney general and future champion of civil rights Earl Warren, endorsed the removal of Japanese and Japanese Americans from the state.[7]

Those in the intelligence field who did not agree with the "military necessity" argument for mass evacuation downplayed the "Japanese problem" and the idea of "undiluted" Japanese "racial strain." Lieutenant Commander Kenneth D. Ringle of the Office of Naval Intelligence in Los Angeles reported to the chief of naval operations in January 1942 that "[at] least seventy-five percent [of Nisei] are loyal to the United States." Ringle also stated that "the large majority" of the Japanese-born Issei were "at least passively loyal to the United States."[8] Ringle supported the findings of the State Department's "Special Representative" Curtis B. Munson, who insisted in his intelligence reports to President Franklin Roosevelt's confidant John Franklin Carter that the "Japanese problem" on the West Coast bore little to no significance.[9] Ringle insisted that "the entire 'Japanese problem' has been magnified out of its true proportion."[10] The Justice Department's director of the Alien Enemy Control Unit, Edward J. Ennis, wrote a memo to the solicitor general in April 1943 in which he suggested that the navy maintained its opposition to mass internment because of its distrust in the Western Defense Command's intelligence capability. In explaining the navy's intelligence view, Ennis cited Ringle's October 1942 article in *Harper's Magazine* that once again disputed the military necessity of the internment and the Japanese problem.[11]

However, in a striking resemblance to DeWitt's amateur intelligence, reports that rejected the Japanese problem nevertheless stuck to the idea that any fifth-column threat would be caused largely by the Nisei educated in Japan. Ringle warned that those Kibei who had spent their childhood in Japan and returned to the United States were "the most potentially dangerous element of all." He even suggested that the Japanese government could have sent these Kibei back to the United States to perform espionage. Although Ringle saw the Japanese problem as no more serious than "the problems of German, Italian, and Communistic portions" in the United States, he was determined that the Kibei in Southern California should be categorized as "enemy aliens" subject to "custodial detention." Ringle's recommendations did not include the mass incarceration of all Japanese Americans. Instead, he recommended detention of "potentially dangerous United States citizens . . . as well as aliens" based on individual case reports submitted by military and naval intelligence officers and the Department of Justice. Instead of singling out Japanese Americans, Ringle's suggested list of U.S. citizens "dangerous to the internal security" included "dangerous Kibei or German, Italian, or other subversive sympathizers and agitators."[12] Thus Ringle's report effectively singled out the Kibei among Japanese Americans as a pro-Axis element that posed the greatest security threat.

Ennis again confirmed Ringle's view that "the only important group of dangerous Japanese were the Kibei." Ennis concluded that the navy intelligence officers' recommendations included evacuation of only three groups from the Japanese American community: the Kibei, the parents of Kibei, and members of pro-Japanese or militarist organizations.[13] Despite their differences, both DeWitt and leading intelligence officers identified the Kibei as the primary group to be rounded up and placed in confinement as enemy aliens. The dominant prewar image of Kibei as a pro-Japan subgroup among Nisei thus compelled even those in the U.S. government who opposed the mass incarceration of Japanese Americans to accept the notion of Kibei as a potential fifth column without much criticism.

Instead of challenging this public indictment of Kibei's alleged loyalty to Japan, many Japanese American community leaders chose to cooperate with the U.S. government's ostracization of the Kibei. By early 1942, the JACL's national vice president and Los Angeles–based leader Ken Matsumoto had established a "close-working relationship" with Ringle.[14] In the wake of Pearl Harbor on December 7, 1941, the JACL leaders used fervently nationalistic rhetoric to seek approval of white Americans and dissociated themselves from Issei and Kibei to win the favor of the U.S. government.

As Michi Weglyn has noted, the JACL at the start of the war was a "politically unsophisticated and neophyte" group that was under the shadow of Issei leadership. Within hours after the attack on Pearl Harbor, federal law enforcement and immigration authorities rounded up Japanese immigrant leaders in California under the suspicion of fifth-column activities and detained them in U.S. Justice Department detention centers. The JACL leaders seized the volatile moment as an opportunity to supplant the Issei leadership and establish themselves as the representatives of all Japanese Americans.[15]

Nisei elites took measures to cooperate with the FBI, the Office of Naval Intelligence, and other federal and local government agencies in identifying potential saboteurs in the Japanese American community. On December 7, forty-eight leading Nisei leaders of the JACL's Southern District Council in Los Angeles established their Anti-Axis Committee. To demonstrate Nisei's loyalty to the United States, the committee deliberately policed and monitored the activities of the Japanese American community and furnished the authorities with a list of any potentially subversive individuals and organizations.[16]

Among the Japanese American groups targeted by JACL leaders were thousands of Kibei who had resettled on the West Coast since their return from Japan. Because of Kibei's transnational education and their perceived ties to Japan, the Anti-Axis Committee members identified the mere existence of Kibei in the Los Angeles area as a potential threat to their loyalty campaign. Regardless of Kibei's social and economic backgrounds or the varied amounts of time spent away from the United States, the committee regarded all Nisei returnees from Japan as a group that needed to be actively policed. The influential chair, Fred Tayama, was instrumental in the Anti-Axis Committee's deliberate targeting of all Kibei in the Los Angeles area. On December 9, 1941, two days after Pearl Harbor, Tayama decided that the committee would raise the question of loyalty among all Kibei members of the JACL and "help them where they see fit."[17]

On December 12, the Anti-Axis Committee summoned David Akira Itami, vice president of the JACL Los Angeles Chapter's Kibei Division and a columnist for the Japanese American newspaper *Kashu Mainichi*. The committee members informed Itami of their intention to assist law enforcement and military authorities and demanded complete cooperation of the JACL's Kibei members.[18] The committee demanded that Itami deliver the Anti-Axis Committee's message to all Kibei Division members, calling for their "complete severance of connection with Japan."[19] Itami and his colleagues at the Kibei Division pledged to "work for the ultimate victory of the United States." At an emergency meeting ten days later, the Kibei Division leaders also passed a resolution to "abolish" the term *Kibei* so that "no differentiation be made among loyal citizens." Moreover, as a demonstration of their sincerity, all Kibei leaders resigned from their positions in the division, surrendered the remaining balance of their financial account, and urged their fellow members to join the Anti-Axis Committee.[20]

However, the Kibei Division leaders' pledge of loyalty proved to be of no avail. In the following month, Fred Tayama and the Anti-Axis Committee decided to turn over the list of all Kibei members of the JACL's Los Angeles Chapter along with names of "pro-Japanese Kibei leaders" to Chief Special Agent Richard Hood of the FBI in Los Angeles.[21] Harry Ueno, a Hawaii-born Kibei who would emerge as a leader of the Mess Hall Workers Union at the Manzanar War Relocation Center, was still embittered more than fifty years after the war by Fred Tayama and the Anti-Axis Committee's wartime cooperation: "People should help their own people. Instead, they betray[ed] their own people."[22] The Anti-Axis Committee's betrayal of the JACL's Kibei members demonstrates just how far the JACL was willing to go to establish their position as the representative voice of the community and gain the trust of white authorities.

Nisei leaders' effort to single out the Kibei did not stop there. In February 1942 the JACL National Headquarters issued a "Kibei survey" and directed each regional chapter to collect responses from local Kibei residents. Seattle's *Japanese American Courier* published the survey on February 20, claiming that the questionnaire would help the JACL provide "assistance" to West Coast Kibei.[23] In Denver the *Rocky Nippon* also obliged the JACL's request to feature the survey prominently in both the Japanese and English editions of the paper, assuring the area Kibei that "every cooperation on their part will serve to insure their welfare."[24] However, as the survey's heading suggested, the foremost purpose that the JACL leaders seemed to have in mind was "the interests of Americanism."[25] The JACL's influential national leader, Mike M. Masaoka, insisted that the survey was "a purely voluntary one," but he also warned in a press release that his organization would closely scrutinize the loyalty of any Kibei who failed to complete the questionnaire. "Certain inferences may be made against you," Masaoka admonished "all Kibei." He emphasized that the JACL would determine "the degree of your loyalty to the United States" on the basis of "the degree of your cooperation" with the JACL's "voluntary" Kibei survey. The JACL's national office also warned each local JACL chapter that a failure to administer the Kibei survey would be "reported to the authorities."[26]

The questions on the Kibei survey looked tailor-made for a report that could be readily furnished to the FBI. The twenty-two questions on the survey solicited detailed personal information about individual Kibei that could help gauge the level of each respondent's cultural and ideological connection to Japan. The survey asked respondents to identify their occupation, age, total number of trips to Japan, and number of years spent in that country. It also asked for details on the respondents' educational experiences in both the United States and Japan. Designed specifically to probe the evidence of male respondents' past and present national allegiance, the survey asked them to list their military service records—years of service, rank, unit, and location—in the United States and Japan. The survey then asked Kibei respondents to list their past and present membership and rank in Japanese religious, prefectural, social, or political organizations. Finally, the survey asked respondents to disclose their dual citizenship.[27] In this way, the Kibei survey of early 1942 served as a lesser-known prelude to the following year's loyalty questionnaire administered by the WRA, which all incarcerated Japanese and Japanese Americans were required to complete by the summer of 1943 in order to become eligible for release from the internment camps.

The JACL's extreme measure of cooperation with the authorities, including their submission of the list of Kibei in Los Angeles, did little to stop the U.S. government's decision to remove all individuals of Japanese ancestry from the Pacific Coast. Secretary of War Henry Stimson successfully lobbied for mass removal of Japanese Americans from the West Coast as an operation under a military command, and Roosevelt's February 19 Executive Order 9066 authorized Stimson to redraw "military areas" and control movements of "any or all persons." Within one month, forced evacuation began and Japanese American leaders pledged full cooperation. Mike M. Masaoka, who avoided wartime incarceration for living outside the "evacuation zone" on the West Coast, led the JACL from Salt Lake City, Utah, during the war. He continued to lobby the U.S. government on behalf of the 120,000 Japanese American internees to accept their loyalty to America.

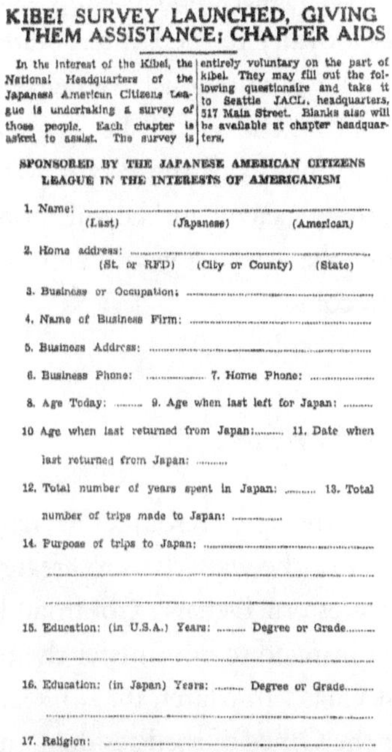

KIBEI SURVEY LAUNCHED, GIVING THEM ASSISTANCE; CHAPTER AIDS

In the interest of the Kibei, the National Headquarters of the Japanese American Citizens League is undertaking a survey of those people. Each chapter is asked to assist. The survey is entirely voluntary on the part of kibei. They may fill out the following questionaire and take it to Seattle JACL, headquarters, 517 Main Street. Blanks also will be available at chapter headquarters.

SPONSORED BY THE JAPANESE AMERICAN CITIZENS LEAGUE IN THE INTERESTS OF AMERICANISM

1. Name: .... (Last) (Japanese) (American)
2. Home address: .... (St. or RFD) (City or County) (State)
3. Business or Occupation: ....
4. Name of Business Firm: ....
5. Business Address: ....
6. Business Phone: .... 7. Home Phone: ....
8. Age Today: .... 9. Age when last left for Japan: ....
10. Age when last returned from Japan: .... 11. Date when last returned from Japan: ....
12. Total number of years spent in Japan: .... 13. Total number of trips made to Japan: ....
14. Purpose of trips to Japan: ....
15. Education: (in U.S.A.) Years: .... Degree or Grade.........
16. Education: (in Japan) Years: .... Degree or Grade.........
17. Religion: ....
18. Military Experience: (in U. S. A.) years: .... Rank.......... Branch.................... Where....................
19. Military Experience: (in Japan) years: .... Rank.......... Branch.................... Where....................
20. Selective Service Order No.............. Classification.............. .... Board No. ....
21. Hobbies: ....
22. Organization membership in past five years (church, Japanese associations, Kenjinkais, Seinenkais, etc. Whether now disbanded or not. If you were an officer in any of them, state the office held and the year, after the name of the organization) ....
23. Dual Citizen. Yes ( ) No ( ) Don't Know ( )

I, THE UNDERSIGNED, do hereby state that the above given statements are true and correct.

.... (Signature)

ATTEST: .... Chapter.

By ....

FIGURE 5 The Kibei Survey. *Japanese American Courier*, February 20, 1942.

The JACL's scare tactics forced the Kibei into the position of demonstrating even stronger manifestations of loyalty than the rest of the Japanese American community. Even these efforts proved far from effective in transforming the prevailing image of the Kibei as the cultural other among the Nisei. In the months before the mass removal of Japanese Americans in 1942, identifying the Kibei among the West Coast Nisei became central to the JACL's campaign to promote Nisei loyalty to the United States. Emerging Nisei leaders such as Masaoka and Tayama might have believed that a sacrifice forced on the Kibei would improve the fate of the Japanese American community during the critical early weeks of the Pacific War. However, the Nisei loyalty campaign would only exacerbate the alienation and stigmatization of many Kibei throughout the war and would embitter many more in the community in the years to come.

The War Relocation Authority and the "Kibei Problem"

The Department of War had no intention of devoting its resources to managing the internment camps for the remainder of the war. Plans to create a new civilian agency were under way as the Western Defense Command's Wartime Civilian Control Administration continued to administer the removal of Japanese Americans from the West Coast. In March 1942, Executive Order 9102 established the WRA under the Office of the President and appointed Milton Eisenhower as its director.[28] Pressure from West Coast politicians and Mountain state governors to ban evacuees from relocating out of the camps forced Eisenhower to manage the internment as long-term detention.[29] However, when Dillon S. Myer took over as director in the summer of 1942, the focus shifted to resettling Japanese Americans. Throughout the war years, Myer insisted that the goal of the WRA was to successfully relocate Japanese Americans from the internment camps back into American society. In his view, the WRA's ten war relocation centers would serve as safe temporary facilities that would "assimilate" Japanese American internees and prepare them to rejoin postwar America. By 1944 Myer was confident in the Nisei's ability to prove themselves as loyal Americans: "I have more faith . . . in the strength of our American institutions. And I feel positive that they have been far more influential in molding the minds of the nisei than the transplanted institutions of Japan."[30]

Driven by his paternalistic idealism, Myer was determined to use his WRA directorship to build his legacy as a civilian administrator who helped assimilate the Japanese in the United States into patriotic Americans. He also fancied himself an educator and operated the WRA camps as social science laboratories for the rehabilitation of Japanese Americans to mold them into a model minority. In developing and evaluating WRA policies, Myer frequently referenced government-sponsored studies in the camps to highlight the internment program as a scientifically proven success. The WRA created the Community Analysis Section (CAS) to assess grievances among the internees in each relocation center. More important, the CAS ethnographers, many of whom were academics with advanced degrees, evaluated and reported on "what the evacuees are thinking on all subjects."[31] The WRA even used the studies conducted by researchers on its payroll to claim that the agency had helped assimilate most Kibei, whom the agency had regarded as the "most acute 'problem group.'"[32]

Prominent camp researchers after the war largely confirmed the positive role of fieldworkers in shaping Myer's academic approach to managing the internment experiment. Anthropologist Edward Spicer, who headed the CAS, suggested that the knowledge and insight of community analysts helped bridge WRA administrators and Japanese American internees.[33] Impressed by Myer's successful "assimilation" project at the WRA, the Truman administration appointed him director of the Federal Public Housing Authority in 1946 and then commissioner of the Bureau of Indian Affairs in 1950. From 1950 to 1953 Myer would spearhead the "termination" program aimed at Native American "assimilation" and "self-sufficiency" by withdrawing federal responsibility from Indian Nations and liquidating native lands. Myer's termination program would have a devastating effect on the integrity of indigenous communities, forcing many Native Americans to relocate from reservations to major urban centers throughout the 1950s.[34]

During the war, JACL leader Mike M. Masaoka's ideal of Nisei assimilation and acceptance found a congenial partner in Myer. A well-connected political lobbyist, Masaoka was instrumental in shaping the JACL's version of the history of Japanese American internment. Throughout the postwar years Masaoka maintained his view that the JACL's wartime policy served the best interests of his community. He proudly told the members of Congress during the hearings on evacuation claims in 1954 that the JACL should be credited for evoking a "generally cooperative attitude assumed by almost every evacuee." Masaoka deployed the Asian American model-minority thesis to emphasize that Japanese American internees' "attitude that bordered on submissiveness" was superior to any "other racial or minority group in the United States."[35] Throughout the war Masaoka and other JACL leaders urged Japanese Americans to prove their loyalty by cooperating with the government's wartime policy. Masaoka declared that the JACL's aspiration was to prove the "assimilation and Americanization of all Japanese Americans." He was determined to convince the American public of Nisei "allegiance through active participation in the war effort."[36]

By the time Myer became the WRA director, JACL members in the internment camps had already been actively liaising between the authorities and the evacuees.[37] With many Issei community leaders incarcerated in the Department of Justice detention centers, Masaoka and the JACL leaders were eager to assert their political leadership and used their campaign to restore the rights of Japanese Americans as a way to emerge from the shadow of Issei leaders.[38] Myer's awareness of the Kibei problem was influenced largely by his relationship with the JACL's leaders, who had identified the Kibei as a threat in their campaign to promote the loyal Nisei image. To both Myer and the JACL, reducing the "Japanese problem" to a "Kibei problem" was of paramount interest to their political goals.

What Myer described as the Kibei problem would emerge as an issue that shaped the WRA's policies of confinement and relocation from mid-1942 to early 1946.[39] He was determined to prove his agency's ability to mold the Japanese American character and struggled with the question of what to do with the Kibei.[40] Myer faced pressure from the military to segregate the Kibei from the rest of the Nisei before the transfer of evacuees from the Western Defense Command to the WRA was completed on October 31, 1942. DeWitt, in his letter to George C. Marshall, the army chief of staff, on August 23, 1942, warned that the "co-mingling" of the Kibei with the rest of the Nisei would expose all Japanese Americans to "Japanese indoctrination." DeWitt reiterated his point in the *Final Report* by asserting that the Kibei remained a threat to national security and to "large numbers" of loyal Nisei. He believed that the task of separating the Kibei from the rest of the evacuees could be achieved by the WRA's collaboration with "cooperative Nisei" informants to identify Kibei in the camps. DeWitt believed that segregation of the Kibei would become necessary in the absence of military supervision after the Western Defense Command's complete release of its jurisdiction over Japanese American internees. He went further by not only recommending that all Kibei be segregated in a separate facility but also stripping them of their U.S. citizenship "through appropriate legal processes or means" under the direction of the Department of Justice.[41]

In August 1942 former JACL Anti-Axis Committee chair Fred Tayama, who had submitted a list of all Kibei JACL members to the federal authorities in January 1942, began fulfilling that role of "cooperative Nisei" by spying on the Kibei in the internment camps.[42] "Recorded by memory the following morning," Tayama prepared a report on a "Kibei meeting" chaired by Ben Kishi in a Manzanar War Relocation Center mess hall on the evening of August 8, 1942. Tayama described remarks made at the meeting on the poor camp conditions as unsolicited complaints. The report began with a description of Raymond Hirai's demands for more doctors, a school for children, and better food. Hirai also demanded union wages for internees who made camouflage nets for the army. To Tayama, perhaps Hirai's most defiant remark was a demand for greater "self-government" for internees by "re-election of all Block Leaders." Tayama's report also claimed that a Hawaiian-born Kibei who had spent thirty years in Japan likened his situation to having been "thrown in this dump like pigs." Then Hirai took the microphone again and proclaimed, according to Tayama, that camouflage work should belong only to the Kibei and that other Nisei workers should be encouraged to quit.[43]

Tayama once again demonstrated his full cooperation with U.S. authorities by submitting his report on the Kibei meeting to the FBI. He then sent the same report on "some dangerous element here within the camp" to Major Richard E. Rudisill of the Office of Naval Intelligence in Los Angeles, urging the office to launch an investigation on the activities of Kibei internees at Manzanar. Karl Goso Yoneda, an influential Kibei communist and labor organizer, also served as an informant at the meeting, which he described in his report as "definitely pro-Axis and anti American." At the meeting, Yoneda's short speech, which was dismissive of a Kibei gathering, was met with a near collective accusation of him being an American and communist spy. After the meeting, Yoneda and Tayama were threatened by a gang of Kibei men led by Ben Kishi, who accused them of being *inu* (dogs), or traitors. The fact that Yoneda himself was a Kibei only added to these Kibei men's indignation toward his "American" disposition.[44] James Oda, a fellow communist Kibei cooperator who was also present at the meeting, believed that the gathering was part of an effort by Kishi and others "with Japanese disposition" to win support of all Kibei at Manzanar.[45]

The conflict between the JACL members and their vocal Kibei critics was enough evidence for military leaders to push for segregation of the Kibei and others sharing any "pro-Japan" sentiment. On October 30, 1942, as the army was transferring the last evacuees to the WRA's ten relocation centers, Assistant Secretary of War John J. McCloy told Myer that the War Department had been alerted of the movement at some camps that might interfere with "the prompt rehabilitation" of the internees. The Kibei and Issei at some internment camps, McCloy stressed, were attempting to "exert heavy pressure on the Nisei" who were "well-disposed toward America." McCloy warned Myer that the War Department would be ready to deploy troops to internment camps in the event of disturbance. To prevent such an "unwelcome" situation, McCloy urged Myer to "deal at once" with the Kibei and other like-minded individuals by planning segregation.[46]

As early as the summer of 1942, the WRA's top administrators also considered favorably the idea of separating the Kibei population from the rest of the Japanese American internees. However, despite the pressure to swiftly deal with the Kibei problem from the JACL, the War Department, and even his own staff, Myer was hesitant to brand such a significant portion of Japanese Americans disloyal and segregate them.[47] Also, rather than military intelligence, Myer placed more trust in his CAS social science experts who monitored the attitudes of the Japanese American internees. Throughout the internment years, Myer turned to the CAS to study Kibei behaviors and attitudes and simultaneously to promote Nisei loyalty.

The CAS reports from 1942 served this purpose by identifying and designating a separate categorization of "pro-Japan" constituents from the rest of the internees. Although the CAS researchers proposed their fieldwork as the basis for policy improvement, they were limited by their own misunderstanding of the Kibei, particularly in their disregard of how the Kibei had been mistreated by the government and the leaders of the Japanese American community since Pearl Harbor.[48] These reports suggested that most of the Japanese American internees were anti-Axis, but they identified adult male "bachelor" Kibei as a group mostly sympathetic to the Japanese Empire. The WRA defined a bachelor Kibei as a man, regardless of his marital status, who had spent "a total of three or more years in Japan since January 1, 1935."[49] Rather than targeting all Kibei, the WRA's focus throughout the rest of the war would be on this gender- and age-specific group of Kibei. Such an attempt to identify and police a problem group from the larger Nisei population was reminiscent of the JACL's singling out of the Kibei after Pearl Harbor as a group that could tarnish the image of loyal Nisei.

Anthropologist and Japan expert John F. Embree led the CAS's effort to study and monitor Kibei thoughts and behaviors in the internment camps. In his first report, "Dealing with Japanese Americans," in October 1942, Embree determined that the internees were generally divided along generational lines in their acclaim of Japanese and U.S. war efforts. As a social scientist, however, Embree warned against swift generalization. He suggested that some Issei who were educated in the United States were more "American in point of view." "Probably," Embree suggested, "many Kibei are culturally Japanese, but by no means all." He posited that those Kibei educated in Japan for "several years and since 1935," including "old bachelors," were mostly likely pro-Japan. These Kibei, according to Embree, were markedly pro-Axis as a result of their education during the years when Japan was moving increasingly toward militarism.⁵⁰ Myer enthusiastically endorsed Embree's report claiming that not all Kibei were necessarily pro-Japan and distributed it to all relocation centers. He encouraged the WRA staff to use Embree's findings on the cultural and racial characteristics of the subgroups within the Japanese American population to design programs aimed at educating and rehabilitating the Kibei.⁵¹

If Embree's report gave Myer a reason to postpone removing all Kibei from the rest of the internees, another CAS report the following summer provided an even more encouraging result that convinced Myer that his assimilation project might work for the Kibei. In the section titled "Are the Nisei Assimilated?" the report suggested that Kibei's education in Japan was not of their own choosing but a result of their parents' desire to "impart" Japanese culture and values to their children. The report claimed that a similar desire for cultural education existed in other immigrant communities. More "privileged" immigrant groups, such as Irish Americans and French Canadians, did not have to send their children to the mother countries because they were able to attend "special 'nationality' schools" in North America. The report asserted that the lack of such privilege forced Japanese American children to embark on their "educational pilgrimage," which had little to do with indoctrination or Kibei's unwillingness to "adopt American ways." The report emphasized that Japanese Americans' "acquisition of American traits" was well documented in studies and that any notion of their inferior assimilation was a "false impression."⁵²

Helping the assimilating process of the most problematic group—adult Kibei—then became one of the most important components of the WRA's overall assimilation project. English classes for Kibei started throughout the relocation centers. The Adult Education Department at the Poston War Relocation Center opened its English classes in October 1942.[53] The Tule Lake War Relocation Center announced its plans to accommodate students with special needs—classes for those "suffering from physical handicaps" and English classes for adult Kibei—in the fall of 1942.[54] The WRA also offered "Americanization classes" to educate adult Issei and Kibei on the culture and customs of the United States to better prepare them for resettlement in American society.[55]

Despite these efforts, the results of the CAS studies were not unanimously assuring. A CAS study in July 1943 reported Kibei's general unwillingness to assimilate on the WRA's terms. This study indicated that Issei and Kibei internees were consistently uninterested in the WRA's adult education program designed specifically for them, including "Americanization classes" called "Understanding America" and "Preparation for Relocation."[56] The conductors of this study seemed puzzled by the disinterest in the Americanization program among the Issei and Kibei. The researchers, however, overlooked the WRA administrators' assumption that a special indoctrination program was needed to Americanize the Kibei, no matter how long they had been back from Japan. This attitude also disregarded Kibei's U.S. citizenship, as the WRA hardly made a distinction between Kibei and Issei, who were Japanese citizens ineligible for naturalization, when designing the Americanization program. To many WRA staff members, most Kibei largely remained perpetual foreigners in the Nisei community. In September 1943 Heart Mountain's English classes for "foreigners" continued to look for Issei and Kibei enrollees.[57] Such attitudes reflected the popular assumption among the WRA staff about Kibei's unassimilability and, ultimately, their disloyalty, as many WRA employees continued to regard the Kibei as the "most dangerous" group.[58]

"Redemption of Kibei"

In February 1943 the WRA required all adult evacuees to complete what was popularly known as the loyalty questionnaire as proof of their readiness for permanent relocation out of the internment camps. Designed initially to register male internees for military service, this program was adopted by the WRA in an attempt to punctuate Japanese American assimilation and loyalty. Myer hoped that positive results of registration would accelerate the loyal evacuees' release from the relocation centers and acceptance by the general American public.[59] Optimism among many Japanese Americans was also high. The WRA staff and JACL members at Tule Lake expected the vast majority of the adult population to sign the loyalty questionnaire.[60] However, questions 27 and 28 on the questionnaire proved to be problematic, as they asked citizens and noncitizens, male and female, young and old, for their willingness to serve in the U.S. military and to swear "unqualified allegiance" to the United States by renouncing any loyalty to the Japanese emperor.[61] Japanese American reactions to these questions varied, from confusion to outrage to enthusiastic support. To Myer's surprise and dismay, the loyalty questionnaire sparked unrest at a number of camps.

Although some internees answered no to one or both of these questions and others refused to answer at all, many "loyal" Nisei and WRA administrators had the impression that the Kibei were leading the charge to resist and sabotage the registration program.[62] Indeed, a few Kibei adamantly opposed registration, but such a wide belief in the Kibei's role in instigating trouble did not emerge out of a vacuum. The term *Kibei* had come to carry such a negative connotation that it was not uncommon for JACL-oriented Nisei to use it as an adjective to camp agitations. Embree documented that at the Topaz War Relocation Center in Utah, the most vocal opposition to registration came from a group of Kibei. According to his report, these Kibei attempted to persuade other internees to vote for a "fight for civil rights" before registering. Only the camp director's invocation of the Espionage Act prevented the vote.[63]

This incident further intensified the widespread mistrust of the Kibei in the internment camps. Moreover, what seemed to be the Kibei-led obstruction of the registration program compounded the WRA's notion of Kibei disloyalty. A group of patriotic Nisei who called themselves Young Democrats complained to Embree that many Kibei were "misrepresenting" the majority opinion about registration at Topaz. The Young Democrats told Embree that the Kibei's "fight for civil rights" was nothing more than an attempt to disturb the registration process because the Kibei had no will to fight against Japan. Other Nisei accused the Kibei gang of being cowards who feared becoming combat casualties.[64]

There were also reports that violent attacks on JACL members by troublemakers intensified during the registration period.[65] Although there were diverse groups of Issei and Nisei resisters in the camps, the Kibei became synonymous with disturbance. JACL members were quick to blame the Kibei for leading any violent camp incident, calling one event a "typical Kibei attack from the rear with a lead pipe."[66] Eric L. Muller has found that a half-century since the conclusion of the war, many elderly JACL members have continued to express their suspicion of those who opposed the registration program. According to Muller, some Nisei critics of resistance continue to believe that any attempt to interfere with registration was an act of "laziness" and "cowardice."[67] Disturbances during the registration also led many WRA staff members to perceive all Kibei as "citizens in name only," who had "almost nothing in common with other second generation Japanese Americans."[68]

As resistance to registration continued, the WRA began to consider more seriously the immediate segregation of "disloyal" internees and to devise a way to separate troublemakers from the rest of the Japanese American population. In July 1943 the WRA announced its segregation plan. Myer stated that the program was designed to ensure the safety of "loyal American citizens and law-abiding aliens" in the relocation centers and to expedite the process of preparing them for post-internment resettlement.[69] Masaoka and the JACL enthusiastically endorsed the segregation policy, which would isolate the "agitators from those who wanted to cooperate with the government."[70] In general, the WRA staff viewed the segregation program as a "means to weeding out potentially dangerous people," including the Kibei.[71] The distrust of the Kibei was so severe that when the segregation program was announced, rumors began to circulate among the internees that all Kibei would be relocated to the Tule Lake Segregation Center in California. The expectation among many WRA staff members on the complete segregation of the Kibei was high. They believed that the segregation of disloyal internees would help alleviate the difficulty of supervising these alleged troublemakers.[72]

And the Kibei were indeed high on the WRA's priority list of disloyal internees who would be transferred to Tule Lake in September 1943. The WRA's administrative instruction issued in July 1943 stipulated the agency's tentative plan on the "separation of evacuees of doubtful loyalty from loyal evacuees."⁷³ The instruction designated "bachelor Kibei" among the disloyal internees who would depart for Tule Lake before "all others" to join those who had applied for repatriation or expatriation.⁷⁴

However, the WRA would reverse its policy in August and eliminate the Kibei category in its official publication explaining the segregation policy, instead using the neutral term "persons."⁷⁵ Myer and WRA administrators had to consider that, despite the negative public perception of the Kibei, it was becoming increasingly difficult for them to cast all Kibei as potential troublemakers. To the ever-paternalistic Myer, who wanted to be remembered by Japanese Americans as a "great white father," Embree's February 1943 report from Topaz included an encouraging episode. The report suggested that with the help of supportive white authority, the Kibei could overcome their difference from other Nisei. Embree found a "very significant development" in Kibei attitudes. He noted that a young Topaz Kibei accused by other Nisei of "misrepresenting" the majority attitude toward registration "brought himself to cooperate with the very government he had attacked." This change in the young man's heart occurred after he met with Embree, to whom he expressed his bitterness and resentment of the WRA. After consultation with Embree, the young Kibei ceased to display militant behaviors and became more "reasonable." Embree called this therapeutic event a "redemption of a Kibei," an important revelation that demonstrated the Kibei's capability to become cooperative and, ultimately, assimilated.⁷⁶

Perhaps the most encouraging evidence of Americanism among the Kibei proved to be the words and actions of patriotic Kibei themselves. During the registration program, a number of Kibei internees stepped forward to announce their desire to fight for the United States. At times, Kibei volunteers were even more articulate than their Nisei counterparts in declaring their intention to join the U.S. war efforts. In fact, some Kibei demonstrated that their overseas experiences had armed them with a sense of internationalism that allowed for a more sophisticated expression of patriotism. For example, a young Kibei volunteer at the Topaz War Relocation Center declared, "To serve in the United States Army, I am thinking not only of defending American democracy against all foes, but also of whatever contribution I may be able to make toward the emancipation of all peoples." He wished to fight for the "common people of Japan," because when he was in Japan, he had "learned the meaning of fascism."[77] Another Topaz Kibei claimed that he wanted to fight not just for the emancipation of Nisei internees but for the "right of the 'common man.'"[78]

Myer's effort to promote Nisei loyalty found help from an unlikely source as the war in the Pacific dragged on. At the same time that McCloy and DeWitt were pushing for segregation of the Kibei, the War Department needed qualified linguists to translate the Japanese code. In October 1942 the army began recruiting male U.S. citizens in the internment camps to sign up for language training at the Military Intelligence Service Language School (MISLS) at Camp Savage in Minnesota. Recruits had to be graduates of a high school in the United States, but preference was given to those who attended elementary and middle school in Japan. Volunteers were required to have a "thorough knowledge" of spoken Japanese and preferably "a fair knowledge of newspaper Japanese."[79] Although volunteers were not guaranteed enlistment in the army, enrollment at Camp Savage offered them an opportunity to leave the camps for the duration of the language training.[80] Ironically, adult bachelor Kibei, who were regarded as the most problematic and disloyal group, had become the most useful for the country and to Myer's goal of proving Nisei loyalty.

These bachelor Kibei's participation in the U.S. war effort interrupted the reputation they had been ascribed. They proved especially useful in the U.S. intelligence warfare in the Pacific Theater. At the same time that the WRA was contemplating segregation of all Kibei bachelors, the U.S. Army was training an increasing number of young Japanese American men to serve in the Military Intelligence Service (MIS).[81] An MIS member observed that the Kibei were overrepresented in the MIS units and that they were the most skilled interpreters translating Japanese documents into English.[82] The rising demand for military interpreters also prompted the army to transfer Kibei soldiers from other combat and medical units to the MIS and ship them to the Pacific.[83] Brigadier General John Weckerling, who was instrumental in establishing the MISLS, praised the Kibei servicemen's role in the Pacific campaigns and insisted that any belief in Kibei's pro-Japan tendency was a mistake.[84] In fact, white officers in the Pacific Theater valued the service of Kibei linguists not only because of their Japanese proficiency but also because of their experiences in Japan. The army even recruited those Kibei who had once been conscripts in the Japanese military, finding them to be among the most valuable assets to the MIS in the Pacific, specifically because of their knowledge of the Japanese army.[85] The increasing number and usefulness of Kibei volunteers, collaborators, and servicemen meant that the WRA could no longer treat internment camp troubles simply as "Kibei problems."

From Enemy Aliens to "New Immigrants": The WRA's Solution to the Kibei Problem

In 1944 Myer looked again to the CAS to produce a study of the Kibei that reflected this complexity and highlight the WRA's positive role in "assimilating" the Kibei. The January 28, 1944, CAS report "Japanese Americans Educated in Japan" provided the WRA with social scientific "proof" of the agency's newest claim that any troublemakers at the relocation centers were a few malcontents among the assimilated Nisei and Kibei. The report's main contributor, Marvin Opler, summarized the complex adjustment experiences of the Kibei upon their return from Japan and how Kibei's reassimilation into America determined their varied responses to the internment experience. The report proved to be more than an anthropological study, as it offered the WRA a new ideological and intellectual tool that could dispel the generalized notion of Kibei disloyalty. This was especially crucial to solving the WRA's public relations problem, because of the widespread notion that the pro-Japan sentiments of the Kibei were the root of camp disturbances. Eliminating loyalty as the central issue would provide the WRA with alternative options for interpreting the Kibei problem and the possibility of eliminating the question of Kibei loyalty once and for all.

The new CAS report helped Myer accomplish this by recasting the Kibei's transnational identity as "new immigrants," highlighting the WRA's positive role in aiding their assimilation. The report asserted adamantly that any sweeping generalization of Kibei's loyalty or cultural disposition was unfounded. According to the report, the Kibei's preference for American or Japanese ways of life represented diverse and complex views based on individual circumstances. However, the CAS researchers confidently claimed that all Kibei at various points in their lives had to go through an experience that made them fundamentally different from other Nisei. The researchers described this common experience among the Kibei as "conflict within themselves" as a result of their experiences in both the United States and Japan.[86]

The report suggested that the Kibei must be regarded as a "new immigrant group" rather than as Americans despite their legal citizenship. As such, the Kibei were subject to assimilation, as were other Japanese immigrants. However, because the Kibei were also Nisei and thus American citizens by birth, the process of their Americanization would be more complex. The report asserted that this complex identity made them a "minority group within a minority." Upon their return to their country of birth, Kibei migrants would undoubtedly experience "conflict in their personal adjustment."[87] The report suggested that the degree of assimilation varied according to the individual's will, ability and social surroundings. Some "drifted off into their own society" and into "non-assimilation." Some extreme cases of "maladjustment" made them "pariahs within the larger minority group."[88]

After the war, Opler elaborated further on maladjusted Kibei in his psychoanalytical study of a Kibei youth at Tule Lake. The troubled young Kibei, whom Opler named Jiro in his study, had spent his childhood in Hiroshima before returning to his native hometown in northern California at the age of 15. Jiro had been a "persona non grata" in Japan, struggling to adjust to life there. Jiro returned to the United States dejected and suffering from an acute inferiority complex.[89] Jiro's troubles grew worse during his readjustment phase, as he "found himself an unwelcome citizen" in his country of birth. He grew even more silent and insecure and developed strong resentment and jealousy toward his Nisei siblings and friends, who rejected his awkward manner and inability to speak English fluently.

After the family's forced relocation to Tule Lake in 1942, Jiro withdrew to a small circle of Kibei friends, with whom he responded yes to the loyalty questions, but he also wrote next to his answer, "if my citizenship rights are restored." Jiro remained at Tule Lake as a segregant, whereas the rest of his family, who had answered positively to the loyalty questionnaire, departed from the camp. Jiro's resentment grew even stronger at this outcome, and Opler declared that he was "confused, depressed, frightened, and inwardly hostile." Opler believed that Jiro demonstrated Kibei's common struggle between two cultures that had made them a unique "class" whose conflict with non-Kibei was exacerbated by the wartime incarceration.[90]

The CAS report suggested three categories of Kibei. First were those who adjusted economically and socially, with stable families and businesses. They tended to be actively pro-American and staunch "flag wavers." They were "conscious-American[s]" and willing to cooperate with the WRA. The report claimed that these Kibei "were assimilated," and little to no difference existed between them and the "majority of the Nisei."[91] The WRA likened them to the JACL members, who tended to be business owners and professionals and worked cooperatively with the WRA.

The second most assimilated group of Kibei were those who used the positive aspects of both American and Japanese culture to "find functions and status." They often contributed to "constructive action in the centers."[92] Based on this assessment, Karl Yoneda's assimilation rate would probably be placed somewhere between the first and second categories, as he was a flag waver and a communist at the same time. This group consisted of quiet, polite, "unobtrusive" Kibei who largely withdrew from society and avoided political or ideological confrontations.

The final type of Kibei were the ones regarded as the problem in the wartime WRA and JACL politics of representation. They included "maladjusted" Kibei, like Jiro, who had rendered their "reputation to the whole" as troublemakers. They had "never accepted American ways" or returned too recently to have been properly Americanized. At the relocation centers they displayed fiercely pro-Japan attitudes and behaviors and attempted any means necessary to secure their chance of returning to Japan. Most Nisei regarded them unfavorably as a "rowdy and uncontrollable group."[93]

Thus the report effectively divided Kibei into good, acceptable, and bad categories. Although the good Kibei included the ones whose degree of assimilation was the most advanced or relatively complete, the second type, or the "unobtrusive" Kibei, were essentially Japanese in culture but harmless to the WRA administration.[94] However, the last type of Kibei were the most dangerous, not because they were culturally or ideologically Japanese but because they were neither Japanese nor American. The report asserted that their misbehavior resulted from the "straddling of two cultures" in ways unfitting to both. They were neither active and productive Americans nor harmless Japanese. Their rebelliousness came from a false sense of what Japan and America meant to them. In short, they were "men without a country" who would soon discover that they had "devoted themselves to an ideal that does not exist," because a "Japan of their own over-heated imagination" was generated by their maladjustment and "lack of status in any society."⁹⁵

The report's new interpretation of loyalty and nation thus acknowledged the influence of Kibei's transnational experiences. It is in this notion of transnational identity that the WRA's criticism of the maladjusted Kibei's "false sense" of nation eliminated the issue of loyalty from the Kibei problem. However, the WRA's notion of transnational adjustment reinforced the binary concept of national loyalty, as the Kibei were expected to choose between the American and Japanese ways, according to the WRA's rearticulation of the two. An idea that one might have multiple loyalties did not fit into the WRA model and was therefore deemed a false sense of nationalism. At the same time, promoting the "good" types of Kibei's transnational adjustment offered new possibilities for highlighting the WRA's version of Americanization and the successful stories of Kibei and Nisei assimilation. These new categories provided an ideal of proper assimilation, which dovetailed with the image of the ideal Nisei promoted by the JACL.

A Model Kibei

In December 1941, when the Anti-Axis Committee was spying on Kibei individuals in Los Angeles, any JACL promotion of loyal Kibei would have been unimaginable. However, by the fall of 1944, things had changed, as the JACL joined in the WRA's rearticulation of good Kibei as successfully Americanized immigrants. The WRA's new concept of the Kibei found an ideal model in an "assimilated" and bilingual veteran of the 100th Infantry Battalion's European campaign. Private First Class Thomas Taro Higa, who had been born in Honolulu and raised in Okinawa, returned to the United States from the Battle of Cassino in Italy in the summer of 1944 to nurse a shrapnel injury.⁹⁶ Upon his recovery, the JACL arranged a nationwide speaking tour that showcased this dynamic and articulate model Kibei whose speeches in fluent standard Japanese and Okinawan dialect inspired primarily Japanese-speaking Issei. The JACL promoted the lectures as an opportunity to "further the war effort" and to "promote national unity."⁹⁷ The JACL believed that Higa's tour convinced many elders of the Japanese American community to support Nisei military service.

The stories of Higa's speaking tour provided the JACL with an opportunity to nationally publicize Japanese American loyalty. In his 120-day tour,

Higa visited 74 cities across the United States, speaking before 20,300 people. The JACL contacted more than eighty newspapers to disseminate the news of Higa's patriotic speeches.[98] Higa delighted the JACL by telling the *New York Times* that Japanese Americans were "as loyal as other groups."[99] The WRA officials were thrilled to find an ideal spokesperson in Higa for their campaign to showcase the successful Americanization of the Nisei to a national audience.[100] The WRA also produced a "moving" film that accompanied Higa's speech.[101]

The WRA's new definition of Kibei Americanization thus needed recasting of all Kibei as an immigrant group, as well as the help of its allies at the JACL. Kibei men were invited to join the WRA-JACL collaboration in promoting the ideal Nisei image. To Myer and JACL leaders, Thomas Higa and other Kibei had proved themselves useful enough to not only alleviate the Kibei problem but also to help their campaign to promote Nisei Americanism. As the WRA-JACL rearticulation of Kibei nationalism and transnational identity demonstrates, federal officials and Nisei elites themselves understood that the Kibei problem was not merely a problem of disloyalty and internment camp militancy. Perhaps these shapers of ethnic self-identity recognized before any scholars that the issues of transnational identity, nationalism, migration, and assimilation were central to approaching the Kibei experience.

Nevertheless, the WRA and JACL's reassertion of Kibei nationalism distorted many historical issues, such as gender, education, and class, that shaped the transnational experiences of the Kibei. Nisei elites and WRA administrators, through deliberate misunderstanding of the Kibei's transborder nationalism, imposed particular brands of immigrant identities on individual Kibei. They assigned new definitions to the notions of Kibei national loyalty and assimilation based on CAS researchers' descriptions of Kibei perspectives. This rearticulation merely transformed a notion of fixed national loyalty into static categories of transnational identities. Those Kibei who did not fit the WRA's concepts of Americanization and Japanization were turned into, in Donna R. Gabaccia's term, historical "nowhere men" who possessed a false sense of nation.[102]

The JACL and WRA's rearticulation of Kibei identity implicitly invoked economic, social, and generational dynamics in a gendered and class-specific language.[103] The notion of national loyalty that persisted throughout the wartime internment had a profound impact on shaping this language implicit in the WRA-JACL articulation of Nisei identity. The glorification of the military service and civic volunteerism of loyal Nisei men highlighted the gendered notion of national loyalty and assimilation invoked by the JACL and the WRA. The JACL glorified the masculinity of the heroic veterans while demonizing the effeminacy of troublemaking and draft-dodging Kibei. According to CAS analyst John F. Embree, Topaz Nisei in 1943 accused a Kibei gang of disturbing the registration program because of their fear of becoming combat casualties in a war that they did not wish to participate in.[104]

Such "gendered limits of social citizenship" were undoubtedly at work in the JACL-WRA articulation of Nisei loyalty.[105] In this context, the heroic Nisei men of the 442nd Regimental Combat Team, the famed all-Nisei unit during World War II, earned back the right of citizenship for the rest of Japanese Americans. The 442nd was so widely praised for its combat records that the 100th Congress named a 1987 resolution H.R. 442 in honor of the Nisei unit; this resolution outlined provisions for redress and reparations for the wartime internment.[106] On the other hand, the militancy of those classified by the WRA as "unassimilated" Kibei denied them a WRA-recognized national identity, as the WRA interpreted their behaviors as the result of bad transnational adjustments and a false sense of nationhood.

The WRA's implicitly class-specific rearticulation of Kibei's identity as new immigrants also demanded social mobility and assimilation of individual Kibei regardless of the differences in their social, economic, and educational backgrounds. The WRA and the JACL promoted middle-class and entrepreneurial Nisei as Americanized models and thus undermined the diverse economic and occupational backgrounds and transnational class formation of the Kibei. Unlike the WRA's new definition of good Kibei, Karl Yoneda, who was deeply influenced by the international labor movement, was neither a self-made businessman nor a socioeconomic misfit. Moreover, the WRA's new interpretation of Kibei transnational experience underestimated the potency of Yoneda's transnational education, which influenced his expression of nationalism and "loyalty." Yoneda's transnational education was a significant factor that influenced his commitment to fight the Axis powers and ally with the JACL. His exposure to radical, anarchist, and socialist literature in Japan made him a staunch denouncer of fascism in Japan.[107] Thus, although the WRA-JACL rearticulation of Kibei's Americanization took into account Kibei's experiences as migrants, it deliberately distorted the nature of their transpacific lives. The WRA-JACL campaign to promote the image of loyal Nisei during World War II cast most Kibei as outsiders without publicly acknowledging the complexity of their transnational experiences and identities. CAS analyst Marvin Opler recognized this in his report, but Myer and his agency never affirmed to the public the diverse range of Kibei responses to the wartime incarceration.

Thus, by the third year of mass incarceration, the question of Kibei loyalty was becoming increasingly complex in the WRA-JACL identity politics. However, even though policymakers and Nisei elites could no longer label all bachelor Kibei as troublemakers, they nevertheless failed to adequately understand that the question of loyalty had affected Kibei individuals in different ways because of their diverse transnational experiences. Kibei volunteers like Yoneda and the JACL might have shared their zeal to cooperate with the American war efforts, but the internationalism that had informed the Topaz volunteers suggests that their version of nationalism clearly distinguished between the Japanese government and the people of Japan. As I demonstrate in the next chapter, although the wartime demand for loyalty had forced them to choose between two countries, it did not compel them to completely sever their connection with all things Japanese.

CHAPTER 4

Beyond Two Homelands

Kibei Transnationalism in the Making of a Japanese American Diaspora

> If America gives her trust to a Kibei like me, I would do whatever it takes to give myself to her. This is what I consider *yamato damashi*—"the true Japanese spirit."[1]

LOCATED IN KAGOSHIMA PREFECTURE on the southwestern island of Kyushu, Kajiki was an obscure rural town when the nearby Mount Sakurajima erupted in early 1914. Like other small Kagoshima Bay towns, Kajiki would have a short-lived fame as a place devastated by one of the most powerful volcanic eruptions in modern Japanese history.[2] Among those who evacuated their homes for a brief escape from the fallout was a 2-year-old Nisei boy named David Akira Itami from Oakland, California, who had arrived in his immigrant father's hometown just a year earlier to be raised by his aunt.[3]

Itami's life would continue to be marked by a series of escapes and unexpected journeys, although the seventeen years he spent in Japan looked as unremarkable as the town where he grew up. Like many of his peers, Itami left Kajiki after graduating from middle school in 1928 to explore the world beyond the mundaneness of the coastal village. He studied philosophy at Daito Bunka Gakuin, a small liberal arts college in Tokyo that was a second-tier institution at best. Less than two years later, he returned to the United States without finishing school, working briefly at a cannery in Alaska before settling in California to work for the Los Angeles–based Japanese American community newspaper *Kashu Mainichi*. Itami was one of more than 10,000 Kibei who returned to the United States before the Pacific War after their sojourn in the Japanese Empire.[4]

Then, like other Nisei in the United States, Itami's life took a drastic turn after the Japanese attack on Pearl Harbor in December 1941 and the mass removal two months later of Japanese Americans from the West Coast by order of President Franklin Delano Roosevelt. In March 1942 Itami wrote his last newspaper column for *Kashu Mainichi* and entered the Manzanar internment camp in California with his wife and 4-year-old daughter.[5] Eight months later, he joined the U.S. Army out of Manzanar, first as a civilian Japanese language instructor and then as an enlistee in the army's Military Intelligence Service.[6] He rose to the rank of master sergeant by the end of the war and won the Legion of Merit award for leading code-breaking missions crucial for the U.S. victory in the Pacific Theater.[7] He returned to Japan with the Allied occupation forces after the war in 1945 to serve as a language monitor at the Tokyo War Crimes Trials, supervising court interpreters for the indicted wartime Japanese leaders, including former prime minister Tojo Hideki. Despite his stellar military record and his critical role during the Tokyo Trials, Itami was far from a celebrated figure in either country; a mere two years after the tribunal, while in Tokyo, Itami shot himself to death the morning after Christmas in 1950 at the age of 39. The news of his death reached few outside his immediate circles of colleagues and acquaintances in Japan and California.[8]

More than thirty years after his death, Itami's life history attracted some attention in Japan when the Japanese national broadcasting company, NHK, aired the *taiga* (historical fiction) drama series *Sanga Moyu* (Mountains and Rivers Are Burning); the series captured over 30% of the country's TV audience in its January 1984 premiere.[9] Based on acclaimed novelist Yamasaki Toyoko's bestseller *Futatsu no Sokoku* (Two Homelands), published in the previous year, the 51-episode series dramatized the wartime struggles of Japanese Americans through the eyes of a Kibei man. While conducting research for *Futatsu no Sokoku*, Yamasaki learned about Itami's work during the Tokyo Trials and used his life as a model to create her novel's tragic hero, Kenji Amo. Like his real-life model, Amo is a U.S.-born Nisei who spent his formative years in Kajiki during the 1920s. Amo leaves Japan at the age of 19 to resettle in Los Angeles before the Pacific War and then joins the U.S. Army out of Manzanar, where his family remained throughout the war. Like Itami, Amo works as a monitor at the Tokyo War Crimes Tribunal and takes his own life after the conclusion of the trials.[10]

For the Japanese audience unfamiliar with the history of Japanese Americans in the United States, Amo's tragic life offered a unique perspective on the war and on what it meant to be Japanese. Throughout the series Amo is torn by his role as a Japanese American soldier caught between his country of birth and the country of his parents. Yamasaki makes ample reference to Kajiki and its location in Kagoshima Prefecture to remind her audience of Amo's upbringing in the region, which is known for its strong identity as the last bastion of Japan's long-lost warrior-scholar traditions. Once the center of Satsuma Domain during the Edo Period (1603–1868), Kagoshima was home to the disenchanted samurai who had led the last armed rebellion against the modern Japanese state after its sweeping military reform had made their status obsolete.[11] In the popular Japanese historical memory, the Kagoshima samurai's failed uprising in 1877 marked the final defeat of the old Japan and its elite warrior-scholar class by the forces of modernization. However, it was not a story of a celebrated samurai but that of a Japanese American soldier that shined the spotlight yet again on Kajiki since the 1914 volcanic eruption. Yamasaki depicts Amo as an American by birth but a Japanese at heart who is steeped in the virtues of the loyal samurai, thanks to his youth spent in Kajiki. In the dramatic finale of *Futatsu no Sokoku*, Amo finds himself unable to overcome his conflicting loyalties to his two homelands. In true samurai-like fashion, he commits suicide as the only way to resolve his "failure to find his own country."[12]

The success of Yamasaki's novel and the NHK drama series sparked a renewed interest among those connected to Kajiki in reclaiming the town's ties to Kagoshima's history through Itami's legacies. Since the NHK drama series ended in December 1984, many of the townsfolk and Itami's former acquaintances made concerted efforts to commemorate the man who made Kajiki famous. In 1995 a memorial was erected at the site of Itami's childhood home, with his portrait engraved on the wall by noted sculptor and Kajiki native Hoga Rokuro.[13] In 2004 the Kajiki Folklore Museum presented the *Futatsu no Sokoku* Exhibit, which showcased Itami's artifacts; the exhibit drew many visitors, including renowned actor Matsumoto Koshiro, who played Kenji Amo in *Sanga Moyu*.[14] Also, since 1984, at least five Kagoshima-based writers inspired by Yamasaki's epic novel have published biographies of Itami. These posthumous accounts of Itami's experiences solemnly, and romantically, celebrate the Nisei man's Kajiki heritage and his diasporic identity as an American citizen who wanted to belong to Japan.[15]

The complex sociopolitical implications of Itami's life as a Japanese American migrant have been overshadowed by this celebratory narrative that claims Itami's Japanese cultural citizenship. Without substantive discussions about the social realities that had shaped Kibei's transnational experiences on both sides of the Pacific, the Japanese biographers' depictions of Itami have largely mimicked Yamasaki's one-dimensional representation of Kenji Amo as a Kagoshima-bred Nisei victimized by the tragic war. Moreover, despite his posthumous fame in Kagoshima, thanks to the popular Japanese novel and TV series based on his life, Itami's name has remained obscure in the United States. Even though Itami's story found an audience in Japan, the dominant postwar historical memory centering on Nisei's loyalty to the United States had little room for the Kibei's multifaceted transpacific life, which complicated the image of Japanese Americans as 100% American.[16]

Also overshadowed in Yamasaki's work is the critical role that Itami and other Kibei played in shaping the politics and social relations in the Japanese American community in the United States during the critical decade before the Pacific War. The traces of his life and work in archival records and historical memories in both countries reveal that the meanings of loyalty and cultural dualism for Japanese American migrants like Itami were far more complex than the simple dichotomy between their American and Japanese identities. More important, these sources illuminate the vital role that Kibei like Itami played in shaping the politics and social relations in the Japanese American community in the United States before, during, and after the war. In short, Itami's diasporic life offers a social history of Nisei's diasporic world.

A Legend of a Kagoshima Gentleman

David Akira Itami was born in 1911 in Oakland, California, to Japanese immigrant shopkeepers from Kagoshima Prefecture. His father, Jojiro, had left Kajiki in 1887 at the age of 20 to become one of the first Japanese settlers in the San Francisco Bay Area. When Itami was born, his parents struggled to keep their East Oakland dry cleaning business afloat amid the mounting anti-Japanese sentiment in the area. Before his second birthday,

Itami was sent to Kajiki, where his paternal aunt would take charge of raising him and ensure that her American-born nephew would receive a proper Japanese education. Although sending their infant child to Japan to be raised by their relatives was far from an easy decision for the Itamis, it was nevertheless a sensible way to ease the family's economic burdens and a practice that would become more common among Japanese immigrants in the United States during the Great Depression.[17]

Yamasaki's novel and the biographical accounts of Itami in Japan largely ignore these critical social circumstances in the Japanese American community that contributed to Itami's separation from his family in the United States. Instead, these works conflate the facts and fiction that shaped the posthumous memories of Kajiki's favorite son. According to these accounts, Jojiro Itami wanted his American-born child to grow up in his ancestral hometown and one day return to California as a Japanese man with a proper Satsuma cultural identity. Allegedly a descendant of an elite samurai family, David Akira Itami demonstrated traits of an ideal Kagoshima man early on. When he turned 5, he joined Kajiki's selective traditional fraternity Seiunsha, a remnant of the local samurai education system emphasizing scholarly and physical discipline. At Seiunsha local youths trained together to develop ethical cultivation, literacy in Confucian classics, physical fitness, and loyalty to scholar-warrior traditions.[18] Inspired by Itami's unique educational background, Yamasaki described her main character as an American-born Nisei transformed into a true embodiment of *Satsuma hayato*—the legendary ancient tribesmen of the Satsuma region and revered ancestors to Kagoshima's samurai class—thanks to his traditional education and Kajiki heritage.

Inspired by *Sanga Moyu*'s idealization of their hometown, the retrospectively glowing memories of Itami's childhood expressed by his former classmates and friends were in line with Yamasaki's fictional account of Kenji Amo. They praised Itami's scholastic excellence as a protégé of Seiunsha's training program. According to their celebratory recollections, Itami learned to read classical texts well before turning 6 and started his compulsory public education at the local Dajo Primary School, where he was said to outperform every native Japanese student. By his fifth year in primary school, his academic achievement and intellectual prowess far exceeded his grade level, prompting his teachers to urge him to forgo his last year at primary school and study at the prestigious Kajiki Prefectural Middle

School. In middle school Itami continued to exhibit excellence in both liberal arts and physical education. Less than three years after *Sanga Moyu*'s last episode aired on NHK, fellow Kajiki middle school alumnus Suiryu Seiko remembered Itami as the most exceptional student, one who made all his older classmates look bad.[19] In 2000, eighty years after befriending Itami in middle school, another former classmate was still mesmerized by the California native's extraordinary skills in deciphering complex classical Chinese texts.[20]

Mindful of his family's financial struggles on the eve of the Great Depression in 1928, Itami opted to apply to tuition-free state-run military officer schools instead of elite universities upon graduating from Kajiki Prefectural Middle School. For Yamasaki and other contributors to Itami's legend, however, Itami's desire to attend a military academy in Japan and pursue a career in the Japanese armed forces served as yet further proof of his Kagoshima samurai roots and his loyalty to Japan.[21] Itami applied to the Imperial Army Preparatory School and the Imperial Naval Academy only to be denied admission by both institutions. Shocked by the unexpected setback suffered by their top student, Itami's teachers and classmates in Kajiki believed that it was his U.S. citizenship that had contributed to the military academies' rejection of the Nisei's patriotism to Japan.[22]

Disheartened but determined to leave Kajiki and pursue a higher education, Itami applied to Daito Bunka Gakuin (Academy of Greater East Asian Culture), a postsecondary liberal arts school in Tokyo that offered degrees in Asian culture and civilization. In addition to tuition-free education, the institution provided stipends that allowed Itami to pay for room and board while going to school in the capital.[23] Itami's decision to study at Daito Bunka Gakuin gave Yamasaki and Itami's biographers in the 1980s yet another reason to speculate that his intellectual pursuit had aligned with his Japanese nationalism. Established in 1923, Daito Bunka Gakuin widely promoted its Asia-centered curriculum as a unique intellectual endeavor to assist Japan's role in fostering unity among Asian societies in their struggles against Western imperialism. With its ambitious offerings in languages and cultures from all major regions of Asia, the school in fact served as an ideal training ground for future cultural experts, administrators, and propagandists for Japan's own imperial aspirations on the continent. The founders of Daito Bunka Gakuin included leading statesmen and industrialists who would emerge as the critical core of the militarist wing of the government in the 1930s. The institution's emphasis on pan-Asianism was part of their effort to promote Japan's euphemistic motto, the "Greater East Asia Co-Prosperity Sphere," which obscured the empire's aggressive colonial expansion in Asia.[24] The school's founding president (and future prime minister), Hiranuma Kiichiro, was a leading advocate of Japan's expansionist foreign policy, and he would be convicted as a Class A war criminal at the Tokyo Trials in 1946.[25] Hiranuma and other founders of Daito Bunka Gakuin envisioned the institute's graduates as serving the interests of Japanese imperialism as colonial administrators, educators, and policy advisers and in other critical political and cultural roles. At Daito Bunka Gakuin Itami studied Chinese classics, arts, and Indian philosophy. He also joined the school's archery team to maintain a healthy balance between books and "soldierly" refinement.[26]

Itami's upbringing and educational background thus inspired his posthumous image in Japan as an ideal Kagoshima warrior-scholar and even evoked a sense of national pride among his peers. In 2000 Itami's Dajo Primary School classmate Kishino Yoshi emphasized that Itami's Kagoshima background and his training in Asian studies were the "backbone" of the Nisei's philosophical and spiritual ethos as a Japanese, even though he ended up serving in the U.S. Army during World War II. Goto Tokuji, a Kagoshima intellectual, believed that Itami's unique educational experience had made him "more Japanese" than most Japanese men of his time. Goto speculated that Itami had suffered from deep remorse for taking arms against Japan and dishonoring his roots by serving in the U.S. Army during the Pacific War, as though he had "aimed his bow and arrow at his own country."[27] Sato Hachiro, an alumnus of Kajiki Prefectural Middle School, believed that, even though Itami had performed his duty to the United States as an American citizen and decorated soldier, he must have felt that he had betrayed his true homeland. Ono Koji, a law professor from Kagoshima, suggested that Itami's samurai ancestry and upbringing had been evidenced by his meritorious service in the U.S. Army but that the Nisei had remained a loyal Japanese all along. Ono went so far as to compare Itami's suicide to *seppuku*—a samurai's ritual suicide to rid himself of shame—and the ultimate expression of his allegiance to Japan.[28] Such romanticization of Itami's suicide contributed to news reports that erroneously claimed that the Kibei had indeed performed *seppuku*.[29]

FIGURE 6 A memorial commemorating David Akira Itami at the site of his childhood home in Kajiki, Kagoshima Prefecture.
Courtesy of the author.

Such a powerful sentiment in these Kagoshima men's collective memory of Itami's Japanese identity did not surprise Yamasaki, who had written her novel with a clear goal of evoking a nationalist historical consciousness. During her speaking engagements after the publication of the novel in 1983, Yamasaki noted that she had wanted to give her readers an opportunity to rethink their collective Japanese identity, which she believed had slowly decayed amid the rapid postwar economic growth and Westernization. She had once considered writing a novel that would depict a search for true Japaneseness through the eyes of a modern-day Japanese man's historical reexamination of Japan's defeat in the Pacific War, the defining moment when Yamasaki believed Japanese society lost its ethos as a nation.[30] However, she feared that such a plot would invite a backlash against her work for breaking a long-standing taboo by depicting Japan as a victim of World War II and potentially evoking nostalgia for Japan's imperialist past. In Itami, Yamasaki found an ideal model for the novel's hero. The emotional struggle of the Kibei educated in Kagoshima allowed Yamasaki to create an image of Japan as a sentimental spiritual home of the Japanese in diaspora. In *Futatsu no Sokoku* Japan emerges as a homeland for all people of Japanese ancestry, especially the Nisei, who are U.S. citizens but are treated like unwanted aliens in their country of birth. Yamasaki's representation of Kenji Amo depicts the Kibei man as a quintessential victim of war and American racism, whose disillusionment with American democracy and longing for a true homeland constantly draw him back to the country of his ancestors. In this way, Yamasaki invites her Japanese readers to rediscover the meaning of Japan as a motherland.

To Yamasaki's delight, her simplistic and yet powerful interpretation of the Kibei's cultural and emotional attachment to Japan touched many of her readers in Japan, including those among the postwar generations. Kono Rikako, a history graduate student at Kyoritsu Women's University, wrote in 2000 that *Futatsu no Sokoku* and its serialization by NHK had helped her gain a greater understanding of how the war had devastated the lives of the Japanese in diaspora. The life story of David Akira Itami had inspired Kono enough that she decided to study the history of the Japanese American community in graduate school.[31] Yamasaki's interpretation of Itami's life in the form of a historical novel also helped an ardent fan of *Futatsu no Sokoku* and *Sanga Moyu* named Kumatani Minako, from Iwate Prefecture, develop an interest in modern Japanese history through the plight of Japanese Americans like Itami.[32] The conflation of facts and fiction in these readers' historical consciousness demonstrates the powerful cultural impact of Yamasaki's work.

Futatsu no Sokoku and *Sanga Moyu* may have inspired many in the Japanese audience to become students of history in their own ways, but Yamasaki's tragic narrative does little to complicate the predictable and polarizing notions about wartime nationalism. Kenji Amo's conflicting loyalties, which lead to his dramatic death, reinforce Kibei's perceived Japanese cultural citizenship and establishes Japan as a hegemonic diasporic home. Fifty years after David Akira Itami's death in Tokyo, his daughter, Michi Itami, responded to this troubling dichotomous interpretation of Kibei's diasporic consciousness. She stated that her late father could very well have had complex personal "circumstances" that had compelled him to take his own life: "No one has been able to give me a simple explanation for my father's sad end."[33] Michi Itami's words serve as a simple reminder that there was much more to Itami's diasporic life than his purported national identities.

Kibei Transnationalism on the Eve of World War II

There was much more to the social realities on both sides of the Pacific that shaped Kibei's lives than the popular posthumous narratives of Itami in Japan. The heavily understudied aspects of Itami's life, from his return from Japan to the attack on Pearl Harbor in 1941, illuminate the indispensable role that Kibei intellectuals played in shaping the politics of and the social relations in the Japanese American community. In the summer of 1931, Itami decided to quit Daito Bunka Gakuin and relocate to the United States after receiving a telegram from Oakland with an urgent message about his mother's illness. In July he returned to his country of birth on the Japanese transpacific liner *Asama Maru*. He had spent more than seventeen formative years of his life in Japan while the Japanese Empire had further solidified its position as a formidable colonial power in Asia under the reign of the young Emperor Taisho.[34]

Itami was a product of the social transformations of the Taisho era (1912–1925) as much as he had been a product of Kagoshima's old samurai traditions. Along with economic prosperity thanks to the post–World War I manufacturing boom, the Taisho era witnessed the rise of unprecedented political liberalism and social unrest, with popular movements led by women's suffragists, political dissidents, and labor unions throughout the archipelago.[35] Cultural transformations were reflected in emerging literary societies, the mass publication of magazines and political commentaries, and a burgeoning interest in popular music, film, and theater, all of which contributed to the wide circulation of new ideas, both homegrown and from abroad. An ardent reader of popular literary magazines since his days at Dajo Primary School, Itami developed a keen interest in literature as a form of social commentary and modeled himself after such leading Japanese modernist writers as Natsume Soseki and Akutagawa Ryunosuke.[36] Itami was a product of Japanese modernity as much as he had been a student of the old Japan.

As he transitioned into his new life in the United States and struggled to pick up English during the first few years after his return, Itami turned to activities that allowed him to use the knowledge and skills he had acquired in Japan. In May 1932 he left Oakland to spend the summer in Alaska as a cannery worker to support himself.[37] He had never been a factory worker in Japan, but being a part of the multiethnic workforce in a frontier province of an empire was not a concept unfamiliar to him. He embraced the Asian immigrant workers' labor activism in Alaska and served as one of the spokespeople for the cannery workers during their wage negotiations that summer.[38] With the money saved from his factory work in Alaska, Itami relocated to Los Angeles to seek new opportunities. Essentially a native Japanese speaker, he sat in on classes at Pasadena High School to improve his English and his familiarity with the American education system. He trained himself to communicate in English effectively enough to study at Los Angeles City College in 1933. In 1934 he started working as a reporter for *Kashu Mainichi* (The California Daily News), a bilingual newspaper in Los Angeles founded by prominent Japanese immigrant businessman Sei Fujii. In 1936 Itami helped found Hokubei Shijin Kyokai (Association of Poets in North America), a group of primarily young Kibei and Japanese immigrant writers who, like Itami, had developed their political consciousness and passion for writing in Japan during the Taisho era.[39] In the first issue of the club's own Japanese-language literary magazine, *Shukaku* (The Harvest), in November 1936, the Kibei writers declared that the magazine was a creative space to reflect on their struggles as sojourners and a means to wrestle with the meaning of their diasporic lives.[40]

Writing functioned as a cultural and political outlet for young Japanese-speaking Kibei like Itami to address issues that they believed were an integral part of the Japanese American transnational experience. One of the contemporary political issues that dominated the pages of the magazine in the second half of the 1930s was the Japanese military expansion in the Chinese subcontinent and its impact on U.S.-Japan relations. The writers feared that the rise of militarism in the Japanese Empire was threatening the well-being of not only the ordinary citizens of Japan but also the Japanese diasporic community in the United States. A number of the magazine's short stories in the second half of the 1930s attributed the heightened anti-Japanese racial hysteria in the United States to the negative image of Japan as an evil empire threatening the peace in the Pacific world. In these stories white Americans used the widely circulated news of Japan's imperialist war depicted in the mainstream Hearst and McClatchy newspapers as justification for their mistreatment of Japanese Americans in the United States. In some stories Japan's colonialism in Asia also shattered the once amicable relationships between Japanese and other Asian immigrant communities as they turned against each other. In other stories related to

Japanese militarism in Asia, the Kibei writers complained that the diplomatic tension in the Pacific caused by the Japanese militarist leaders had tarnished the image of the Japanese in the United States.[41]

Itami devoted considerable energy to voicing his concerns over the impact of international relations on the anti-Japanese sentiment in his *Kashu Mainichi* articles. Within four years after being hired as a reporter in 1934, Itami started his own daily column, titled "Air Mail," in the Japanese section of the newspaper. Sei Fujii, who was also the respected president of the Japanese Association of America, gave Itami his complete trust and considered the young Kibei an ideal columnist whose transnational education had given him a nuanced understanding of geopolitics in the Pacific world and its implications on Japanese Americans' political future.[42] In his columns from 1939 to 1941, Itami used his multilingual reading skills to analyze articles and editorials published in newspapers in the United States, Japan, and China. He claimed that conflicting views on Japan's war efforts in Asia in different countries and languages had led to misunderstandings among diverse groups of people across these nations. He also argued that the mainstream U.S. media outlets' demonization of the Japanese Empire had led to the deteriorating U.S.-Japan relations and anti-Japanese hostility in the United States.[43]

Itami was frustrated by the negative public opinion of Japan, which he believed had much to do with the yellow journalism practiced by the mainstream U.S. press. Itami phrased his criticism carefully in order to direct his readers' attention to what he viewed as American newspapers' "fearmongering tactics" that seemed to violate "democratic principles and journalistic integrity." Refraining from criticizing U.S. government policies or the American public for their anti-Japanese sentiment, he emphasized the American media's "concerted effort to push for a war" between the United States and Japan. In early 1940 Itami wrote in "Air Mail" that the American newspapers had refused to report a statement by the U.S. Department of State earlier that year that had assured the continuation of normalized trade relations between the two countries even in the case of suspended diplomacy over foreign policy differences.[44]

Itami also hoped to convince his readers that Japan's activities in Asia had done little to pose a threat to the security of the United States. In his effort to downplay Japan's imperial aggressions in Asia-Pacific, he risked using his column as political propaganda to portray U.S.-Japan relations as an alliance rather than a source of belligerence. He argued that the United States and Japan had shared geopolitical interests in fighting communism. Itami went so far as to portray Japan's war efforts in China as a necessary action to prevent the spread of Soviet communism in Asia. In January 1940 Itami reported that, although the U.S. government had planned to increase the naval budget to bolster its Pacific fleets, the plan did not represent a potential preparation for a war against Japan. Instead, Itami suggested a "not-too-farfetched" scenario of a possible U.S. strike on the Soviet Pacific ports with Japan's assistance. Itami argued that the real threat to the U.S. national defense was the Soviet Union, not Japan.[45]

Despite his naïve optimism about U.S.-Japan relations, Itami emerged as a leader in the growing community of Kibei in Southern California in the late 1930s. Itami's work as a leading political columnist for a Japanese American community paper and his relationship with Sei Fujii earned him enough respect among the Kibei in Southern California, who formed their own caucus within the Japanese American Citizens League (JACL). Founded in 1929 by emerging Japanese American professionals, the JACL was an exclusive organization open only to U.S.-born Nisei. JACL leaders sought to emerge out of the shadow of the Japanese immigrant generation and assert their position as the new leaders of the Japanese American community. The Kibei in the JACL's Los Angeles Chapter voted Itami into the position of vice president of the "JACL Kibei Division" in April 1939.[46]

However, not all Kibei approved of Itami's view that the positive portrayal of the Japanese Empire could improve the Japanese American community's respectability and curtail widespread anti-Japanese sentiment in the United States. Through his *Kashu Mainichi* columns uncritical of Japanese imperialism in Asia, Itami had earned the title "pro-Axis Kibei" from Japanese American writers at *Doho*, a leftist newspaper critical of Japanese imperialism. Itami's critics at *Doho* included vocal Kibei members of the Communist Party, such as James Oda and George Ban, both of whom, like Itami, were products of the Taishio era liberalism in Japan. However, even though all three of them had read political and literary magazines in Japan in the 1920s, Oda and Ban had been ardent followers of the Marxist literature and labor activism in Japan. Both of them returned to the United States in the 1930s ready to join the radical leftist and antifascist movement in the United States. They saw Itami as an apologist for Japan's "Greater East Asia Co-Prosperity Sphere." In early 1940 a growing number of vocal Japanese American leftists joined the JACL to push anti-Axis and pro-union agendas.[47] Oda and Ban joined the JACL's Kibei Division in Los Angeles to wage a political battle against Itami in the emerging Nisei community organization. Over the next ten months, the tension between Itami and his antifascist rivals on the Japanese American left did enough to divide the Kibei community in Los Angeles. In October 1940 Itami used his authority as vice president to expel Oda and Ban from the JACL's Kibei Division. Itami's drastic measure stamped his reputation among the Japanese American left as a dangerous sympathizer of the Japanese Empire.[48] Many *Doho* readers found Itami's action deeply offensive and accused him of betraying his own background as a former cannery worker and labor organizer.[49]

The War, Kibei Transnationalism, and the Question of Japanese American Loyalty

The mounting diplomatic tension between the United States and Japan that culminated in the Pacific War in December 1941 further exacerbated divisions among the Kibei and the Japanese American community as a whole. Itami found himself mired in this tension when the JACL leaders seized the volatile moment as an opportunity to supplant the Issei leadership and establish themselves as the representatives of all Japanese Americans. As discussed in Chapter 3, the JACL's Anti-Axis Committee in Los Angeles pressured Itami to pledge complete loyalty and cooperation from all Kibei JACL members in Los Angeles. According to the committee's meeting minutes from December 12, Itami and his fellow Kibei representative, Ted Okamoto, were "very confused and skeptical and were quite undecided about" their course of action. Itami's skepticism about the committee's tactics was not unfounded. He read with suspicion the Japanese version of the committee bulletin, which had been translated from its English version for distribution among the Japanese-speaking Issei and Kibei. A section from the original English text that read "We pledge our unequivocal repudiation of Japan" had been translated into Japanese as "We declare complete severance of connection with Japan."[50] The English version allowed the "repudiation of Japan" to be interpreted simply as Nisei's denouncement of Japan's aggression. However, the Japanese version's call for "complete severance of connection with Japan" required that the Japanese-speaking Issei and Kibei exercise a vigorous form of self-rejection, based on the assumption that they had more heavily invested personal and cultural ties with Japan. The Anti-Axis Committee's demand also meant to many Issei and Kibei that they would have to terminate correspondence with their relatives in Japan. Moreover, the committee members notified the FBI and the United States postmaster general that the JACL would monitor and "control" Japanese American community newspapers.[51] Itami's *Kashu Mainichi* columns thus became a target of censorship for the first time, and by none other than the leaders of his own community.

Intimidated by the JACL leaders' determination to report those who failed to adhere to the Anti-Axis Committee's patriotic manifesto, Itami agreed to urge other Kibei to submit to the committee's policy. The committee's public relations chairman and the JACL national office's number two man, Ken Matsumoto, reported on December 16 that Itami was confident in the Los Angeles Kibei's loyalty and that all Kibei members of the chapter would "work whole-heartedly" with the Anti-Axis Committee.[52] In addition to encouraging other Kibei to cooperate with the JACL, Itami used his writings in *Kashu Mainichi* to deflect negative images of Japanese Americans amid increasing racial hysteria on the West Coast. In the absence of *Kashu Mainichi*'s publisher and editor Sei Fujii, who was detained at the Department of Justice camp in Santa Fe, New Mexico, along with other Issei community leaders, Itami took charge of the paper's publication. Under Itami's supervision, *Kashu Mainichi*'s alleged pro-Japan commentaries all but disappeared.

With his own name and identity as a Kibei leader turned over to the FBI, Itami faced a dire situation that called for the best of his sense of urgency.[53] Itami decided that the best course of action was to turn to the language of patriotism. Despite the Anti-Axis Committee's treatment of Kibei, and perhaps because of the JACL's determination to continue its unequivocal cooperation with federal authorities by any means possible, Itami sought means beyond his Japanese-language columns to profess his loyalty to the United States. In a letter titled "Nisei's Duty" to *Time* magazine on March 16, 1942, Itami expressed his support of the military necessity of Japanese American evacuation from the West Coast. Without acknowledging his Kibei status, he wrote that he believed that the cooperation with evacuation plans was Japanese Americans' "duty" to help the army defend the coast by not getting in the troops' way. He also believed that the evacuation would relieve the "worry and anxiety of our fellow Caucasian citizens on the coast." Itami seemed apprehensive of what he perceived to be a near certain consequence of the West Coast Nisei's failure to perform this task: "We have [no] desire to be charged responsible if and when any single [Japanese] bomb is dropped here." He reasoned that "it is quite certain that enraged public will look for a scapegoat in us on such event."[54]

In the absence of Sei Fujii, Itami and his colleagues at *Kashu Mainichi* devoted their last effort to avoid the branding of their paper as a pro-Japan publication. In *Kashu Mainichi*'s final editorial before its suspension on March 21, Itami joined acting publisher Kazuo Terada and English section editor Robert Hirano in urging Japanese Americans to cooperate wholeheartedly with Roosevelt's executive order. The editorial claimed that the situation was the "supreme test" of the Japanese American community's loyalty to the American government. The editors did not forget to pay tribute to the freedom of the press and the democratic system in the United States that had allowed their paper to serve its bilingual community for years. They finally announced that *Kashu Mainichi* would terminate wartime publication and cease to function as a community newspaper during the Japanese American "exodus" to relocation centers. The readers were advised to trust the Wartime Civilian Control Administration under the direction of the U.S. Army for the dissemination of necessary information.[55]

Itami demonstrated his pledge of loyalty beyond the limits of newspaper columns. He was among the first to volunteer to join the advance working party, which arrived at the Owens Valley Reception Center in Manzanar, California, on March 23, two days after *Kashu Mainichi* suspended publication.[56] Despite his repeated messages of cooperation and his volunteerism, Itami's critics at the Japanese American leftist weekly *Doho* viewed his presence at Manzanar with suspicion. Itami's patriotism did little to change his label as a "pro-Japan" writer, as Japanese American leftists did not forget how Itami had mistreated Kibei communists in the JACL's Kibei Division before the war. The paper dedicated to "complete victory over Japanese militarism and Nazi fascism" reported in early April that "rabid pro-Axis 'Air Mail' columnist . . . Kibei Akira Itami" had been assigned as the head of the evacuee information office at Manzanar, which included another former *Kashu Mainichi* staffer, Roy Takeno. The *Doho* article portrayed the transition of the working crew and their family members as otherwise being smooth and pleasant. And despite inconveniences inevitable in what the paper described as a "pioneering project," families reported little complaints. The paper claimed that even the elderly Issei began to appreciate the "democratic" process of evacuation and the daily provision they received at the camp.[57]

Rather than responding to the *Doho* writers, Itami again turned to the national audience to improve the public image of Japanese Americans and perhaps his own image as well. In his second patriotic letter to *Time*, which he wrote from Manzanar after his arrival at the camp, Itami could not have agreed more with the *Doho*'s positive portrayal of mass incarceration. In fact, his words sounded even more pro-American than those featured in the *Doho*. In the letter Itami reported that the Japanese American evacuees at the Owens Valley Reception Center enjoyed excellent treatment and high morale. Itami depicted camp life as a positive experience, with sufficient food and support from the army and federal staff. He also stressed that young Nisei in the camp maintained high spirits and pride, as they were mindful of their American identity and citizenship. Apart from "occasional sandstorms," Itami's letter even depicted the climate at Manzanar as being "very good to our health." "Under the snow-covered High Sierra mountains," Itami wrote, the evacuees were enjoying a life of leisure in their "new home."[58]

Itami's articulation of loyalty and cooperation, and, more important, his ability to articulate himself in both English and Japanese did enough to convince the Wartime Civilian Control Administration staff to put him in charge of the evacuee information office at Manzanar. Among those who looked suspiciously at Itami's enthusiastic cooperation with internment authorities was James Oda, who remained bitter toward Itami for expelling leftists from the JACL's Kibei Division. Not only was Oda "alarmed" to find Itami working with Manzanar administrators, but he also was certain that Itami was quietly awaiting the right moment to muster the pro-Japan faction and instigate a disturbance at Manzanar. That summer, Oda joined his leftist associates in warning WRA administrators of Itami's potential as a leader of pro-Japan elements, but their warning did little to convince camp authorities.[59]

As more Japanese American internees arrived and more vocal JACL members assumed leadership of the camp population, Itami kept a relatively low profile at Manzanar. He largely avoided getting involved in camp politics and kept enough distance from both avid JACL members and leftists. He was absent when JACL leaders, such as Togo Tanaka and former Anti-Axis Committee members Fred Tayama and Joe Masaoka, joined forces with Kibei communists James Oda and Karl Yoneda and others to form the Manzanar Citizens Federation in June 1942. According to Yoneda and Oda, the formation of the Manzanar Citizens Federation came out of the anti-Axis Nisei's attempt to retaliate against what they saw as the growing influence of pro-Japan activities led by the Manzanar Black Dragon Association, which was headed by a Kibei named Ben Kishi.[60] Kibei leftists like Karl Yoneda proved to be a great asset to the Nisei campaign to prove loyalty, and ironically these antifascist Kibei were among the most active informants for U.S. government authorities on the activities of other Kibei in the camp.[61]

The war fostered a strange alliance between the JACL and Japanese American communists. Soon after the attack on Pearl Harbor in December 1941, experienced San Francisco Bay Area labor organizer and Communist Party member Yoneda actively spoke out against imperial Japan. Not only did he encourage other Kibei groups to support the war against Japan, but he also joined Japanese American communists in recommending that the JACL in northern California follow the lead of their Southern California brethren by forming an anti-Axis committee of its own. He also encouraged JACL national secretary Mike M. Masaoka to lead the Japanese American community even more forcefully in the direction of patriotism. Among the first volunteers to the internment camp, Yoneda took charge of leading "the participation in war efforts" for the Manzanar Citizens Federation. Before Masaoka and JACL leaders pushed for the creation of an all-Nisei combat unit in the U.S. Army, Yoneda proposed that the JACL make a public proclamation of the Nisei's desire to serve in the American military and take arms against the Axis powers. In July 1942 Yoneda and Nisei communists led a campaign to petition President Roosevelt to allow Japanese Americans to join the U.S. Armed Forces. Itami was among the 218 signers of the petition.[62]

Itami's days at Manzanar did not last long. When the U.S. Army's Military Intelligence Service Language School (MISLS) moved from San Francisco to its new facility at Camp Savage, Minnesota, in June 1942, he volunteered to become one of the first wartime Japanese-language instructors. After Itami left for Minnesota, some allegedly pro-Japan Black Dragons at

Manzanar who discovered his departure branded him a traitor. They even attempted to harass Itami's wife and daughter, who remained temporarily at Manzanar. Those sympathetic to Itami protected his family from the attackers.[63]

What motivated Itami to take a patriotic turn in 1942? Was he an opportunist who was able to simply abandon his prewar loyalty to Japan to gain a favorable position when mass incarceration had become an unavoidable fate of Japanese Americans? Was he a pragmatist, as his one-time associate and fellow Los Angeles–area Kibei writer Masao Yamashiro suggested after the war, who saw that teaching Japanese at Camp Savage would secure him and his family permanent leave from the camp? James Oda, who volunteered for the U.S. Army's Military Intelligence Service and was sent to the MISLS in November 1942 for language training, was "flabbergasted" to find himself sitting in Itami's class. Soon, however, the former enemies put their past differences aside, as Oda was convinced of Itami's sincerity in "changing horses." Oda was especially impressed by Itami's decision in early 1944 to give up his position as a relatively high-paid civilian chief language instructor to voluntarily enlist for active military service. Oda even criticized Yamashiro for considering Itami as a mere pragmatist. Even Itami's prewar writings sympathetic to Japan's military aggression in China, Oda reflected, could simply have been the young Kibei journalist's obligation as an employee of the Japanese immigrant-run newspaper.[64] No matter the intention, Itami could only prove his loyalty to the United States through his actions, just as other Nisei during the war were asked to. What Itami, Oda, Yoneda, and other Kibei did during internment proves that to many Nisei the war complicated the question and meaning of loyalty. To many Kibei, articulation of loyalty had as much to do with survival as with a means to fight fascism.

Nisei Linguists in the Pacific

Itami's proficiency in both Japanese and English placed him high on the list of linguists who would play a critical role in military intelligence during the Pacific War. He worked for the Military Intelligence Service (MIS) in Washington, D.C., intercepting and deciphering Japanese codes. He excelled at this task not only because of his ability to comprehend coded conversations but also because of a remarkable coincidence that proved to be crucial in making him the most qualified man for the job. In 1944 the officials at the Ministry of Foreign Affairs of Japan selected some of the most complex regional Japanese dialects to conduct their coded international communications so that these conversations would be almost incomprehensible for the Allied linguists trained in the standard Tokyo dialect. One of the dialects selected for this purpose was the southern Kagoshima dialect, which was extremely difficult even for native Japanese speakers outside the region to understand. What the Japanese officials could not have expected was that the MIS had David Itami, a Kibei who grew up in Kagoshima and had been educated in the region's traditional classical studies since age 5.[65]

One of the Japanese officials who managed communications during the war was Maki Hideji, who headed the Broadcasting Section of the Foreign Ministry's Intelligence Bureau. A Kagoshima native, Maki communicated with Japanese diplomats abroad to gather reports from outside the Japanese sphere of influence. In 1944 the MIS in Washington, D.C., intercepted Maki's phone conversation with a Japanese attaché in Germany in the heavily coded Kagoshima dialect. Itami was summoned immediately to decipher the phone call, which consisted of a report from the European Theater and a discussion about the strategic positioning of the Japanese fleet in the Pacific. During this assignment, Itami would learn that the Japanese diplomat in Berlin at the other end of the phone conversation was Sogi Takateru. Sogi had been Itami's mentor in Kagoshima who had arranged financial help for Itami's return trip to California in 1931.[66]

Itami and Sogi would meet again in Japan under the Allied occupation, as Itami's career as a linguist would eventually take him back to Tokyo at the end of the war.[67] Before his arrival in Tokyo, however, Itami made stops on Iwo Jima and Okinawa, where he stayed with the U.S. occupation forces for four months after the conclusion of the war in August 1945. On Iwo Jima Itami compiled the information gathered from more than 800 Japanese prisoners of war who had been interrogated by Nisei members of the MIS. By early 1945 the U.S. War Department had deployed hundreds of Japanese American soldiers in the MIS to the Pacific Theater. In early 1945 the Honolulu-based Joint Intelligence Center, Pacific Ocean Area (JICPOA), sent more than fifty Japanese American MIS soldiers to Iwo Jima to assist the Marine Corps's invasion of the island.[68] On Iwo

Jima, Terry Takeshi Doi, a Kibei graduate of the MISLS, searched caves "with only a flashlight and knife persuading many enemy soldiers to come out and surrender." The army awarded Doi a Silver Star for his bravery on Iwo Jima.[69] Although trained to be interrogators, MIS soldiers such as Doi often found themselves on the front lines, exposed to the same dangers that the Marines faced. "The Nisei were brought here for office work," a Marine battalion commander on Iwo Jima told the press in April 1945, "and by golly, they've done better in the field than anyone."[70]

These sporadic accounts of Nisei linguists in the Pacific were largely overshadowed by the storied campaigns of the all-Nisei combat unit in Europe that had graced the pages in both national and Japanese American community newspapers since 1943. In fact, because of the sensitive nature of Nisei linguists' intelligence work and the overrepresentation of Japanese-speaking Kibei in the MIS, the army did not even publicly acknowledge Nisei's military service in the Pacific until February 1944.[71] As discussed in Chapter 3, the popularity of the 100th Infantry Battalion and the 442nd Regimental Combat Team even allowed the WRA and the JACL in 1944 to make Thomas Higa, a wounded Kibei veteran of the Italian campaign, a national hero and spokesperson for Nisei loyalty by organizing a nationwide speaking tour.[72] In the following year, Higa, a fluent Okinawan speaker, agreed to join the MIS in Okinawa to help persuade Japanese civilians in hiding to surrender.[73] His service as a linguist, however, went almost unnoticed by the press, and no welcome ceremony or speaking tour awaited Higa when he returned from his duty in Okinawa. Any serious effort to document the varied experiences of MIS servicemen in the Pacific would emerge only many years after the war.[74]

However, one MIS linguist's heroic service in the Pacific did receive national attention in early 1945. Frank Hachiya, a Kibei from Hood River, Oregon, participated in the "liberation" of the Marshall Islands in 1944, spending five months translating Japanese military documents.[75] After his service in the Marshall Islands, Hachiya was scheduled to return to the JICPOA in Hawaii, but he instead volunteered for one more combat tour. In December 1944 he led a team of linguists attached to an infantry division on Leyte in the central Philippines, where fierce battles had continued for days. Two nights before new year's day, Hachiya was caught in an ambush and shot in the abdomen while returning to his unit after interrogating a Japanese prisoner. According to newspaper reports, Hachiya crawled his way "out of the valley and up the hill, through the grass and the scrub," and completed his duty as "he was dying when he finally reached his lines" by making "his report while they bound his wound."[76] Five days later, Hachiya died and the Silver Star was awarded to him posthumously for his valor on the battlefield.[77]

The story of Hachiya's heroic service and tragic death stirred a nationwide controversy, as the press also exposed an incident that had taken place a month before in Hachiya's hometown of Hood River, Oregon. American readers learned that the American Legion of Hood River on November 29, 1944, in a blatant act of prejudice, had removed the names of all Japanese American inductees from the county's roll of honor. Readers who were moved by Hachiya's death responded to this discovery with outrage, and a campaign to restore the honor of Nisei soldiers from Hood River ensued. An editorial in the *New York Times* in February 1945 lamented, "Perhaps some day what is left of [Frank Hachiya] may be brought back to this country for reburial among the honored dead."[78] Two months later, the Associated Press's Joe Rosenthal, who photographed the famous flag raising on Iwo Jima, called the Hood River American Legion's decision a "crying shame."[79] In April 1945 mounting public pressure forced the American Legion in Hood River to restore the names of Nisei inductees to the roll of honor. Hachiya's identity as a Kibei, however, remained unannounced to the public.[80]

Itami, too, had to wait a full year after the war for any public recognition of his service in the MIS. In August 1946 Itami received his Legion of Merit award for having translated over 4,000 wartime Japanese documents.[81] However, no community celebration or speaking tour had been planned for him by the JACL. Nor did any Japanese American community newspaper break the story that Itami was back in Japan to serve at the Tokyo Trials when he received the award in his commander's office at Washington Heights, the Allied powers military complex in the Yoyogi neighborhood. In Itami's absence from home, the *Minneapolis Morning Tribune* interviewed his wife, Kimiko, who had remained at the family's wartime home in Minnesota, where Itami had worked as a U.S. Army language instructor. She mended military clothes for sale at a local army surplus store to support herself and her daughter, Michi. "When people said, 'You are [a]

NISEI WINS FIGHT TO 'PROVE SELF'

Downs FBI Distrust, Gets Merit Award

By RAY WIELAND
Minneapolis Tribune Staff Writer

A slight, modest Nisei woman told the story in Minneapolis Sunday of how her husband overcame the suspicion and distrust of the FBI in World war II to win the legion of merit and a high position of trust in the war crimes court in Tokyo.

Sgt. Akira Itami, 513 Eighteenth avenue N., she said, is a Kibei.

(Kibei is the name given Japanese-Americans sent to Japan for education. They were top priority suspects for the FBI at outbreak of the war.)

GETS INTELLIGENCE POST

At Camp Savage, where he taught for a year in the Japanese language school, Itami soon grew tired of constant questioning and investigation. He enlisted in the army to "prove himself."

Sgt. Itami

He soon convinced one officer after another of his loyalty. Importance of his work increased until he went to Washington to develop an intelligence library for the war department.

MRS. AKIRA ITAMI AND MICHIKO
Language expert's daughter tries Tokyo kimono

FIGURE 7 The Itami family. David Akira Itami's wife, Kimiko, and daughter, Michi, planned to join him in Tokyo in late 1946.
Minnesota Morning Tribune, September 16, 1946.

Kibei. We can't trust you,' it hurt him as if he had been called a traitor," she reflected on her husband's struggle to "prove himself" and his loyalty to the United States. "Now they know."[82]

Loyalty Has Many Faces

Itami and other Kibei's prewar life and education in Japan was the reason that the U.S. government and military authorities had suspected them as a pro-Japan group. Ironically, it was their education in prewar Japan that made them the most ideal linguists in the MIS in the Pacific during the war. Because of Itami's role in handling sensitive intelligence work, not much is known about his activities in the Pacific before his arrival in Tokyo four months after Japan's surrender. When he shot himself to death in Tokyo in 1950, he had told no one of the circumstances that led him to end his own life.

When Itami's wartime experience became a model for a popular Japanese novel in 1983, however, it added yet another dimension to the interpretation of Japanese American loyalty and nationalism. Because Itami himself left no written traces of his experiences, any attempt to recreate the narrative of his life story beyond a few available fragmentary sources has been difficult. The dearth of records on Itami's combat mission and personal life prompted the author of *Futatsu no Sokoku* to search for another real-life model to sustain her dramatic storytelling about a tragic Kibei hero. In a chapter titled "Brothers," Yamasaki invented a story of two Nisei brothers who encounter each other on a battlefield as enemies. Instead of David Itami, the real-life model that inspired Yamasaki's depiction of the main character Kenji Amo in this chapter is Harry Fukuhara, a Kibei MIS linguist from Seattle. In 1933, 13-year-old Fukuhara moved to Japan with his mother and brothers. In 1938 he returned to the United States by himself to attend college, leaving his mother and three brothers in Hiroshima. With his family stranded in Hiroshima during the Pacific War, Fukuhara joined the MIS. Although he had spent just five years in Japan, Fukuhara possessed excellent language skills, and upon completing the MISLS training, he emerged as one of the most reliable U.S. Army linguists. In April 1943 Fukuhara left for the Pacific with no basic military training; he served in New Guinea and the Philippines, where he became a commissioned officer in August 1945 just a couple of weeks before Japan's surrender.[83]

As the 33rd Infantry Division in northern Luzon prepared for the planned invasion of Japan in early August 1945, Fukuhara's worst fear was that he might encounter his brothers on the battlefield, as they would likely have been conscripted into the Japanese armed forces. To Fukuhara's relief, the U.S. deployment of atomic bombs on August 6 and August 9 made the invasion seem no longer necessary. However, he was soon horrified by the news that one of the bombs had been dropped on Hiroshima, where his family lived. He became anxious about finding his mother and three brothers. When Emperor Hirohito announced Japan's surrender on August 15, Fukuhara was determined to return to Japan to look for his family. In the following four weeks in the Philippines, the 33rd Infantry Division rapidly transformed itself "from attacker to peacekeeper," and the unit assigned Fukuhara the task of educating the American soldiers on the culture and customs of Japanese people before it left Luzon to occupy Japan.[84]

Two weeks after his unit landed on Wakayama in western Japan in September 1945 as a part of the Allied occupation forces, Fukuhara obtained permission to travel to Hiroshima to find his family members. In early October he returned to his family home in the destroyed city. His mother had found shelter in time to narrowly escape the blast from the atomic bomb, but his older brother Victor had fallen victim to the blast and radiation. Just as Fukuhara had anticipated in Baguio City in Luzon, his two younger brothers, Pierce and Frank, had been conscripted into the Japanese army. They had returned to Hiroshima shortly after the end of the war and thus avoided the atomic bombing. Fukuhara learned that his younger brother Frank had been trained for a kamikaze mission in Miyazaki Prefecture on the southern Japanese island of Kyushu, the place where the 33rd Infantry Division had originally planned to invade.[85] The atomic bomb that destroyed his family's hometown and killed thousands of Japanese people thus prevented the Fukuhara brothers from pointing rifles at each other on the battlefield.

Harry Fukuhara's story did wonders for Yamasaki's formulation of Amo's dramatic wartime experience in the Pacific. The author of *Futatsu no Sokoku* interviewed Fukuhara in Japan as part of her research for the novel before 1983.[86] Fukuhara's vivid description of the 33rd Infantry Division's liberation of Baguio in Luzon in 1945 combined with his fear of facing his brothers on the battlefield offered Yamasaki perfect material that could add more drama to her story and fill the void between David Itami's Washington and Tokyo years. In the "Brothers" chapter, Yamasaki twists Fukuhara's story to set up a dramatic scene in which U.S. Army lieutenant Kenji Amo meets his younger brother Tadashi, a stranded Nisei in Japan who had become a private in the Japanese Imperial Army, face to face in the Battle of Luzon in 1945.[87]

Yamasaki put together bits and pieces of Itami's and Fukuhara's life stories to set up Kenji Amo, the novel's heroic and tragic representation of Itami, as a linguist officer attached to the U.S. Army's 33rd Infantry Division, which landed on Luzon in early 1945. Yamasaki also set up the scene to highlight Amo's emotional dilemma, as he is torn between his Japanese consciousness and his allegiance to the American government. On the eve of the U.S. attack on Baguio, Amo sees on a list of Japanese POWs the name of a young soldier from Kajiki, Kagoshima, where Amo and his siblings had grown up. Amo decides to interrogate this Japanese prisoner, named Isa Shinkichi, hoping to learn the whereabouts of his brother Tadashi. When the interrogation commences, not only does Isa know Amo's younger brother, but he also recognizes Amo: "Aren't you Amo Otoshichi's son Kenji, the one who moved to America?" When Amo denies this adamantly, Isa continues, "Well, you look just like him. . . . I've heard from everybody in Kajiki that although Kenji Amo was an American-born Nisei, he was a fine Satsuma gentleman with true Japanese spirit, even better than ordinary Japanese. No way he would be interrogating Japanese prisoners of war." As a feeling of guilt swells up inside Amo, Isa presses harder, "Well, you look like you're well fed and your hair is shiny. And you're wearing that dandy American uniform. But do you have any idea what Tadashi's going through now?" Amo finally gives in: "Tell me about my brother." At Amo's request, Isa reveals that Tadashi Amo is a member of the Japanese army's Asahi Division on Luzon.[88]

The drama continues as Amo volunteers to join the patrol units on the front line to look for his brother, hoping he can persuade Tadashi to surrender. Meanwhile, Yamasaki's plot places Tadashi Amo in a small scouting party stranded on the American side in Baguio and desperately trying to catch up with their unit. While Tadashi's group goes into hiding, Kenji arrives at the scene accompanied by Caucasian soldiers, who soon discover the Japanese soldiers and start shooting. In this chaotic moment, the eyes of the two brothers meet and the stunned Tadashi murmurs in English, "Really you?" Kenji calls to his brother, "Tadashi, surrender! You'll be killed!" He then turns to his comrades, "Cease fire! He's my brother!" A Japanese sergeant, realizing what is happening, points his rifle at Tadashi's back, determined to shoot him if he surrenders to his brother in the American uniform. Tadashi has no intention of surrendering and certainly has no desire to provoke his sergeant by showing any sign of disloyalty. As both sides exchange fire, Kenji throws himself in front of his brother, rescuing him in a most dramatic fashion and capturing him as a prisoner of war.[89]

Yamasaki thus appropriated dramatic elements from the experiences of Itami and Fukuhara to allow her readers to see Kibei as perpetually torn between two sides. At the same time, the nature of Kibei's split loyalty becomes clearer as the story progresses, for the novel emphasizes Amo's emotional and cultural ties to his family and his "hometown" in Kagoshima. His connection to Japan by blood and his upbringing as a virtuous Kagoshima man would always outweigh his duty to the United States as a legal citizen.

The next climactic part in Yamasaki's reinterpretation of Itami's and Fukuhara's life experiences revisits Hiroshima in 1945. As the story moves toward its ending, Yamasaki continues to add more drama to convince her readers that the Kibei's emotional struggle between the two homelands directly contributes to his suicide. The story that follows Amo's battlefield encounter with his brother takes place in August 1945 in Manila when Kenji Amo receives a top secret account that an atomic bomb has been dropped on Hiroshima. The news of the atomic bombing brings back the memory of his intelligence work in Washington, D.C., the previous year, when he had been assigned to decode an intercepted telephone call between Tokyo and Berlin. In this dramatization, inspired by David Itami's real-life experience of intercepting Japanese diplomat Sogi Takateru's transmission from Berlin, Yamasaki reinvents the content of the coded conversation in Kagoshima dialect to set up the prelude to the novel's tragic ending. Amo recalls that the Japanese official in Berlin had hinted to Tokyo in coded language that the scientists who had worked on developing a devastating weapon in Germany had fled to England and America and potentially worked for the Allied powers. Could that devastating weapon have been an atomic bomb? Amo drives to a church outside Manila, kneels before the altar, and wonders whether his report on that coded phone conversation had been responsible for the U.S. government's development and hasty deployment of the atomic bomb that claimed thousands of Japanese lives. A pipe organ sounds solemnly in the empty cathedral, and Amo trembles in utter remorse for what he could only conceive as an unforgivable act committed by a person of Japanese ancestry.[90]

Throughout the novel these traumatic moments make Kenji Amo's emotional struggle between his two homelands grow stronger and, eventually, strong enough to kill him. As the story reaches the main character's return to Japan as a member of the occupying forces, Amo's guilt and anguish for his role in causing Japan's suffering become unbearable. His loyalty and dedication to his country of birth has only torn him and his family apart. Amo feels "lost between the two homelands—America, the country of his citizenship, and Japan, the land of his ancestors to which he was connected by blood." Disillusioned, Amo turns to death as the final solution to his suffering. To the last page, Yamasaki makes it clear that it is the Kibei's inability to find his own country that claims his life. In Tokyo Amo shoots himself in the head, and in his dying moment the images of the Stars and Stripes and the Red Sun appear before him. He reaches out his hand but cannot grasp the flags of his two homelands.[91]

Yamasaki's imaginative and dramatized portrayal of a Kibei man's deep attachment to Japan nevertheless evokes nostalgia for what other Japanese writers exploring Itami's life story romanticized as the image of a patriotic warrior-scholar. These commentators on Itami's Kagoshima upbringing assert that even Itami's fulfillment of his duties as an American citizen during the war must have been inspired by his roots in Japanese culture and moral tradition. They portray Itami's suicide as an ultimate expression of his loyalty to Japan. For many Japanese readers and especially for those who appreciated Itami's background as someone who had spent his childhood in Kajiki, the renewed interest in the Kibei man's life and death offered them the pleasure of rediscovering the meaning of Japanese nationalism decades after the country's defeat in the Pacific War.

Nisei Loyalty and the Sanga Moyu Controversy in the United States

Three decades after the war, David Akira Itami was a long-forgotten figure in the Japanese American community and the postwar narrative of Japanese American history. However, the popular Japanese novel and TV series based on his transpacific life created a heated controversy in the Japanese American community in the mid-1980s, when the movement for redress and reparations was in full swing. Encouraged by the popularity of Yamasaki's *Futatsu no Sokoku* in Japan, NHK scheduled the U.S. premiere of *Sanga Moyu* on West Coast Japanese-language cable stations for the spring of 1984. Both Yamasaki and the NHK executives anticipated that the drama's plot, centering on the Japanese American wartime experience, would be a natural fit for the U.S. audience. On the contrary, NHK's announcement of the series' U.S. debut was met with a fierce backlash from the Japanese American community on the West Coast. In particular, the story of a Nisei with split loyalties did not sit well with the leaders of the JACL. For the three decades after the war, the organization had vigorously promoted the history of Japanese Americans' 100% Americanism in their campaign for redress and reparations for the wartime incarceration. JACL leaders publicly protested what they viewed as Yamasaki's gross distortion of Japanese American history. "There are no torn loyalties," claimed the JACL's executive director, Ron Wakabayashi. Clifford Uyeda, a respected leader of the JACL's redress campaign, called the novel "an anti-American piece." The organization's national president, Floyd Shimomura, added, "We spent three generations trying to prove our loyalties. I'd hate to see a TV show undo all of that."[92]

The stakes were high for Shimomura and the JACL's influential lobbyists, such as the organization's former national secretary Mike M. Masaoka, who had worked closely with Washington politicians to push for a redress legislation. In early 1983 the bipartisan Commission on Wartime Relocation and Internment of Civilians (CWRIC), directed by the U.S. Congress, released a report after nearly three years of investigation and hearings on the impact of the wartime incarceration of Japanese Americans. The commission unanimously recommended a formal government apology and monetary reparations for the unjust detention of Japanese American civilians based on "race prejudice, war hysteria and a failure of political leadership."[93] Masaoka believed that the Nisei's continued demonstration of unquestioned loyalty to the United States would be crucial for American society's broad support for the commission's recommendations. He was determined to prevent *Sanga Moyu* from airing on American television, even if the viewership would be limited to Japanese-speaking cable subscribers. He demanded that NHK withdraw its plan to premiere *Sanga Moyu* in the United States, warning that the series "could jeopardize good relations on all sides."[94]

The heated public outcry and controversy prompted the network to cancel the series' premiere in the U.S. market. It would take six years before *Sanga Moyu* eventually debuted on the Japanese-language cable channel Nippon Golden Network in Hawaii in 1989. Bewildered and frustrated by the backlash against *Sanga Moyu*, Yamasaki accused her Japanese American critics of censoring the work based on the five years of what she described as sincere and rigorous research and writing. She complained that those outspoken Japanese American objectors in the United States did not even know how to read Japanese and thus could not have engaged her work properly.⁹⁵ Yamasaki's preparatory work for *Futatsu no Sokoku* had included research on Japanese American history during her brief stint as a visiting scholar in Hawaii in 1978. There she learned the history of Japanese American wartime incarceration, which became an important part of the novel's plot. However, she failed to grasp the centrality of Nisei's loyalty to the United States that had shaped the dominant collective historical memory in the Japanese American community and its postwar movement for redress and reparations.

The volatile historical developments in the 1930s and 1940s that shaped Itami's transpacific life and the wartime exigencies that engendered diverse responses from Kibei show that the postwar efforts for redress were similarly reductive about the role of Nisei as Yamasaki's simplistic narrative. Although Yamasaki's characterization of Itami as essentially a Japanese failed to consider his complex diasporic consciousness, the redress activists' rejection of Kibei's cultural duality also operated within a nationalistic framework. Itami lived through complex and unpredictable circumstances engendered by a war that had a lasting impact on the lives of Japanese Americans beyond these dichotomous narratives centering on national loyalty. But he did not live long enough to have a voice in this controversial debate over Kibei's split national allegiances inspired by his own transnational life.

CHAPTER 5

Between Two Empires

Nisei Citizenship and Loyalty in the Pacific Theater

IN A COLUMN PUBLISHED in the Japanese magazine *Kaigai no Nippon* in August 1942, Tokyo-based journalist Tamotsu Murayama urged his fellow Nisei in Japan to show their support for Japan's "Greater East Asia War." Murayama called on U.S.-born Japanese Americans to "return to the consciousness of their race" and demonstrate their undivided loyalty to the country of their parents.¹ In another article Murayama's expression of allegiance to Japan went even further. He claimed that Japanese Americans in Japan were ready to dedicate their lives to fulfilling the duties of their diasporic citizenship with "great perseverance and spirit of sacrifice necessary for the construction of a Greater East Asia." He deftly adopted the "pioneer" narrative of Japanese emigrants to depict the U.S.-born Nisei as the new group of migrants making inroads into Japan's march toward a pan-Asian empire.²

A seasoned reporter who had worked for American and Japanese news outlets before the war, Murayama understood the cultural and political nuances of national loyalty in both countries. The Seattle native had received his middle school education in Nagano Prefecture and returned to the United States to finish high school and college in San Francisco. By the early 1930s he had begun his career in journalism at the *San Francisco Chronicle* and joined the editorial staff of the San Francisco–based *Shinsekai Asahi* (The New World Sun).³ An emerging voice for the Bay Area's Japanese American community, Murayama actively professed Nisei's Americanization and undivided loyalty to the United States during the period of intense anti-Japanese hostility. In early 1935 he led a speaking circuit consisting of West Coast Japanese American community leaders to promote the positive image of Nisei to mainstream American society. Before an audience of prominent local political elites in Phoenix, Arizona, Murayama stressed Japanese Americans' U.S. citizenship by birth, declaring that Nisei's "loyalty is pledged to the United States."[4] Murayama relocated to Japan at the beginning of 1937 to pursue more lucrative career opportunities at state-run outlets there. Despite being away from the United States, Murayama commanded enough respect among San Francisco's Nisei that they elected him president of the city's Japanese American Citizens League (JACL).[5]

That Murayama quickly switched his national allegiance when the Pacific War began in 1941 illuminates how the volatile historical circumstances made the question of loyalty and citizenship fluid and fragile for Nisei migrants. Although 120,000 Japanese and Japanese Americans in the United States endured mass incarceration, the war also had a significant effect on the lives of more than 20,000 Japanese Americans who were stranded in the Japanese Empire. The Nisei in Japan did what they could to endure wartime hardships away from their families back home: surviving the firebombing, confronting the fear of living in wartime Japan as U.S. citizens, and wrestling with their uncertain future after the war. They also grappled with the ever fluid question of loyalty during the tragic war between the United States and Japan. Although the Japanese government never treated U.S.-born Japanese Americans as enemy aliens, the Nisei in Japan nevertheless faced mounting pressure to demonstrate their support for the Japanese war effort against their country of birth. For instance, despite U.S.-born Nisei's purported ethnic and cultural ties to Japan, the Japanese press scrutinized the national allegiance of Japanese American residents in Japan because of their U.S. citizenship. To Japanese Americans in the Pacific, the war made the issue of their legal and cultural citizenship ever more complicated and elusive. More than seven decades after World War II ended, the diverse stories of Japanese Americans in the Pacific Theater remain largely unexplored.

In this chapter I examine the various ways that Japanese American migrants negotiated the issue of wartime loyalty and citizenship outside the dominant U.S.-centered context of the Japanese American internment. In Japan some Nisei were able to deploy their cultural dualism, which allowed them to negotiate their fluid allegiances to the two nations during and after the war. For instance, many graduates of the Japanese state-run school Heishikan worked for Japanese intelligence, monitoring wartime English-language shortwave radio programs intercepted from Allied nations. Unlike the Nisei men in the Japanese military who lost their American citizenship for bearing arms against the United States, the noncombatant and clandestine nature of the Japanese American radio monitors' wartime service to Japan largely allowed them to avoid being branded traitors by the U.S. government. Moreover, many of these Nisei radio monitors argued after the war that their Heishikan training and their wartime intelligence work for the Japanese government had given them greater insights into U.S.-Japan relations, which allowed them to contribute to the postwar alliance between the two nations.

For many Nisei male dual citizens in wartime Japan, the price for their service to the Japanese Empire was their American citizenship; the Japanese government's claim of their loyalty forced these Japanese American men to fight the United States against their will. As the battles in Asia-Pacific dragged on, the Japanese government drafted an increasing number of Nisei men in Japan to serve in the military, especially during the final phase of the Pacific War in 1944 and 1945. These Nisei servicemen's fate illuminates an important gendered dimension of loyalty and citizenship. After the war the U.S. government stripped the birthright citizenship of the Nisei men for bearing arms against their country of birth. Their military service, generally under duress, not only cost them their legal citizenship as Americans but also permanently excluded them from the dominant public narrative of Japanese American loyalty and Americanism.

Collaborators or Innocent Helpers?
Diasporic Citizenship and Nisei Loyalty During World War II

Murayama's case offers an opportunity to explore how complex and salient the issue of loyalty—to the Japanese government—was to thousands of stranded Japanese Americans in wartime Japan. After brief stints at the Alliance News Agency and the Associated Press in the United States, Murayama relocated to Japan at the beginning of 1937 to work for the state-run Domei News Agency and Nippon Hoso Kyokai (Japan Broadcasting

Corporation; NHK). Intent on remaining in Japan, Murayama resigned from the JACL presidency one week after he had won the election.[6] In Japan his career thrived as an English-language correspondent for the state-run news outlets.

As soon as Japan's war with the United States began in December 1941, the Japanese press began to scrutinize Nisei's nationalism. Influential Japanese journalist Tomomatsu Toshio admonished Japanese Americans to abandon any lingering allegiance to their American citizenship: "Wise Nisei have probably recognized that the land of their birth is but a false and base foreign country." He told Nisei in his 1942 essay that "their birth certificate is only a scrap of paper."[7] Propaganda writers in Japan even wrote pieces that demanded Japanese Americans behind barbed wire in U.S. internment camps cultivate a pro-Japanese consciousness. When reports from the United States about Nisei's induction into the U.S. Armed Forces and the creation of the 100th Infantry Battalion reached Japan in 1942, Kanda Yoshi claimed that "good" Nisei would never dream of fighting against their parents' homeland. Government official Kawamura Masahei was confident that at least the good Nisei in Japan whom he personally knew would rather commit suicide than serve in the U.S. Armed Forces.[8]

Murayama was not the only Japanese American in wartime Japan who enthusiastically professed allegiance to the Japanese government. Noboru "Fred" Miike echoed the sentiment of Japanese writers who believed that all Nisei's racial and cultural consciousness should compel them to proclaim their loyalty to Japan. Miike joined the Japanese wartime propaganda effort, which was critical of racial discrimination in the United States, and reiterated the notion of the Pacific War as Japan's anti-imperial quest to liberate racial minorities in the U.S. territories. No reasonable "person of any color skin—white, black, yellow, red, brown—would want to fight for a country that does not grant him equality," claimed the Hawaii-born Nisei in 1942.[9]

Although many Japanese Americans in the U.S. internment camps faced a dire situation that forced them to prove their loyalty to the U.S. government, pressure was also on Nisei in Japan to demonstrate their allegiance to the Japanese government. There were signs that Japanese policymakers and political commentators were suspicious of Japanese American residents' ability to become loyal Japanese citizens. For instance, policy analyst Nakase Setsuo in early 1942 was far from convinced that the Nisei could readily abandon their "American life-styles."[10] As the war dragged on, another analyst, Murakami Tsugio, was extremely doubtful of Nisei's ability to emerge as pioneering leaders in an expanded "Co-prosperity Sphere." Murakami went so far as to claim that Nisei's "American character" disqualified them from becoming productive Japanese citizens, "however much they are made to know about their ancestral land's divinity and however much is cultivated in them the spirit of sincerity."[11]

Although none of these Japanese thinkers held a radically negative view of the Japanese Americans in Japan or branded them as enemy aliens, their cautious distrust of the Nisei residents was enough to alarm Murayama. In his wartime writings in Japan, Murayama persistently urged Japanese readers to recognize the Nisei as the legitimate heirs to the "vanguard of the Japanese race" and as "loyal citizens and soldiers."[12] In *Kaigai no Nippon* he implored the readers to remember that the Nisei in Japan were children of "pioneer" emigrants who were enduring "the inhuman treatment" in the form of mass incarceration in the United States. Although "Japan had been so unkind and heartless" in her suspicion of Nisei's loyalty to Japan, Murayama announced that the Japanese Americans in Japan were determined to dedicate themselves to the "victory of [Japanese] Imperial forces."[13]

Murayama's patriotic language was not far removed from his articulation of Japanese American loyalty to America before the war as a Nisei community leader in San Francisco. Moreover, it bore a striking resemblance to the language of unquestioned loyalty to the U.S. government expressed by such JACL-oriented Nisei as Mike M. Masaoka in the United States during and after World War II.[14] As a matter of fact, it was not a secret that Maruyama held a high regard for Masaoka, as the two men first encountered each other in 1936 in Masaoka's hometown of Salt Lake City. Masaoka, then a young University of Utah student, impressed Murayama with his exceptional public debating skills at a meeting to establish a JACL chapter in Utah.[15] During World War II, Masaoka emerged as an articulate spokesman for the Japanese American community in the United States, championing the notion of Nisei's unquestioned American patriotism and shaping the image of a loyal Japanese American. Similarly, in wartime Japan Murayama spoke on behalf of Japanese American residents in Japan, depicting them as loyal and patriotic members of the Japanese Empire. Murayama's emphasis on unconditional Nisei loyalty, cooperation, and sacrifice during the war almost sounded like a Japanese version of Masaoka's "allegiance through active participation in the war effort," although Masaoka certainly would not have approved of Murayama's allegiance to the Japanese government.[16]

Just as Masaoka had won the trust of Dillon S. Myer of the U.S. War Relocation Authority (WRA), Murayama's expression of loyalty allowed him to work closely with Japanese authorities during the war. In late 1942 the Japanese Foreign Ministry's Intelligence Bureau invited Murayama to render his service as an editor of war intelligence reports based on the translations of English-language shortwave radio programs from the Allied territories. Murayama's extensive experience as a bilingual journalist in the United States and Japan made him an ideal candidate for the wartime intelligence work.[17] Earlier that year, the Intelligence Bureau had created a team of radio monitors consisting mainly of English-speaking Nisei residents in the Tokyo area. These Nisei monitors' primary task was to transcribe the English radio broadcasts transmitted from Allied territories, such as the U.S. and British colonies. When the war suspended Japan's diplomatic channels with the Allied powers and isolated the Japanese Empire from the rest of the world, the Intelligence Bureau relied on overseas radio programs to gather the latest information on sociopolitical developments in the U.S. and British empires.[18] The Intelligence Bureau operated its "radio room" twenty-four hours a day and dispatched Nisei monitors on designated shifts to intercept Allied broadcast programs, such as *Voice of America*, *Radio Australia*, *All India Radio*, and *BBC News*. By late 1945 about fifty monitors worked in the radio room, including Nisei journalists who worked for Japanese press outlets, such as the *Japan Times*.[19]

Although the Nisei monitors dispatched to the radio room took on the rigorous task of spending many hours carefully listening to shortwave broadcasts, the extent of their service was strictly limited to transcribing the broadcasts. It was never their job to translate or analyze the transcripts, as they were effectively excluded from the task of summarizing and interpreting the gathered information. Based on the information compiled from the notes taken by the monitors, the Intelligence Bureau's Broadcasting Section put together a sixty-page daily report called the "Shortwave News," copies of which were delivered to the cabinet ministries and military branches.[20] Kabayama Sukehide, the head of the Broadcasting

Section, led a team of Japanese analysts to edit transcripts prepared by the young Nisei monitors. Murayama was the only Nisei on the editorial team whose qualifications and loyalty were trusted by bureau officials.[21]

Nevertheless, the labor of Nisei monitors was indispensable for the preparation of the "Shortwave News." Ikeda Norizane, a veteran insider of the Japanese intelligence community, supervised these young Nisei employees. A Tokyo native who had studied in Britain, Ikeda was a member of the Japanese diplomatic mission in Australia when the Pacific War broke out in December 1941. His boss, the Japanese first minister in Melbourne at the time, was none other than Kawai Tatsuo, the founder of the all-Nisei school Heishikan.[22] Upon repatriation to Japan in October 1942, Ikeda was transferred to the Intelligence Bureau's Broadcasting Section to work with the Nisei monitors.[23] According to Ikeda, the young Japanese Americans who had studied at Heishikan stood out as the most productive group among the forty Nisei wartime radio monitors. They aptly applied their Heishikan training in stenography to transcribe live broadcasts, whereas others used typewriters, until the Broadcasting Section obtained recording devices in 1945.[24]

Heishikan remained open throughout the war and recruited new students among young Nisei residents in Japan. The school continued to offer Japanese language, culture, and law classes in English and sponsored cultural excursion programs. Heishikan students lived in the school's dormitory in Nakano Ward on the outskirts of Tokyo and continued to receive stipends. They took classes during the day and took night shifts as monitors in the radio room. After the air raids by the Allied powers destroyed the railways, the Nisei monitors walked or hitchhiked to the radio room in the remote rural section of western Tokyo.[25]

In general, Heishikan's Nisei students, who had become stranded in Japan after Pearl Harbor, saw the school as a haven that enabled their survival. Fumiko Tabata, a stranded Nisei in Japan who enrolled at Heishikan after Pearl Harbor, thought it "remarkable" that classes were held in English, the "language of the enemy," which had been banned elsewhere in Japan.[26] When the Foreign Ministry called on Nisei Heishikan students to work in the Broadcasting Section as radio monitors, they considered it an obligation to render their service to their benefactor.[27]

Masao Ekimoto, a Nisei college student from Southern California, was running out of money in 1942 and applied for a Heishikan scholarship.

He was admitted to the school in December 1942 and immediately started working in the radio room.²⁸ Ekimoto's experience illuminates how the war between the United States and Japan complicated the issue of citizenship and loyalty for the Nisei Heishikan students. Ekimoto was 21 years old in 1939, when he learned about Heishikan from Sei Fujii, his father's friend and the publisher of the Los Angeles–based newspaper *Kashu Mainichi*. The chance of getting a two-year government scholarship to study in Japan intrigued Ekimoto, who had to give up on pursuing a higher degree in the United States because of financial difficulties. Ekimoto was a top student at high school and an experienced writer and editor for the school newspaper. Like many other applicants for the Heishikan scholarship, Ekimoto saw education in Japan as a way out of the Japanese American community in California, where few Nisei enjoyed the prospect of building a career outside the ethnic community. By the time Ekimoto drove to the Japanese American Consulate General in Los Angeles to apply for the scholarship in the fall of 1939, however, Kay Tateishi, Sam Masuda, and two other Nisei had already been selected from Southern California to attend Heishikan. Unswayed, Ekimoto left for Japan shortly after his twenty-second birthday in January 1940, as his determination to continue his education convinced the president of a local Japanese American bank to provide a $2,000 loan without security.²⁹

Ekimoto boarded the Japanese ocean liner *Tatsuma Maru* in January 1940 at a moment of heightened U.S.-Japan diplomatic tension, as the Sino-Japanese war dragged on. In fact, when the ship left San Francisco on January 18, 1940, some twenty-three months before Pearl Harbor, the war in Europe and Asia had already jeopardized the safety of transpacific voyages between the United States and Japan. In December 1939, more than 500 seamen had scuttled the German cruise liner *Columbus* off the coast of New Jersey to escape capture by a British destroyer. They traveled by train to San Francisco to board the *Tatsuma Maru* on January 18, 1940, bound for Yokohama, where they would embark on a return passage to Germany. This plan was canceled at the last minute for fear that the presence of German passengers might cause the British Navy to intercept the Japanese vessel en route to Yokohama.³⁰ As the *Tatsuma Maru* set sail, Ekimoto saw two British cruisers approaching the ship to check whether German nationals were on board. A week later, while docking at Honolulu, Ekimoto and other passengers on the *Tatsuma Maru* learned that British naval vessels from Hong Kong had stopped the *Asama Maru* out of Yokohama and seized two German passengers.[31] To avoid any confrontation with the British naval forces, the *Tatsuma Maru* stayed off the direct path to Yokohama and took an alternative route through Micronesia, reaching Yokohama in February 1940. After arriving in Japan, Ekimoto enrolled in a Japanese immersion program at Nichibei Home, a boarding school for Nisei students, before fulfilling his goal of attending college classes at Waseda University. On December 8, 1941, he went to school as usual, only to learn that the Japanese attack on Pearl Harbor had stranded him and the forty members of Waseda's international student club in Japan.[32]

A former dual citizen, Ekimoto had renounced his Japanese citizenship before relocating to Japan in 1940 and thus had no obligation to serve in the Japanese military. After Pearl Harbor, however, he felt uncertain about what his legal status as a citizen of the enemy nation might do to his chance of sitting out the war in Japan. When he secured admission at Heishikan, however, he could feel safe as a student at a government-run institution for foreign nationals of Japanese ancestry.[33] This circumstance provided him and other Heishikan students with little room to consider their service to the Foreign Ministry's Intelligence Bureau during the war as a breach of their loyalty to the United States.

For Susumu Saiki, a Stockton, California, native who graduated from high school in Hiroshima and moved to Tokyo in August 1943, the education at Heishikan offered him the opportunity to brush up on his English. While his family in the United States spent the war years behind barbed wire, being stranded in Japan actually allowed Saiki the luxury of continuing his education. Norio Hide from Wapato, Washington, who joined Heishikan in April 1944, worked as a radio room monitor and transcribed *Voice of America* broadcasts after taking classes during the day. When he visited a friend's home in a rural town in Fukuoka during the summer break, he was stunned to find that almost all the men from the village had been conscripted into the military. His enrollment at Heishikan and service to the Foreign Ministry had allowed him to avoid the possibility of being drafted and taking arms against the country of his birth.[34]

However, the role of Japanese Americans in wartime intelligence work at the Japanese Foreign Ministry became the basis for the assertion made by some postwar critics of Heishikan that Kawai's brainchild essentially had been a clandestine spy school. Ten years after the war, a former student using the pseudonym Ikuro Hiroda, who claimed that he had been born in Great Britain and studied at Heishikan, recalled that the school had been nothing but a "modern" training facility for spies.[35] In an article published in the monthly news magazine *Gendai* in 1997, Shimojima Tetsuro, a nonfiction writer, accused the Ministry of Foreign Affairs of the wartime "crime" of using young second-generation Japanese Americans for espionage. Shimojima used his interview with former Heishikan student George Ogishima to claim that the young Nisei students had been deceived and manipulated by the Intelligence Bureau officials into serving the Japanese war effort.[36]

However, more recent research by Kumei Teruko and the testimonies of former Nisei Heishikan students and radio room monitors have rejected any allegation against the Nisei's wartime service in the Japanese Foreign Ministry as espionage work. Moreover, the former monitors have maintained that their employment by the Foreign Ministry should not be considered an act of disloyalty against the United States.[37] More than fifteen years after the closure of the school in 1945, the alumni stood firm in their belief in the bridge-building ideal of Heishikan's mission: "The purpose of Heishikan, at the time of its establishment, was to have the students train themselves well, to enter society, and, in the end, to stand between Japan and the United States and . . . to erect a shining, golden bridge across the Pacific Ocean, a bridge over which the traffic will be not one-way but in both directions."[38] Ekimoto, a member of the school's second class, told his fellow alumni during a reunion luncheon in 2006 that Shimojima's accusation against Heishikan was a "regrettable case" stemming from ignorance and misunderstanding. Ekimoto argued that, because the school had been founded by the Foreign Ministry's Intelligence Bureau on the eve of the Pacific War and the Nisei graduates did work for the Bureau's Broadcasting Section, it was easy for critics like Shimojima to conclude that the Japanese government had established the school as a spy-training facility. Heishikan, Ekimoto reminisced, was "truly a warm . . . 'home away from home' in a strange land during a difficult period."[39]

In fact, Ekimoto and other Heishikan students even saw their work in the radio room as a way to fulfill the bridge-building purpose of their transnational education. They hoped that the work of monitoring radio programs from the Allied nations during the war would somehow help ameliorate the U.S.-Japan relations by providing the Japanese Foreign Ministry with accurate information from home. Norio Hide, who worked for the U.S. Department of Defense after the war, wrote to his fellow alumni in November 2006 to stress that his education at Heishikan during the war had strengthened his "international understanding" through his service to both Japan and the United States. Hide believed that the "spirit of Heishikan" and the knowledge of Japan he had gained from the school had allowed him to build a career in the U.S. government after the war and enabled him to serve effectively as a liaison between U.S. and Japanese forces for forty-seven years.[40]

The controversial role of Nisei monitors in the Broadcasting Section remains largely unknown to the public at large. This is in stark contrast to the sensationalized story of Iva Toguri. Toguri was a Japanese American who appeared in the wartime Japanese propaganda radio broadcast *Zero Hour*, and she was notoriously dubbed Tokyo Rose, a moniker that actually had been coined by Allied troops listening to Japanese radio broadcasts before Toguri's appearance. Los Angeles native Toguri went to Japan in July 1941 to visit her relatives, only to be stranded in Tokyo when the Pacific War broke out in December 1941. She was working as a typist for Radio Tokyo when Charles Cousens, the Australian prisoner of war placed in charge of *Zero Hour*, recruited her in November 1943 to host the show. Cousens had gotten to know Toguri while he was an inmate at a Tokyo POW camp. Toguri had helped Cousens and other Allied inmates by smuggling food into the prison. Cousens was impressed by Toguri's outgoing personality and impeccable American English accent. Toguri initially refused to work on the radio program but agreed to join the *Zero Hour* team when Cousens promised that she would not have to make anti-American comments on the show.

Although Toguri's role during *Zero Hour* broadcasts was limited largely to announcing music and telling funny stories under the nickname Orphan Ann, after the war the American media and government accused her of betraying her country. Even though she was one of more than a dozen female propaganda broadcasters—all Japanese citizens except Toguri—on wartime Japanese radio, Toguri's American citizenship made her appearance on *Zero Hour* an act of treason against the United States. Largely swayed by the public hysteria surrounding Tokyo Rose, the U.S. government convicted Toguri of treason, stripped her U.S. citizenship, and sentenced her to ten years in prison.[41]

Numerous news reports and studies have since restored Toguri's honor by exposing the fallacy of the Tokyo Rose legend that had led to her being wrongfully accused of performing propaganda work for the Japanese government.[42] These works have revealed that the treason case had scapegoated Toguri, whom the media had established as the voice representing all wartime English-language propaganda radio announcers in Japan, and essentially handled her case as a trial against the mythical character of Tokyo Rose rather than against Iva Toguri's actual deeds. Ironically, it was Toguri's decision to keep her American citizenship during the war that allowed the U.S. government to try her for treason. Despite the pressure from her superiors in the Japanese Foreign Ministry's Intelligence Bureau to renounce her American nationality as a measure to prevent potential future repercussions, she was adamantly loyal to her citizenship by birth.[43]

Unlike Toguri, in the immediate postwar years the former Heishikan students and radio room monitors faced virtually no public allegation against their wartime involvement with the Japanese Foreign Ministry's intelligence work. A few published sources, testimonies of former Nisei radio room employees, and a U.S. government investigation have suggested that the Nisei monitors' role was too limited to warrant any evidence that would incriminate them as spies. Also, Heishikan's curriculum included no special training that would have qualified its students as intelligence agents. Moreover, American intelligence experts after the war did not view young Nisei's wartime activities in the Japanese Intelligence Bureau as spy work. In 1949 a State Department report from the U.S. political adviser in Kobe dismissed the idea of Heishikan as a training facility for spies. According to the report, the school had been decidedly "liberal" and nonmilitaristic in its pedagogical approach. The adviser claimed that the Heishikan curriculum, which included history, politics, law, classics, and calligraphy, resembled that of any standard diplomatic training course, including the American version.[44]

The report signified that the U.S. government did not consider the wartime employment of young Nisei by various Japanese press outlets, as well as the Japanese Foreign Ministry, as evidence of their service to the Japanese emperor. According to the 1940 U.S. Nationality Act, "performing the duties of any office, post, or employment under the government of a foreign state" could become a basis for one's loss of one's U.S. citizenship.[45] This provision did not apply to the Japanese American monitors in the

Japanese Foreign Ministry's Intelligence Bureau. Several former Nisei Heishikan graduates and Broadcasting Section monitors had little trouble obtaining American passports soon after the war's end and returned to the United States.[46] Susumu Saiki, a member of Heishikan's third class and former Broadcasting Section monitor, remained in Japan after the war to continue his education at Meiji University. He returned to California in 1958, facing no legal obstacle to his loyalty to the United States, and resettled in San Francisco. Consequently, Saiki was appalled by postwar Japanese articles alleging that the Heishikan students' employment as shortwave broadcast monitors for the Foreign Ministry could have been a sign of treason against the United States.[47]

Fighting for the Emperor: Nisei Draftees in the Imperial Armed Forces

Although the former Heishikan students and Japanese American civilian monitors in the Japanese Foreign Ministry's Broadcasting Section had little trouble retaining their U.S. citizenship, the same could not be said about the Nisei men who were conscripted into the Japanese military during the Pacific War. After the war the U.S. government strictly enforced the provisions in Section 401 of the 1940 Nationality Act. According to this law, the Japanese Americans who served in the Japanese military during the war had "serv[ed] in the armed forces of a foreign state" without authorization of the U.S. government and thus had committed the treasonous act of "bearing arms against the United States."[48]

Because Japanese military records do not specify whether or not their servicemen held foreign citizenship, it is difficult to ascertain the number of Nisei who were forced to fight against the Allied forces during World War II.[49] Nisei male dual citizens of military age in Japan could have numbered well over 2,000, but only a handful of accounts of former Japanese American servicemen in the Japanese armed forces emerged in the latter half of the twentieth century.[50] Kay Tateishi, a Heishikan graduate who avoided conscription by working for Domei News Agency during the war, suggested that almost all the military-age Nisei male dual citizens in Japan served in the imperial armed forces against their will during World War II.[51] Many of the Nisei men like Tateishi who did not serve in the military had acquaintances who entered the army or navy during the war. Shigeo Yamada, a Nisei officer in the Japanese navy during the last two years of the war, remembered to visit his fellow Japanese American friends in Tokyo, including radio room monitor Masao Ekimoto, whenever he was on leave. One of Ekimoto's fondest wartime memories was seeing his Nisei friend return to Tokyo alive and spending a few days together in the city despite the firebombing.[52]

Yamada, who grew up on a potato farm in Idaho, moved to Japan in 1939 after graduating from high school to enroll in a Japanese immersion program at Nichibei Gakuin and later to study at Keio University in Tokyo. Although university students were initially exempted from military service, the Japanese government reversed this policy and started to conscript young men out of colleges in December 1943, when the Japanese battlefield casualty rate was reaching a staggering 20%.[53] Yamada left Tokyo in the fall of 1944 to start training in the Navy Signal Corps, where he specialized in decoding enemy wireless transmissions. He was commissioned as an ensign on Christmas Day, and on completion of his training, was dispatched to the cruiser *Yahagi*, which joined the 10th Destroyer Squadron near Sumatra.[54] Joining him on the *Yahagi* was another Nisei ensign, Shigeaki Kuramoto, who had played football at Meiji University before joining the navy.[55]

On April 6, 1945, five days after the American invasion of Okinawa, which signified the near complete victory of the Allied forces, the *Yahagi* escorted the famed battleship *Yamato* into the South China Sea in what would turn out to be the Japanese navy's final desperate sortie. Yamada and Kuramoto's main task was monitoring radio traffic between the Allied fleet and pilots and translating the transmissions simultaneously.[56] The next day, hundreds of American planes joined the Allied submarines and destroyers in a one-sided battle that nearly wiped out the Japanese squadron. Yamada miraculously survived, despite being an "Idaho potato" who didn't know how to swim. He clung to debris from the destroyed ships to stay afloat until a Japanese destroyer that had escaped the battle rescued him and other survivors. Fellow Nisei officer Kuramoto was not as fortunate; he drowned with nearly 3,000 other Japanese sailors aboard the ships.[57]

Brawley, California, native Iwao Peter Sano was another Nisei serviceman in the Japanese military who lost his U.S. citizenship after the war. Sano left for Japan in the summer of 1939 at the age of 15 to become a *yoshi*, or an adopted son, of his childless uncle and aunt in Yamanashi Prefecture in central Japan. Sano's adoption into his uncle's household was entirely his parents' decision, but he accepted it without protest and held no resentment at the prospect of being separated from his family in Imperial Valley. Instead, he wondered how he would learn Japanese, which he spoke very little, and adjust to new customs and surroundings. Sano managed to learn enough Japanese that summer to enroll in middle school and relocated to Tokyo to attend high school.[58] After the Pacific War broke out, Sano returned to Yamanashi to wait for the draft order. When he was drafted into the army and reported to the assembly center in Tokyo in March 1945, the possibility of dying on the battlefield abroad did not affect him much, as he looked forward to leaving the city ravaged by air raids and food shortages. Sano and fifteen other draftees traveled through the Korean Peninsula to join the 118th Regiment of the Kwantung Army in Manchuria to be trained as suicide bombers. Sano felt relieved that he was not assigned to a unit in the South Pacific, where he would have been forced to fight against the American forces. Sano's fear was that his own brother, Patrick, who had remained in California with his parents, could well have been drafted into the U.S. Army. For Sano, the prospect of becoming a human bomb felt less dreadful than the possibility of facing American troops on the battlefield.[59]

Sano served in the Kwantung Army when the Japanese military was desperately scraping through the final phase of the war. By the time Sano arrived in Manchuria, the 118th Regiment had shipped its artillery to the Pacific front, where the Allied forces were scoring decisive victories. With their arsenal virtually empty, Sano and other troops of the regiment went through the training as suicide bombers to carry the remaining bombs and dive under Soviet tanks. By the time they prepared for the final showdown in August 1945, however, the war had come to an end and the regiment surrendered to the Soviet army. For Sano, the end of the war was the beginning of his three-year ordeal in a Soviet POW camp in Siberia. As a prisoner of war in Krasnoyarsk, he was forced to perform heavy labor, including coal mining and factory work producing tank tracks. What threatened the prisoners' chance of survival, however, turned out to be hunger and the bitter cold. Sano was constantly preoccupied with securing food, but he also observed that the camp's Russian employees were in a similar plight, as the war had devastated the Soviet Union.[60] Sano was one of 650,000 Japanese POWs detained in Soviet camps after World War II.

Although most of the 3.5 million Japanese POWs who had surrendered to the American forces in the Pacific and China were repatriated to Japan in 1946, it took Sano and other POWs in Siberia another two years until they were allowed to return to Japan.[61] Finally, in June 1948, Sano arrived at Maizuru in western Japan, one of the coastal cities designated as repatriation ports.[62]

When the war forced many Nisei men in Japan to fight the United States against their will, the question of loyalty affected them in different ways. What they shared in common, though, was that, however reluctant they were about serving in the Japanese military and taking arms against the United States, the stranded Nisei had little choice but to fulfill their duty as Japanese citizens. Although Nisei veterans of the Japanese military could recover their U.S. citizenship after the war, the onus was on them once again to convince the U.S. government that they had been forced to serve the Japanese emperor under duress.

From the Stateless to Citizens: Loyalty, Citizenship, and Belonging in the Japanese American Diaspora

For Shigeo Yamada, Peter Sano, and other Nisei men who served in the Japanese military and returned to Japan alive, their ability to speak English offered them an opportunity to work for the Allied occupation forces in charge of governing Japan after the war. Japan under occupation had quickly transformed these Nisei veterans of the Japanese military from traitors to important assets for America's cold war empire in the Pacific. Despite their act of "disloyalty" to the United States during the war, the U.S. occupation government embraced their service in various civil staff sections, as their language skills proved to be valuable. After his discharge from the Japanese navy, Shigeo Yamada returned to Tokyo and worked for the Civilian Intelligence Section at the General Headquarters of the Supreme Commander for the Allied Powers (SCAP). According to the report prepared by SCAP, the Civilian Intelligence Section operated as "a sort of F.B.I. for the Occupation." Yamada's background as a Japanese naval officer helped secure this employment in 1946. Yamada conducted security surveillance by analyzing the activities of "radically inclined" Japanese groups, such as organized labor and right-wing "militarist" organizations.[63]

After his return to Yamanashi Prefecture in June 1948, Peter Sano translated local newspapers at the Civil Information and Education Section of the Occupation Office in Yamanashi. He transferred to the section's Tokyo office, where he met his future wife, Minako Hirata, also a translator at the Civil Information and Education Section.[64] Because their service in the Japanese armed forces had stripped their U.S. citizenship, both Yamada and Sano were employed by SCAP as Japanese civilian staff.

Jim Yoshida, another former Nisei serviceman in the Japanese army, worked as a civilian employee for the British Commonwealth forces that occupied Mizuba in Yamaguchi Prefecture, procuring local workers for the postwar rebuilding of infrastructure in the region. A son of a Japanese immigrant businessman in Seattle, Jim Yoshida had accompanied his mother on a vacation to Japan in April 1941. The Yoshidas did not intend to settle permanently in Japan, as Jim had a college scholarship waiting for him in the states. However, as the family prepared their return trip to Seattle in early August of that year, the escalating U.S.-Japan diplomatic tensions would forever change the course of Yoshida's life. The Japanese government's decision to suspend all shipping to the United States on August 1, as a response to the U.S. embargo of aviation fuel to Japan, forced Yoshida and other Japanese Americans who had wished to return to the states to be stranded on the archipelago. For the next few months, Yoshida anxiously waited in his father's hometown in Yamaguchi Prefecture, hoping for the news of normalized diplomacy between the two countries. Instead, the news of the Japanese attack on Pearl Harbor on December 7 shattered his hope of returning to Seattle and starting college.[65]

What Yoshida did not know was that, at the time of his birth in Seattle in July 1921, the Japanese government had claimed his citizenship and allegiance on the basis of *jus sanguinis* (citizenship by blood). A dual citizen, Yoshida was subject to conscription into the Japanese military for its war against his country of birth. Although the revised Japanese Nationality Law in 1924 allowed Nisei in the United States to renounce their Japanese citizenship, Yoshida's parents were oblivious to this changed policy and their son remained a dual citizen.[66] Neither they nor Yoshida could have foreseen a war between the United States and Japan and how it would affect the lives of Nisei in Japan. In the fall of 1942 Yoshida was summoned by the Japanese army to report for a physical examination. As a member of the 42nd Division out of Yamaguchi, Yoshida would spend the rest of the war years on the Manchurian front before his repatriation to Japan, joining hundreds of Nisei men in the Japanese military who automatically lost their U.S. citizenship as a result of their service to the emperor during the Pacific War.[67]

In his memoir, Yoshida emphasizes that he had had no desire to fight for the Japanese military during World War II and was torn by the "helluva fix" in which he found himself. When the Korean War broke out in June 1950, he was eager to show his loyalty to the country of his birth. He volunteered to work as a civilian interpreter for the U.S. Army in Korea, where he spent more than six months in combat zones. Yoshida hoped that helping the American war efforts in Korea would boost his chance of recovering his U.S. citizenship, which he had lost as a result of his service in the Japanese military against his will. Yoshida took great pains to regain his citizenship, as he navigated the bureaucratic red tape to obtain a special visa that allowed him to travel to Hawaii and file a civil suit against the U.S. government for taking his citizenship away. In 1953 Yoshida regained his U.S. citizenship and resettled in Hawaii.[68]

On the other hand, for Shigeo Yamada, the question of loyalty was not a simple matter of choosing sides. Like Yoshida, the thought of fighting in the war against the United States had deeply troubled Yamada's conscience, and he obeyed the conscription order only to avoid being thrown in jail. Nevertheless, Yamada also accepted military duty for the Japanese emperor as his service to people "of the same blood." Yoshida reflected that two years of education in Japan had "rather brainwashed" him to give service to the Japanese navy. After the war, Yamada decided not to recover his U.S. citizenship. "I don't consciously feel it's right," Yamada told Michael Hirsch of the Associated Press in 1990, "[because] I did take arms against my country of birth."[69]

Peter Sano returned to the United States in 1952 as an immigrant and soon became an American citizen again. Having lost his U.S. citizenship in Japan as a result of his military service in the Imperial Army during the final year of the Pacific War, Sano had to apply for naturalization. He went through the citizenship test, interview, and pledge of allegiance, as part of the procedure designed to assess foreign-born immigrants' loyalty and Americanization. Back in California, the former suicide bomber became an architect and a passionate peace activist who participated in antiwar demonstrations throughout the Vietnam War era. Sano also refused to work on any project related to the military and continued until 2013 to talk publicly about his wartime experiences as a cautionary tale against military indoctrination.⁷⁰

World War II in the Pacific altered the lives of many Japanese Americans in the former Japanese Empire, as those who survived the war faced difficult decisions on where and how to pursue their future. Many Nisei decided to stay in Japan permanently and live the rest of their lives as Japanese, whereas others returned to the United States. Like Sano, the Japanese American migrants who had lost their U.S. citizenship abroad were confronted with the American legal system that once again scrutinized their loyalty. For these Nisei to return to the United States and reunite with their families, recovering their U.S. citizenship involved entering into the complex postwar system of U.S. immigration and naturalization policies as foreigners. Their new legal status as immigrants then allowed them the right to become U.S. citizens through naturalization.

The postwar experiences of Peter Sano and other Japanese American survivors of Japan's war in the Pacific show that these transnational individuals shaped the intersected histories of the U.S. occupation in Japan, postwar immigration, and the Asian American social movement. Peter Sano's emergence as an American peace activist after the war was a culmination of his exile as a Japanese prisoner of war and his struggle to navigate the postwar American system of immigration and citizenship to reclaim his place in Japanese American history through his diasporic identity.

Reclaiming America

Tamotsu Murayama remained in Japan and continued working for the *Japan Times* after the war, but his career as a propagandist was over as soon as Japan lost the war in August 1945. He quickly shed his identity as a pro-Japan writer and established a new career as a philanthropist and administrator, which allowed him to work closely with Americans. Murayama became known for his dedication to building the Boy Scouts Federation of Japan during the three decades after the war.⁷¹ He died in 1968 at the age of 63 on a trip to Hong Kong for an international Boy Scouts conference, and his wartime activities as a propaganda writer have remained long forgotten in Japan and the United States.⁷²

FIGURE 8 A 1954 story featuring Tamotsu Murayama's postwar transformation was headlined "Japan Editor Takes His Boy Scouting Seriously."
Honolulu Advertiser, June 6, 1954.

Murayama's passionate expression of loyalty to Japan and his cooperation with Japanese intelligence work during World War II did not seem to affect his relationship with Bill Hosokawa, an influential JACL historian. Like Mike M. Masaoka, Hosokawa was instrumental in shaping the postwar public narrative of Japanese American loyalty to the U.S. government and 100% Americanism.[73] Murayama and Hosokawa had become acquainted before the Pacific War, when Murayama was working as a journalist in San Francisco. Despite Murayama's pro-Japan sentiment during the war, no animosity existed between the two men in the summer of 1960 when Murayama visited Hosokawa in Denver as the leader of the Japanese delegation to an international Boy Scouts jamboree in Colorado. Hosokawa helped Murayama meet Denver mayor Dick Batterton, who agreed to establish a sister-city relationship between Denver and Takayama, a small mountainous city in central Japan.[74] Perhaps Hosokawa, who, like Murayama, had once moved to Asia to seek work as a journalist before the war, understood that like the Japanese Americans in the United States,

Murayama and other Nisei in wartime Japan had faced a situation in which they needed to take extreme measures to proclaim their loyalty to a nation.

The diverse experiences of Japanese Americans in various corners of the Pacific during World War II demonstrate that the meaning of loyalty was far more complex and fragile than the matter of choosing between two countries. For many stranded Nisei in Japan, the war blurred the cultural, political, and even legal boundaries of their citizenship, as they found themselves in situations in which they had little room to negotiate their national allegiance. The Japanese government's treatment of American citizens of Japanese ancestry during the war never amounted to the mass incarceration endured by Japanese Americans in the United States. Nevertheless, the loyalty of Nisei migrants to their ancestral land was under close scrutiny, and they responded in various ways to render their service to the Japanese war effort against the Allied forces.

CHAPTER 6

Buried Wounds of the Secret Sufferers

Memory, History, and the Japanese American Survivors in the Nuclear Pacific

BORN IN PASADENA, CALIFORNIA, in 1927 to a well-to-do immigrant family, Kaz Tanaka Suyeishi followed her Japanese parents' return migration to Hiroshima as a toddler and grew up in the city's Minami Kannonmachi neighborhood.[1] By 1941 the Japanese exclusion movement in the United States had driven some 11,000 U.S.-born Nisei to their parents' hometowns throughout Hiroshima Prefecture, which had sent the largest number of Japanese emigrants to the United States in the late nineteenth century and the early 1900s. Suyeishi was one of the 3,000 Nisei from the United States who lived within Hiroshima's city limits at the start of the Pacific War.[2] Although she spent the war years in the city with a major military garrison and some of Japan's largest munitions plants, Suyeishi did not fully grasp the lasting implications of the bitter conflict between her two homelands on her life as an American citizen living in Japan. From time to time she even waved at the B-29 bombers flying over her house on their way to Tokyo and other firebombing targets, calling those planes her American "silver angels."[3]

Nevertheless, the war deeply transformed Suyeishi's daily life as it drew closer to its tragic end. Upon graduating from Hiroshima First Girls' Prefectural High School in the summer of 1945, Suyeishi joined her peers in the Women's Volunteer Citizens Corps, which was mobilized throughout Japan by national decrees to sustain industrial and military production during the final phase of World War II.[4] Working part-time at a Mitsubishi Heavy Industries factory in Hiroshima exposed Suyeishi to the devastating impact of Japan's "Greater East Asia War" on the lives of the conscripted laborers and their families from Korea, the country Japan had annexed in 1910. She witnessed the physical toil and social discrimination that the hundreds of Korean workers were subjected to on a daily basis.[5] A few of her own neighbors were Koreans who visited her home from time to time to see her father, a well-known benefactor around the neighborhood who generously gave food and money to the poor during the war.[6]

However, nothing would alter Suyeishi's life more than the destruction that befell Hiroshima, which had the heaviest concentration of U.S.-born Nisei. On the morning of August 6, 1945, while fetching water in the backyard of her family home, Suyeishi spotted one of her "silver angels" flying close by. This time, she saw a strange "white spot falling away" from the American B-29 bomber. Not one minute had passed after she had lost sight of the plane when the blast from the atomic bomb explosion threw her upside down to the ground. When she regained consciousness, she found her body cut and bruised by flying debris. Suyeishi was one of the thousand U.S.-born Japanese Americans who survived the atomic bombing in Hiroshima that day.[7]

Suyeishi fell ill within a few months after the bombing and would spend the rest of her life battling the aftereffects of the radiation exposure. In 1949 she returned to the United States to study fashion, determined to rebuild her "second life." Soon she would be joined by hundreds of fellow Nisei A-bomb survivors from Hiroshima and Nagasaki who left Japan to pursue second lives of their own in their country of birth.[8] The tragic end to the war marked one of the critical moments of diasporic upheaval that would continue to shape these American atomic bomb victims throughout the postwar decades. Back in the United States, despite their hope for a new start upon their return migration, they found themselves in a country that refused to acknowledge their existence as American civilian victims of the atomic bombing. Without recognition as survivors of wartime atrocities, they struggled to gain access to resources for proper medical treatment for their radiation illnesses.[9]

In this chapter I examine the struggles of Nisei A-bomb survivors to illuminate the limits of the postwar regime of compensatory justice and the politics of the Japanese American redress movement. Japanese American A-bomb survivors remain excluded and are essentially stateless in the historical memories of a war shaped by the exigencies of U.S. geopolitical interests as a cold war empire. The U.S.-centered liberation narrative of the atomic bomb and the dominant domestic framework of the Japanese American wartime experience have had little room for Nisei A-bomb survivors' perspectives on the transnational impact of wartime violence committed against Japanese Americans on both sides of the Pacific. Yet these survivors never disappeared from history. Their negotiation with the postwar politics of citizenship and historical memory challenges the narratives of the war, the postwar Japanese American redress movement, and the meaning of loyalty.

Living with Buried Wounds: Nisei Atomic Bomb Survivors and the Postwar Regime of Compensatory Justice

For years Kanji Kuramoto endured the haunting memory of rummaging through the streets of Hiroshima in the days after the atomic bombing in search of his father. The Hawaii-born engineering student had barely escaped the immediate impact of the bomb on the morning of August 6, 1945, thanks to his Volunteer Citizen Corps assignment in the navy yard outside the city. However, the devastation that he witnessed during those few days after the bombing became inescapable scenes of living hell in his memory. As soon as he finished college in 1948, he left Japan to resettle in California. "I wanted a new life," Kuramoto reflected years later. "I have tried to forget this tragedy. It gave me great relief [to return] to the United States."[10]

Kuramoto was not alone in his pursuit of a new life in the United States after the war. By the mid-1950s hundreds of Japanese American A-bomb victims returned to the United States to escape the tragic memories of surviving the atomic bombing in a country ravaged by physical, psychological, and socioeconomic devastation.[11] Among those Nisei returnees was Mary Yano, who left Hiroshima and returned to her hometown of Los Angeles in 1954, hoping to rebuild her life.[12] Yano had gone to Hiroshima with her family in the spring of 1940 with a goal of studying Japanese and returning home to Los Angeles in time to start tenth grade. When the war forced Yano to extend her stay in Japan, she continued to commute to Hiroshima Jogakuin, a Christian mission school in central Hiroshima, from her home on the city's northern outskirts. Minutes before the atomic bomb fell on August 6, 1945, she boarded the streetcar in Teramachi, just a mile away from the city center. Soon after the trolley left the station, the intense heat and dust from the blast filled Yano's "ears, eyes, nose and mouth," but she managed to find her way back home without suffering serious burns. Despite the deep emotional trauma of having survived the atomic bombing that had claimed at least 110,000 lives, she felt healthy enough to forgo any medical treatment and work as an interpreter for the Allied occupation forces in the nearby town of Kure in the following years.[13] It was not until her family returned to the United States in early 1954, shortly after the end of the U.S. occupation of Japan, that she began to suffer from fatigue and acute pain that never left her body.[14]

That the symptoms of Yano's radiation illness did not appear until her postwar resettlement in the United States made it all but impossible for her to receive proper diagnosis and medical care as an A-bomb victim. Japanese American atomic bomb victims like Yano, Kuramoto, and Suyeishi would soon find out that their return home further compounded their lifelong struggles for survival, as their country of birth steadfastly remained silent about their existence. Without recognition of their victimhood and survival from the atomic bombing, the Nisei A-bomb survivors' bodies, maimed by the blast and radiation, remained the sites of their suppressed memories.[15]

Yano's real battle with the A-bomb's delayed medical effects began when she thought she had finally found peace at home. Despite her detailed explanations about how she had survived the Hiroshima bombing, the medical professionals and administrators at Los Angeles County Hospital in charge of Yano's case were dismissive of the possibility that her illness was connected to her exposure to the A-bomb blast and radiation. Yano made numerous attempts to convince her doctors that her pain must have been caused by the aftereffects of radiation, to no avail; they diagnosed her condition as a "congenital" motor neuron disease. In 1961 Yano developed a tumor in her right breast. Yet her doctors believed that the cancer had nothing to do with the atomic bomb. For fifteen years after her return from Hiroshima to California, she battled the delayed and excruciating progression of her illness, which culminated in the cancer spreading to her throat.[16] In 1969, after "four trips to the hospital and an operation for throat cancer," Yano's body finally gave in. She was 44 years old.[17]

Yano's mother, Toshiko, who had clung to the hope that her daughter would one day regain her health and get married, was devastated to outlive her. "I had bought a beautiful Japanese wedding dress for Mary before we came back to America but she was never able to wear it," she lamented in an interview in 1972. "It was such a waste." Yet more devastating to Toshiko was that her daughter had lived through the pain, fear, and isolation without recognition from her country, her community, or even her physicians that she had been crippled by the atomic bomb.[18]

In contrast to the postwar American society's indifference to the plight of Nisei A-bomb victims, in Japan the U.S. government funded medical treatments and studies of survivors beginning in 1947. Under the auspices of the U.S. Public Health Service and the National Academy of Sciences, the Atomic Bomb Casualty Commission (ABCC) treated 300,000 Japanese A-bomb survivors in Hiroshima and Nagasaki. Although the ABCC served primarily as a medical research program to study long-term genetic effects of radiation, it also was the first large-scale program to provide routine medical and psychiatric examinations of atomic bomb victims. Jack D. Kirshbaum, a pathologist at West Valley Community Hospital in Los Angeles who had worked with the ABCC in Hiroshima during the 1960s, was appalled to learn that hundreds of American citizens like Mary Yano were dying without medical care. "These people are suffering," he told *Newsweek*'s Paul Brinkley-Rogers in 1972. "If this government is funding a program for Japanese citizens over there, I see no reason why it should not do the same for Americans here."[19]

Mary Yano did not live long enough to witness the limited attention that Nisei A-bomb survivors began to receive from the likes of Dr. Kirshbaum and U.S. media outlets in the early 1970s. By the fall of 1971, two years after Yano's death, a growing number of Nisei survivors in the United States, frustrated by their inability to secure proper medical care, had begun to organize.[20] A group of Japanese American A-bomb survivors in California organized the Committee of Atomic Bomb Survivors in the United States of America (CABS).[21] Kaz Suyeishi and Kanji Kuramoto, childhood friends in Hiroshima, were among the leaders of the group's effort to bring to California from Japan doctors who possessed the knowledge and experience of working with patients with radiation illnesses.[22] Thomas Noguchi, a Japanese immigrant doctor and noted Los Angeles coroner, joined the Nisei survivors' movement to gain public support for this medical care program. He volunteered to write letters to politicians and medical professionals in both the United States and Japan. "It is incredible that I, as a

Japanese, did not know of this problem before now," the outspoken physician told newspapers in 1972, "and even more incredible that the U.S. government did not realize these people are living here."[23]

That year, the efforts of Nisei survivors and their supporters even compelled a few members of the U.S. Congress to sponsor a bill for the creation of a government-funded medical treatment program for atomic bomb victims residing in the United States. Ranking Democratic representative Edward Roybal of California introduced a bill, H.R. 1123, in the House of Representatives on January 3, 1973. Within three weeks Roybal secured fifteen co-sponsors and reintroduced the bill during the House session on January 24. The bill called for "reimbursement of certain individuals" for the bodily damage caused by the atomic bomb explosions and the resulting fallout in Hiroshima and Nagasaki in August 1945. However, Roybal's bill omitted the critical information about who those "certain individuals" were.[24] It provided no explanation that the primary beneficiaries of the proposed medical treatment program were American citizens of Japanese ancestry who had survived the nuclear weapon deployed by their own government. The bill did not pass, having little chance in the first place to overcome the long-standing opposition from the U.S. Defense and State Departments to any direct aid associated with the atomic bombing.[25]

Nevertheless, encouraged by this first legislative attempt on their behalf, the Nisei A-bomb survivors persevered in their continued effort to secure U.S. government-sponsored medical compensation. In August 1975, thirty years after the atomic bombing of Hiroshima and Nagasaki, Kuramoto and Suyeishi traveled to Washington, D.C., as representatives of the CABS to petition Congress to sponsor their legislative campaign.[26] Roybal responded again, this time joined by another California Democrat, George Danielson. Between the two of them, Roybal and Danielson wrote ten bills over the next six years. However, only two of those bills made it out of House committees. On January 6, 1981, during the 97th Congress, Roybal introduced a new bill that featured much clearer language than what he had written almost a decade earlier. This new bill called for direct aid to "a United States citizen or permanent resident suffering from any illness caused by the atomic bombing in August 1945."[27] Two weeks later, on January 22, Danielson introduced an identical bill in the House authorizing the U.S. Department of Health and Human Services to provide medical treatment to the U.S. A-bomb victims.[28] Like its predecessor in 1973,

Roybal's and Danielson's bills in 1981 stood little chance of gaining enough votes, and in the end, they served as a symbolic call for historical recognition of Nisei A-bomb survivors. The bills also marked the end of the A-bomb survivors' unsuccessful legislative campaign for compensatory justice in the United States, as no sponsor of such a bill would emerge again.[29]

It is not an accident that the Nisei survivors of the atomic bombing remained secret sufferers. The U.S. government has consistently refused to acknowledge these American citizens with faces of the enemy whose existence challenged the prevailing narrative that the bomb was a liberator that had saved millions of lives and prevented further bloodshed in the Pacific Theater. The exigencies of the U.S. cold war alliances in Asia-Pacific based on nuclear proliferation shaped the American master narrative of the "good war," which depicts the atomic bombing as a necessary end to the brutal war.[30] The U.S. occupation forces that ruled Japan from 1945 to 1952 with near absolute power censored Japanese reporting on the effects of radiation and restricted foreign journalists' access to sources related to the atomic bombing. For many decades after 1945, popular narratives and memories of war in both the United States and Japan have depicted the casualties of the bomb singularly as Japanese and rendered a significant number of non-Japanese victims invisible. The notion that Japanese were the "sole sufferers of this terrible dawn of the nuclear age" helped downplay Japan's colonial past as well as the horrific implications of nuclear violence at the hands of the U.S. military, which had contributed to the deaths of thousands of non-Japanese A-bomb victims, including the U.S.-born Nisei.[31] Not only did this serve post–World War II U.S. interests in the rapid rehabilitation of Japan as America's cold war ally in the Pacific, but it also allowed many Japanese themselves to cope with the tragic legacies of their country's own militarist past by embracing a deep sense of victimhood. As a consequence, it took the world many decades after the war to recognize the tens of thousands of Korean victims of the atomic bombs, most of whom were conscripted laborers and their families in Hiroshima and Nagasaki. The American citizens of Japanese ancestry like Yano remain the only group of non-Japanese victims excluded from the U.S.-centered postwar discourse on compensatory justice.[32]

The post–World War II U.S. design for immediate rehabilitation of Japan largely dictated the terms of the international regime of reparations that also made it all but impossible for the Nisei A-bomb survivors to seek redress. The emergence of the U.S. cold war empire in the Pacific depended not only on the ruins of the former Japanese Empire but also on rebuilding Japan as an economic power and a bulwark against communism in Asia. As Lisa Yoneyama has argued, such directives of the victor's justice shaped the role of the United States as the sole executioner of compensatory justice that determined "the aggrieved and the aggressors, the redressable and the unredressable, the forgiven and the unforgiven."[33] For instance, the 1951 San Francisco Peace Treaty, which officially brought peace between Japan and the Allied powers, minimized Japanese indemnities for its war responsibilities by firmly establishing the limits of legal and political parameters for the compensatory rights of the victims of wartime atrocities. Article 14 of the treaty "waivered" the rights of individual citizens of the Allied nations or former Japanese colonies to seek compensation from the Japanese government, effectively denying their ability to demand redress for the damage they had suffered during the war.[34] Neither aggrieved nor redressable, the hundreds of thousands of non-Japanese atomic bomb victims, including the Japanese American survivors, remained excluded in the postwar state regimes of compensatory justice.

Instead of treating the lasting human cost of the atomic bombing of Hiroshima and Nagasaki as an international war crimes issue, such exigencies of the U.S. cold war geopolitical realignments limited the scope of the compensation program for atomic bomb victims to the realm of the Japanese domestic health and welfare system. For the Nisei survivors, their U.S. citizenship became a liability that denied them access to medical care for the treatment of their radiation illnesses. When the Japanese government enacted the Law Concerning Medical Care for the Victims of the Atomic Bombing in 1957, which established a pension and medical care program based on a narrow definition of *hibakusha*, the Japanese term for atomic bomb victims, the law covered exclusively the Japanese citizens who could prove their presence in the areas directly affected by the atomic bombs in August 1945.[35] Although a small number of Nisei survivors in the United States who were able to establish dual citizenship and had resources to go back to Japan could take advantage of this Japanese government program, the 1957 Japanese law all but excluded the majority of Nisei survivors in the United States from the only state regime of care in the world created for the victims of the 1945 atomic bombing.

In a country without universal health care, Nisei A-bomb survivors in the United States found themselves confronting the multi-billion-dollar

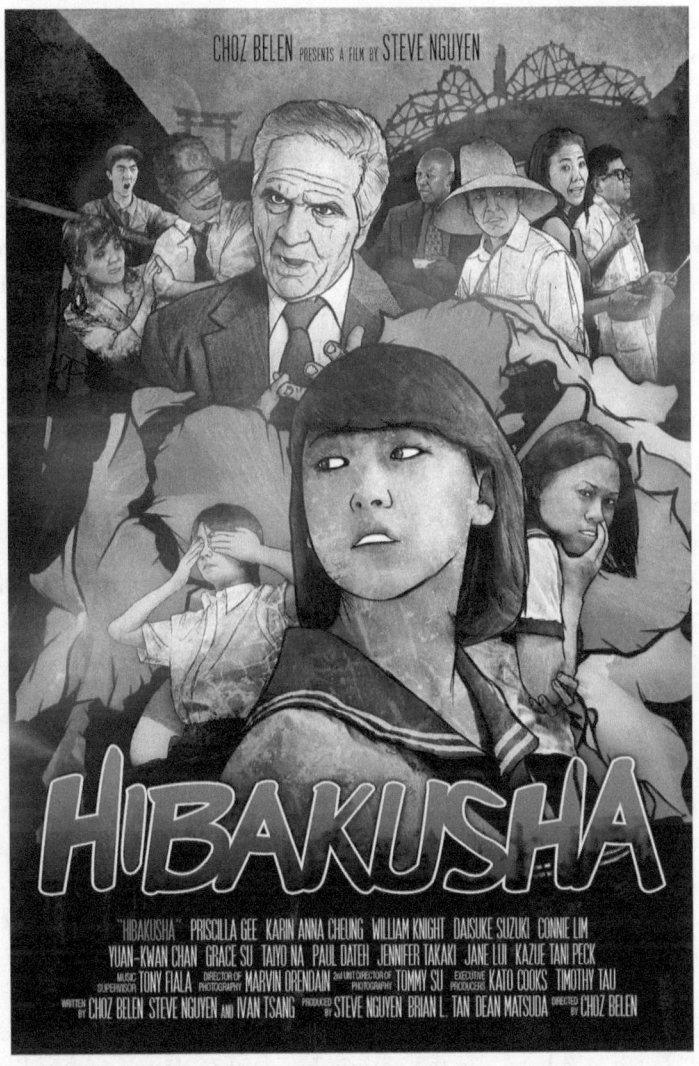

FIGURE 9 In *Hibakusha*, a 2012 animated short film, Kaz Suyeishi revisits the earliest memories of her survival of the atomic bombing.
Courtesy of Steve Nguyen and Choz Belen, Studio APA.

medical industry run by private insurance companies that refused to cover the A-bomb patients because of their "preexisting" radiation illnesses. Without means to pay expensive medical bills, Kaz Suyeishi traveled back to Hiroshima for medical treatment whenever her conditions worsened. It was not until she turned 65 in 1992 that she finally became eligible for a

U.S. government-sponsored medical insurance program when she qualified for Medicare.³⁶ Through her lifelong struggle for survival and her activism for redress on behalf of her fellow Japanese American victims of the atomic bombing, Suyeishi developed a unique perspective on the historical legacies of the bomb that forever altered her diasporic life as an American citizen of Japanese ancestry who experienced multiple forms of racial and state violence on both sides of the Pacific. From time to time she remembered her Korean neighbors in Hiroshima who might not have survived the atomic bomb. "I am not naïve to think that all Japanese who had experienced racism in America sympathized with Koreans in Japan [during the war]," she reflected, "but I saw how my father treated Koreans with respect and it had an impact on my life." Seventy years after the atomic bombing, Suyeishi was able to articulate how American racism, Japanese colonialism, and the legacies of the tragic war converged in her transpacific life: "I could understand the hardship [that Koreans in Japan] must have suffered when I came back to America and realized that my country wouldn't help me treat my illness [caused by] the atomic bombing."³⁷

Surviving Internment and Surviving the Atomic Bomb:
Japanese American Diaspora and the Politics of Redress

In November 1953, eight years after surviving the atomic bomb in Hiroshima, Stockton, California, native Yoshiko Sogawa returned to the United States.³⁸ She had gone to Hiroshima during the war, in late 1943, when she left the Gila River War Relocation Authority (WRA) camp to join the group of Japanese repatriates from the WRA and U.S. Department of Justice detention camps who were exchanged for American hostages held by Japan. Had it not been for the atomic bomb that destroyed her life, she would have lived the rest of her life as a Japanese in her family home in Hiroshima. However, like many Nisei A-bomb survivors, Sogawa, a struggling part-time English tutor in Hiroshima's south-central neighborhood, sought a second life in her country of birth to escape the deep emotional trauma of being an American victim of the atomic bombing. Sogawa was "happy to be back home" one last time for a chance to start anew at the age of 33.³⁹

Sogawa's story of survival adds even more to the complex diasporic dimensions of Japanese American migrants' encounters with prewar anti-Japanese xenophobia in the United States, the wartime mass incarceration of Japanese Americans, and the aftereffects of the atomic bombing that intimately intersected in their experiences. Living with the buried wounds from the atomic bombing was only one part of Sogawa's lifelong struggle to survive multiple forms of racial and state violence throughout her transpacific life. She was born in Stockton to potato farmers from Hiroshima in 1920, when the overwhelming majority of California's voters helped enact the most exclusionary alien land law in history, which completely banned Japanese landownership. In 1923, when Sogawa had turned 3, her family lost their potato farm in San Joaquin Valley after the U.S. Supreme Court upheld the 1920 California Alien Land Law.[40] Her immigrant parents decided that the time had come for the Sogawa family to give up on their American dream. In 1925 young Yoshiko accompanied her mother and infant sister to Hiroshima to enroll in school and start a new life; her father remained in Stockton to work as a farmhand as long as he could, to make enough money to send to his family in Japan.[41] After graduating from high school in 1938, Yoshiko Sogawa made a temporary return to California to help her father finish preparing for his return migration to Japan. The father and daughter hoped that they would be back in Hiroshima in three years to reunite with the family.[42]

However, the outbreak of the Pacific War in December 1941 shattered their plan and extended the family's separation indefinitely. Within the next five months the U.S. government's proclamation of Executive Order 9066 removed Sogawa and her father from their home in Stockton and forced them into incarceration, first at the nearby San Joaquin County Fairgrounds and then at the Gila River War Relocation Center in the Arizona desert.[43] Sogawa grew restless in the American internment camp, as she looked for ways to communicate with her mother and sister in Hiroshima. As soon as they arrived at Gila River in the summer of 1942, the 18-year-old Kibei and her father applied for repatriation to Japan as a way to leave the camp early and rejoin their family. Earlier that year the U.S. State Department and the Japanese Ministry of Foreign Affairs had agreed to trade civilian "enemy aliens" at a neutral port in the Indian Ocean as part of the wartime prisoner exchange program. The U.S. government then rounded up prisoners for exchange by soliciting applications for repatriation from the detainees throughout the WRA and Department of Justice internment camps.[44]

Despite being a U.S. citizen, Yoshiko Sogawa was selected for repatriation, whereas a clerical error resulted in the rejection of her Japanese immigrant father's application. On August 28, 1943, she said good-bye to her father, who remained at Gila River for the remainder of the war, and left for New York Harbor to join 1,512 other repatriates from the detention camps all over the country.[45] On September 3, Sogawa set sail on the Swedish ocean liner MS *Gripsholm*, bound for Goa in Portuguese India through the South Atlantic and the Indian Ocean. She was one of 149 Nisei citizens aboard the repatriation vessel.[46]

Six weeks later, Sogawa and the other Japanese repatriates landed on Mormugao in southern Goa to be traded for American and Canadian civilians from Asian territories under Japanese occupation. Sogawa's group then sailed on the Japanese exchange liner *Teia Maru*, which made stops at Singapore and Manila to pick up more Japanese passengers before arriving at Yokohama in November 1942.[47] After her 75-day voyage, Sogawa reunited with her mother and sister in Hiroshima. They sat out the rest of the war in their home in the city's Kannonmachi neighborhood, two kilometers away from the hypocenter where the atomic bomb was dropped on August 6, 1945. Sogawa had just stepped out of her house on that fateful morning when the blast from the A-bomb explosion shattered glass doors and windows, propelling shards that tore into her flesh.[48]

How does one contextualize the multiple forms of state and wartime violence that shaped Yoshiko Sogawa's life on both sides of the Pacific? These moments of diasporic upheaval experienced by Sogawa and other Nisei survivors of the war in Japan have yet to find a place in the dominant historical memories of the Japanese American wartime experience and the postwar Japanese American politics of redress. The Civil Liberties Act, enacted by the U.S. Congress and signed by Ronald Reagan in 1988, mandated the U.S. government to issue an official apology and provide monetary compensation of $20,000 to each surviving former Japanese American internee.[49] It took the Japanese American community more than four decades after the war to see their redress campaign come to fruition, a rare feat in the history of reparations movements in the United States. However, as noted by Alice Yang Murray and as discussed in Chapters 3 and 4, the success of the Japanese American redress movement largely depended on "a single type of narrative" of loyal Japanese Americans, "who suffered heart-wrenching losses but endured internment with quiet dignity and perseverance."[50] This representation of the Japanese American triumph would become the hallmark

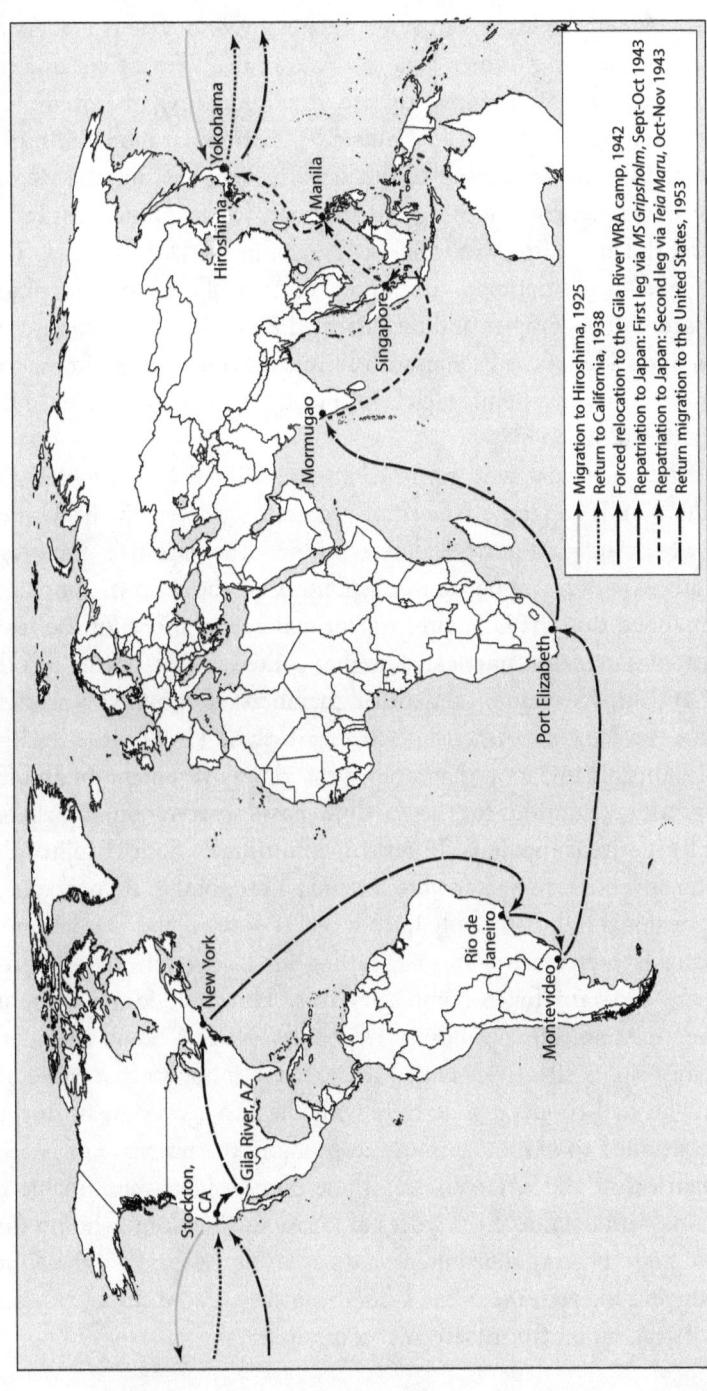

MAP 2 Yoshiko Sogawa's transpacific journeys.
Map by Bill Nelson.

of the Asian American success story in the post–World War II era. As A. Naomi Paik argues, the former Japanese American internees became the "assimilated mascot" of "progress toward racial equality," the exemplary model for other groups of color to emulate.[51] The popular model-minority trope emerged from this, a result of the narrative emphasizing the victory for American democracy that mitigated the tragic legacy of the mass incarceration and the long history of racial oppression in the United States. This "oversimplified" yet "emotionally appealing" history of Japanese Americans further obscured the complex and multifaceted Nisei lives and responses to the war on both sides of the Pacific, such as Yoshiko Sogawa's confrontation with multiple forms of systemic racial violence and wartime atrocities in the United States and Japan.[52]

Those Nisei survivors who returned to the United States joined the post–World War II Japanese American redress movement in the United States as a way to gain historical recognition. The Japanese American A-bomb survivors were important contributors to the redress campaign, which demanded that the U.S. government make reparations for the mass internment of Japanese Americans in the United States during World War II. Suyeishi, Kuramoto, and other members of the CABS worked closely with the Japanese American Citizens League (JACL), the leading Nisei civil rights organization that lobbied the U.S. government for an official apology and reparations for the wartime mass incarceration, to help organize its legislative campaigns. In return, according to Sodei Rinjiro, the 1976 JACL convention in Sacramento featured a proposal to support a separate congressional bill, eventually introduced by Roybal and Danielson in the House of Representatives in 1981, calling for a government-sponsored medical care program for A-bomb survivors. However, formal support from Japanese American community leaders for Nisei A-bomb survivors' compensatory rights effectively ended there. JACL lobbyists like Mike M. Masaoka, who had cooperated actively with the U.S. government during the war, continued to work vigorously to promote the narrative of Nisei's wartime patriotism and perseverance. These Nisei leaders were unable to come to grips with including the voices of Japanese American A-bomb survivors who might portray the United States as an aggressor. Like the Kibei internees during the war, the Nisei A-bomb survivors faced stubborn resistance and ostracization from their own community.[53]

A Japanese American Diaspora in the Nuclear Pacific

On May 10, 2016, the White House announced that on May 27 Barack Obama would become the first sitting American president to visit Hiroshima to commemorate the victims of the August 1945 atomic bombing.[54] During those seventeen days leading up to this unprecedented visit, a debate emerged about whether or not Obama would use the occasion to issue some form of apology for the destruction of Hiroshima, despite the seven decades of the U.S. government's firm unapologetic position on its deployment of nuclear weapons. Led by Fox News Channel contributors Michelle Malkin and Mike Gallagher, Obama's critics on the right called the president's planned trip to Hiroshima an "apology tour" that would diminish America's prestige by changing the narrative of World War II as the "good war."[55] Although the White House assured the public that the president did not intend to "revisit" the U.S. decision to drop the atomic bomb to end the war, speculation about an expression of remorse from Obama arose, and not just among conservative pundits. Some atomic bomb survivors in Japan admitted that Obama's decision to visit Hiroshima had increased their hope for an apology from the American president.[56]

Barack Obama's long history of peace activism contributed to such wide speculation—critical or hopeful—about a public apology to Hiroshima victims. Not only had he participated actively in the nuclear disarmament movement in the early 1980s as a young student at Columbia University, but also both his senatorial (2004) and presidential (2008) campaigns included plenty of antinuclear rhetoric.[57] Moreover, in one of his first speeches given overseas as U.S. president on April 5, 2009, in Prague, Obama declared "America's commitment to seek the peace and security of a world without nuclear weapons."[58] His vision for a nuclear-free world seemed to launch a new doctrine for permanent U.S. nuclear disarmament based on multilateral diplomacy, adding to the charismatic president's worldwide popularity. He hinted at pushing for the U.S. government's ratification of the Comprehensive Test-Ban Treaty (CTBT), a 1994 international resolution signed by Bill Clinton but rejected by the U.S. Congress. The sense of global optimism created by Obama's nuclear-free agenda helped him emerge as the surprise winner of the Nobel Peace Prize in his first year in office.[59] Seven years later, on the eve of Obama's visit to Hiroshima in 2016, the

United States remained one of the eight countries with nuclear capabilities, along with China, Iran, Israel, and North Korea, that had yet to ratify the CTBT.[60] Yet, although the president had failed to make good on his promise in Prague, the announcement of the historic visit to Hiroshima in his final year in office suggested that he was determined to make reconciliation for the 1945 atomic bombing a part of his legacy.

However, Obama visited Hiroshima on May 27, 2016, not as a peace activist but as the sitting president of the country, which for the past seven decades had justified its possession of the world's largest nuclear arsenal as a means for global peacekeeping. His commemorative remarks at the Hiroshima Peace Memorial Park that morning included no words of apology. In fact, the president's speech contained not a single mention of the term *atomic bomb*. Instead of the 15-kiloton uranium-fueled bomb dropped from an American B-29 bomber, he attributed the destruction of the city nearly seventy-one years ago to "death [that] fell from the sky" and "a flash of light and a wall of fire." Obama's speech in Hiroshima that day also omitted a key aspect of the atomic bomb's legacy. Although his speech paid tribute to "over 100,000 Japanese men, women and children, thousands of Koreans, [and] a dozen Americans held prisoner" in Hiroshima on August 6, 1945, he failed to acknowledge the more than 3,000 U.S.-born Japanese American civilians trapped in the city that morning when the bomb was dropped.[61]

The speech's critical omission of such a significant number of American atomic bomb victims escaped most listeners' notice, as much of the world had yet to even hear about the existence of U.S.-born Nisei migrants in Japan during the war, let alone those Nisei who were victimized by the atomic bomb. The invisibility of Nisei atomic bomb survivors in the seven decades since Hiroshima and Nagasaki is symptomatic of the nation-centered narrative's exclusion of rightless subjects from the state regime of legal, civil, and human rights.[62] Just as the Nisei migrants' complex transnational experiences contradict the narrative of the United States as a country of immigrants in pursuit of freedom and opportunity, the struggles of Japanese American atomic bomb survivors complicate the narrative of the atomic bomb as the force of good that saved millions of lives.[63]

Throughout the postwar decades these American survivors have remained excluded from the dominant historical memories of the war shaped by U.S. cold war geopolitical interests. Their struggles for survival and historical recognition reveal the complex ways in which historical forces in and between two Pacific empires converged in their lives at various conjunctural moments, demonstrating the impact of colonial and state violence beyond the political borders of nation-states. The Japanese American A-bomb survivors' stories of survival after World War II hinge on their negotiation with the legacies of brutal Japanese colonialism, which intensified anti-Japanese sentiment and racial discrimination in the prewar United States, the shifting geopolitical dynamics of the post–World War II Pacific, and the politics of race, citizenship, and historical memory.

For the Nisei A-bomb survivors, their bodies remain sites of living memories. The permanent damage inflicted on their bodies is a reminder that their American citizenship by birth was the liability that denied them access to the postwar regime of reparations in both Japan and the United States. These American migrants thus became essentially stateless in the postwar state regime of care and compensatory justice. Nevertheless, the Japanese American A-bomb survivors became a lesser known but critical constituent of Asian American social movements of the 1970s and 1980s. Their unique position as Americans who once lived in the former Japanese Empire allowed them to articulate their support for the postwar Japanese American redress movement in a language of anti-colonialism and transnational reconciliation. As demonstrated by Kaz Suyeishi's perspective on the impact of Japanese imperialism on the lives of non-Japanese A-bomb survivors in Hiroshima such as Koreans and U.S.-born Nisei, Japanese Americans who survived the war in Japan did not simply dwell on their own victimhood. Rather, their campaign for compensatory justice called for broader, transnational consideration of the tragic impact of Japanese colonialism, institutional racism in the United States, and nuclear proliferation. In this way the postwar Asian American social movements and the legacies of war have intersected in the diasporic lives of Japanese Americans in the nuclear Pacific.

Epilogue

IN AN INTERVIEW for the HBO documentary series *Axios*, which aired in November 2018, U.S. president Donald J. Trump expressed his strong objection to granting birthright citizenship to the children of immigrants. "How ridiculous [is it that] we are the only country in the world where a person comes in, has a baby, and [that] baby is essentially a citizen of the United States," Trump said, decrying America's time-honored institution of *jus soli* (birthright citizenship), the legal principle commonly shared in countries throughout the Americas and elsewhere with strong identities as "nations of immigrants."[1] Trump signaled that he would sign an executive order to eliminate the birthright citizenship of U.S.-born children of nonresident aliens, insisting that he had the power to effect such a policy, which would be in violation of the Fourteenth Amendment. Since early 2017 his administration had already used executive orders to institute harsh anti-immigrant measures in the name of national security, granting "enhanced vetting capabilities" to the U.S. Refugee Admissions Program and establishing the notorious travel ban on individuals from several Muslim-majority nations to prevent "foreign terrorist entry."[2]

Trump's position on citizenship and immigration sparked renewed public debates about the sanctity of the Fourteenth Amendment's birthright citizenship clause.[3] However, this attack on birthright citizenship was far from new. As examined in the first two chapters of this book, anti-immigrant agitators during the first half of the twentieth century campaigned vigorously to strip U.S.-born Nisei's birthright citizenship. Decades before the World

War II mass incarceration of Japanese Americans, these exclusionists had already argued that Nisei's alleged loyalty to Japan and their unassimilability posed a threat to the country's security and well-being. The call for removal of Nisei's citizenship and American identity was an integral part of the fierce movement to exclude all individuals of Japanese ancestry from American citizenry.[4] At various historical moments since then, representations of Asian Americans, Latinx Americans, and, more recently, Middle Eastern, Muslim, and Arab Americans as perpetually foreign and undesirable have continued to drive anti-immigrant sentiment and xenophobic politics aimed at limiting the racial boundaries of American citizenship. As Mae M. Ngai has argued, even if race-based exclusion is not always an intended result of the campaign to eliminate birthright citizenship, it is always a certain outcome.[5]

The transpacific displacement of 50,000 Nisei citizens was one such outcome of the ferocious exclusion movement in the American West that sought complete elimination of Japanese Americans' constitutional rights to their citizenship. Although the narrow domestic frame of Nisei Americanism has dominated Japanese American historiography, these Nisei migrants' transnational experiences throughout the twentieth century were the norm rather than the exception. In this book I have explored the history of a large contingent of American-born Nisei as migrants and sojourners who moved in multiple directions between the American West and the former Japanese Empire. The prevalence of Nisei's movements and transnationalism in the Pacific not only illuminates the intersection of legal and sociopolitical developments in both the United States and Japan but also reveals the fallacy of the essentialized and dichotomous distinctions between the categories Issei, Nisei, and Kibei. As Eiichiro Azuma has noted, the "alleged differences, rifts, and struggles" among these groups that "became manifest" during the Pacific War have shaped our understanding of their backgrounds and of their purported political and cultural dispositions.[6]

Japanese American migrants' complex transnational experiences as citizens, immigrants, and the stateless shaped how they conceptualized their own diasporic identities and sense of belonging outside the dominant celebratory narrative of the United States as a country of immigrants. In 1976 former Heishikan student Masao Ekimoto returned to his hometown in Southern California for the first time since his voyage to Japan in 1940.

A special guest at his high school reunion, Ekimoto stood surrounded by his old classmates and their families when a curious attendee asked him whether he "felt to be more American or more Japanese" after spending thirty-six years of his adulthood in Japan. Ekimoto responded without hesitation, "I feel I'm seventy-percent American and seventy-percent Japanese; it doesn't add up mathematically, but that's the way I feel." The bemused expressions of those surrounding him suggested that they did not quite know what to make of the way Ekimoto articulated his self-identity. Not only did this formulation of his cultural dualism fail to add up to one hundred percent, it also defied common expectations that he must be either "more American" or "more Japanese."[7] As demonstrated in the preceding chapters, many Nisei migrants on both sides of the Pacific articulated their citizenship in ways that challenged the dominant narrative of Nisei loyalty in Japanese American historical memory.

A diasporic history of Japanese Americans also challenges us to rethink the multiple meanings of home and belonging for Nisei migrants, their descendants, and their extended transnational families across borders beyond the disciplinary boundaries of ethnic and area studies. In the spring of 2008, Kanda Minoru, a Japanese businessman and independent scholar, reflected on his own search for a Japanese American diaspora. Kanda's grandmother and granduncle, both of whom had been born and raised in Hawaii, had gone to Japan to study in the 1920s and 1930s. Kanda's granduncle, Jiro Kato, returned to Hawaii after completing his studies and football career at Meiji University. His grandmother, Kimie Kato, remained in Japan, got married, and lived the rest of her life in that country. Kanda was fond of his Nisei grandmother, who helped raise him in his native hometown in Nara Prefecture.[8]

Although his grandmother had lived the rest of her life as a Japanese, Kanda believed that the legacy of her "American heritage" had been passed onto him and his family. His grandmother had claimed that no one around her knew that she had come from America.[9] She spoke Japanese impeccably, but Kanda noticed from time to time signs that suggested to him that his grandmother was not an ordinary Japanese woman. He remembered her humming the American national anthem while watching Olympic medal ceremonies on television. Her American upbringing also influenced the lifestyle of her Japanese grandsons. "My brother and I could've been the only boys in Nara Prefecture in the sixties eating oatmeal for breakfast," Kanda quipped during a talk on his family history.[10]

The memory of having the daily oatmeal breakfast prepared by his Hawaii-born grandmother inspired Kanda to explore the legacy of his own family's transnational history and the meaning of diaspora. He reached out to his relatives in Hawaii and attended family reunions there to meet his granduncle's children and grandchildren, the Hawaii-born *Sansei* (third generation) and *Yonsei* (fourth generation). Kanda wondered how the generational designations—Issei, Nisei, Sansei, Yonsei—used by Japanese Americans in the United States would apply to his grandmother and himself. After all, his grandmother spent most of her life in Japan, and Kanda himself was a Japanese native. Both of them have lived at the margins of the linear immigrant narrative that has shaped both Japanese emigration history and Japanese American history. He concluded that a new framework was needed to examine the multidirectional movements that shaped the experiences of diasporic individuals like his grandmother. He proposed the concept of "transnational Japanese" (*ekkyo nihonjin*) rather than the conventional Issei and Nisei for studies of Japanese return migrants and U.S.-born Japanese Americans who settled in Japan.[11] Kanda's new framework still privileges Japan as a diasporic home to his grandmother and other Japanese American migrants from the United States. Nevertheless, his approach to studying Japanese American transnational families and the varied experiences of the Japanese American transnational generation remind us of the critical need to rethink the geographic and conceptual boundaries of Asian American history. Future studies of migration and transnational families must consider Asian American history beyond the U.S.-based immigrants and their descendants whose experiences are presumed to be confined to their respective ethnic communities within U.S. political borders.

As Arif Dirlik has argued, Asian America is not merely a place in the United States but a multiple location in the world in constant transition. This concept of Asian America that defies a fixed, U.S.-centered spatial and temporal context allows us to reconsider "nationalities, racial affinities and ethnicities" as ideas that are constantly reshaped by historical and political developments in both the United States and Asia-Pacific.[12] The making of a Japanese American diaspora before, during, and after World War II demonstrates a critical intersection of the histories of nations and empires, human migration, and transnational families and communities on both sides of the Pacific.

Notes

Introduction

1. "Ko-a no shinzen kekkonpu," *Asahi Shimbun*, April 7, 1939.
2. Michael Jin, "The Japanese American Transnational Generation: Rethinking the Spatial and Conceptual Boundaries of Asian America," in *The Routledge Handbook of Asian American Studies*, ed. Cindy I-Fen Cheng (New York: Routledge, 2017), 246. Several newspapers in the Anglophone world reported on the Japanese brutality in Nanjing throughout late 1937 and 1938 based on accounts submitted by their Shanghai-based correspondents. See, for example, "Terror in Nanking," *The Times* (London), December 18, 1937; "Butchery Marked Capture of Nanking," *New York Times*, December 18, 1937; "Japanese Troops Kill Thousands: 'Four Days of Hell' in Captured City Told by Eyewitness," *Chicago Daily News*, December 15, 1937; "Survivor Tells of Nanking Fall," *Seattle Daily Times*, December 16, 1937; "Witness Tells Nanking Horror as Chinese Flee," *Chicago Daily Tribune*, December 17, 1937; "Japanese Atrocities Marked Fall of Nanking After Chinese Command Fled," *New York Times*, January 9, 1938; and "Nanking's Fall to Be Told," *Los Angeles Times*, March 18, 1938.
3. Jin, "Japanese American Transnational Generation," 246–47; "Ko-a no shinzen kekkonpu." See also Chapter 1.
4. Su Chung (Lucille Davis), *Court Dishes of China: The Cuisine of the Ch'ing Dynasty* (Rutland, VT: Charles E. Tuttle, 1966), 11–12; Fuyuko Kamisaka, *Mitsu no sokoku: Manshu ni totsuida nikkei amerikajin* (Tokyo: Chuo Koronsha, 1996); U.S. Air Force Passenger Manifest TYO-56–0708, Travis Air Force Base, Fairfield, California, February 25, 1956, Records of the Immigration and Naturalization Service, RG 85, National Archives and Records Administration, Washington,

D.C.; U.S. Social Security Administration, *Death Master File*, database (Alexandra, VA: National Technical Information Service).

5. The Japanese Consulates General in the United States counted 40,000 U.S.-born Nisei from the contiguous United States and Hawaii who had gone to Japan by the mid-1930s. This number represented one-fourth of the total Japanese American population, based on the 1930 U.S. Census, and one-fifth based on the number of Nisei counted by the Japanese Foreign Ministry in 1935. Although other unofficial sources, such as the vernacular Japanese American newspapers in Hawaii, Los Angeles, and San Francisco, throughout the 1930s and 1940s suggested an even larger number of U.S.-born Nisei in the Japanese Empire, I use the Japanese government's figures and the total number of U.S.-born Japanese Americans based on the 1940 U.S. census to estimate that about one-fourth (50,000) of Nisei (200,194) had gone to the Japanese Empire by the eve of Pearl Harbor to work, study, join their parents' return migration to Japan, or for other reasons, such as short-term study tours and personal visits that turned into long-term stays. See Teruko Kumei, "1930 nendai no kibei undo: Amerika kokusekiho to kanren ni oite," *Imin kenkyu* 30 (1993); and Paul R. Spickard, *Japanese Americans: The Formation and Transformations of an Ethnic Group* (New York: Twayne, 1996), 89, 167. See also Robert Lee's introduction to Mary Kimoto Tomita, *Dear Miye: Letters Home from Japan, 1939–1946*, ed. Robert Lee (Stanford, CA: Stanford University Press, 1995), 18–19; and Yuji Ichioka, "Introduction," in Karl G. Yoneda, *Ganbatte: Sixty-Year Struggle of a Kibei Worker* (Los Angeles: Asian American Studies Center, University of California, Los Angeles, 1983), xii.

6. Kumei, "1930 nendai no kibei undo"; U.S. Department of Commerce, Bureau of the Census, *Sixteenth Census of the United States: 1940* (Washington, DC: U.S. Government Printing Office, 1943).

7. Manu Karuka, *Empire's Tracks: Indigenous Nations, Chinese Workers, and the Transcontinental Railroad* (Berkeley: University of California Press, 2019), xii.

8. See Moon-Ho Jung, "Seditious Subjects: Race, State Violence, and the U.S. Empire," *Journal of Asian American Studies* 14, no. 2 (June 2011): 221–47; and Paul A. Kramer, "A Complex of Seas: Passages Between Pacific Histories," *Amerasia Journal* 42, no. 3 (2016): 32–41.

9. Shelly Chan, *Diaspora's Homeland: Modern China in the Age of Global Migration* (Durham, NC: Duke University Press, 2018), 8. See also Stuart Hall, "Cultural Identity and Diaspora," in *Identity: Community, Culture, Difference*, ed. Jonathan Rutherford (London: Lawrence & Wishart, 1990); and Paul Gilroy, *The Black Atlantic: Modernity and Double Consciousness* (Cambridge, MA: Harvard University Press, 1993).

10. The most notable Asian American theorist who has articulated the potential pitfalls of "denationalization" is Sau-ling C. Wong. See Saul-ling C. Wong,

"Denationalization Reconsidered: Asian American Cultural Criticism at a Theoretical Crossroads," *Amerasia Journal* 21, no. 1–2 (1995): 16–17. See also Rhacel Salazar Parrenas and Lok C. D. Siu, "Introduction: Asian Diasporas—New Conceptions, New Frameworks," in *Asian Diasporas: New Formations, New Conceptions*, ed. Rhacel Salazar Parrenas and Lok C. D. Siu (Stanford: Stanford University Press, 2007), 1–28.

11. A. Naomi Paik, *Rightlessness: Testimony and Redress in U.S. Prison Camps since World War II* (Chapel Hill: University of North Carolina Press, 2016).

12. See, for example, Madeline Y. Hsu, *Dreaming of Gold, Dreaming of Home: Transnationalism and Migration Between the United States and South China, 1882–1943* (Stanford, CA: Stanford University Press, 2000); and Charlotte Brooks, *American Exodus: Second-Generation Chinese Americans in China, 1901–1949* (Berkeley: University of California Press, 2019). Brooks's work examines the migration of a significant number of U.S.-born Chinese Americans to southeast China during the first half of the twentieth century.

13. "The Formation of a Diasporic Intellectual: An Interview with Stuart Hall by Kuan-Hsing Chen," in *Stuart Hall: Critical Dialogues in Cultural Studies*, ed. David Morley and Kuan-Hsing Chen (London: Routledge, 1996), 504.

14. As discussed in Chapter 1, by the first decade of the twentieth century, the widespread nineteenth-century xenophobic violence against Asians in the United States, manifested in race riots, lynching, and expulsion of the Chinese and South Asian immigrant communities, had evolved into well-organized political campaigns at local, state, and national levels, with Japanese immigrants as the primary targets of Asian exclusion. Built on the earlier Asian exclusion movement that had resulted in the Chinese Exclusion Acts, the new legislative and judicial campaigns mobilized nativist and anti-immigrant groups across class lines to effect the enactments of laws systematically aimed at complete exclusion of the Japanese and other Asian groups from American citizenry. For the manifestation of anti-Chinese violence in the late nineteenth and early twentieth centuries and its influence on other xenophobic movements, see, for example, Beth Lew-Williams, *Chinese Must Go: Violence, Exclusion, and the Making of the Alien in America* (Cambridge, MA: Harvard University Press, 2018); and Erika Lee, *At America's Gates: Chinese Immigration During the Exclusion Era, 1882–1943* (Chapel Hill: University of North Carolina Press, 2003).

15. Mae M. Ngai, "The Architecture of Race in American Immigration Law: A Reexamination of the Immigration Act of 1924," *Journal of American History* 86, no. 1 (June 1999): 70–71.

16. For contemporary accounts documenting the legal and socioeconomic discrimination that affected second-generation Japanese Americans' socioeconomic outlook in the western United States, see Junichi Takeda, *Zaibei hiroshima*

kenjinshi (Los Angeles: Zaibei Hiroshima Kenjinshi Hakkojo, 1929); and Isamu Nodera, "A Survey of the Vocational Activities of the Japanese in the City of Los Angeles," Master's thesis, University of Southern California, 1936).

17. Mikiso Hane, *Modern Japan: A Historical Survey* (Boulder, CO: Westview Press, 1986).

18. See Chapter 2 for a detailed examination of case studies. See also Michael Jin, "Americans in the Pacific: Rethinking Race, Gender, Citizenship, and Diaspora at the Crossroads of Asian and Asian American Studies," *Critical Ethnic Studies* 2, no. 1 (Spring 2016): 128–47.

19. See the accounts of Frank Hirahata, Sen Nishiyama, Kay Tateishi, and Nobuyo Yamane in *Amerasia Journal* 23, no. 3 (1997): Frank Hirahata, "Fifty Years After the Pacific War: 'Molded to Conform, But . . .'" (pp. 145–63); Sen Nishiyama, "Unexpected Encounters" (pp. 125–42); Kay Tateishi, "An Atypical Nisei" (pp. 199–216); and Nobuyo Yamane, "A Nisei Woman in Rural Japan" (pp. 183–96). Although the Japanese American transnational experience remains heavily understudied, a number of memoirs and autobiographies written by individual Nisei migrants emerged in the mid-1990s. Examples include Tomita, *Dear Miye*; Minoru Kiyota, *Beyond Loyalty: The Story of a Kibei*, trans. Linda Klepinger Keenan (Honolulu: University of Hawai'i Press, 1997); and Iwao Peter Sano, *One Thousand Days in Siberia: The Odyssey of a Japanese American POW* (Lincoln: University of Nebraska Press, 1997).

20. See Jin, "Japanese American Transnational Generation," 246–47. See also Zaibei Nihonjinkai, *Zaibei Nihonjinshi* (History of Japanese in America), which in 1940 reported that 10,000 Nisei had returned to the United States from Japan, which left the number of Nisei remaining Japan at 20,000; see Zaibei Nihonjinkai, *Zaibei Nihonjinshi* (San Francisco: Zaibei Nihonjinkai, 1940), 1117–18. Brian Masaru Hayashi notes that figures suggested by contemporary estimates were probably too low; see Brian Masaru Hayashi, *Democratizing the Enemy: The Japanese American Internment* (Princeton, NJ: Princeton University Press, 2004), 44–45, 238n11. Despite their diverse socioeconomic backgrounds, ages, and life experiences on both sides of the Pacific, Nisei migrants are predominantly viewed as those who had gone to Japan as infants or young children for educational purposes. During World War II, these Kibei were ostracized for their education in prewar Japan and their alleged Japanese cultural orientation. In this book I focus on the multiplicity and complexity in Nisei migrants' transpacific experiences beyond this simple formulation of their collective identity.

21. Commission on Wartime Relocation and Internment of Civilians, *Personal Justice Denied: Report of the Commission on Wartime Relocation and Internment of Civilians* (Washington, DC: U.S. Government Printing Office, 1982), 66.

22. Naoko Shibusawa, "The Artist Belongs to the People: The Odyssey of Taro Yashima," *Journal of Asian American Studies* 9, no. 3 (October 2005): 259.

23. Eiichiro Azuma, *Between Two Empires: Race, History, and Transnationalism in Japanese America* (Oxford, UK: Oxford University Press, 2005), 209.

24. For a discussion on the production of multiple scholarly, popular, and artistic representations of the history of the Japanese American internment, see Alice Yang Murray, *Historical Memories of the Japanese American Internment and the Struggle for Redress* (Stanford, CA: Stanford University Press, 2008).

25. These multiple perspectives of transnational individuals illuminate the interconnections between historical memory and the role of the nation-state in perpetuating representations of the past that emphasize dominant institutions, values, and identities. In light of the present-day war on terror and its historical parallel to the anti-Japanese movement in the first half of the twentieth century, I build on the recent work of A. Naomi Paik, who examines the ways in which "rightless" subjects have been systematically excluded from national narratives and the state regime of legal, civil, and human rights. Paik argues that rightlessness has been rendered external to the dominant narrative of the United States as a champion of rights home and abroad. See Paik, *Rightlessness*.

Chapter 1

1. Kay Tateishi, "An Atypical Nisei," *Amerasia Journal* 23, no. 3 (1997): 203.

2. "Visit of Prime Minister Nobusuke Kishi of Japan," *Department of State Bulletin*, July 8, 1957.

3. "The Forgotten Nisei," *Pacific Citizen*, December 19–25, 1975.

4. Yuji Ichioka, "Japanese Immigrant Response to the 1920 Alien Land Law," *Agricultural History* 58 (1984): 162–63.

5. "The Forgotten Nisei."

6. Ichioka, "Japanese Immigrant Response."

7. In 1906, the year Toyoji Chiba arrived in California, the San Francisco Board of Education forced Japanese American students to attend the city's segregated Chinese school. The school board rescinded the segregation order the following year when President Theodore Roosevelt intervened to prevent diplomatic tension with Japan. In exchange for the cancellation of school segregation, Roosevelt agreed to take more proactive measures to restrict Japanese immigration to the United States through a series of negotiations with Japan. These negotiations resulted in the Gentleman's Agreement of 1907, which stipulated that the Japanese government seize the passports of migrant laborers bound for the United States. See "For Heaven's Sake Do not Embarrass the Administration," *Harper's Weekly*, November 10, 1906; and Roger Daniels, *The Politics of Prejudice: The Anti-Japanese*

Movement in California and the Struggle for Japanese Exclusion (Berkeley: University of California Press, 1962), 35–36.

8. "The Forgotten Nisei"; Mori Takemaro, "Colonies and Countryside in Wartime Japan," in *Farmers and Village Life in Twentieth-century Japan*, ed. Ann Waswo and Nishida Yoshiaki (New York: Routledge Curzon, 2003), 183–84.

9. "Bunkan koto shiken gokakusha ichiran: Bunkan koto shaken gaikoka," http://kitabatake.world.coocan.jp/rekishi25.2.html (accessed January 16, 2018); Yukio Suzuki, *Keibatsu: Kekkon de katamerareru nihon no shihaisha shudan* (Tokyo: Kobunsha, 1965), 89.

10. Ministry of Foreign Affairs of Japan, "Waga kuni to kakukoku no aida no shomondai," *Waga gaiko no kinkyo*, no. 7 (November 1963); "Envoy Here Soon," *Canberra Times*, December 31, 1965.

11. "The Forgotten Nisei"; "Visit of Prime Minister Nobusuke Kishi of Japan."

12. See Eiichiro Azuma, *In Search of Our Frontier: Japanese America and Settler Colonialism in the Construction of Japan's Borderless Empire* (Berkeley: University of California Press, 2019), 153–82, 242–60. For Nisei's role envisioned by Japan's settler empire, see Eiichiro Azuma, *Between Two Empires: Race, History, and Transnationalism in Japanese America* (New York: Oxford University Press, 2005), 111–34.

13. My reconceptualization of diaspora borrows from Shelly Chan's formulation of the "temporalities of diaspora." I examine the emergence of the transpacific community of U.S.-born Japanese American migrants as a process contingent on complex, unpredictable, and unexpected convergences of multiple historical developments and social realities across national borders at different conjunctural moments. See Shelly Chan, *Diaspora's Homeland: Modern China in the Age of Global Migration* (Durham, NC: Duke University Press, 2018), 12–14; and Michael Jin, "Americans in the Pacific: Rethinking Race, Gender, Citizenship, and Diaspora at the Crossroads of Asian and Asian American Studies," *Critical Ethnic Studies* 2, no. 1 (2016): 130.

14. "Chinese Immigration: The Social, Moral, and Political Effect of Chinese Immigration; Policy and Means of Exclusion; Memorial of the Senate of California to the Congress of the United States," *Daily Alta California*, August 23, 1877.

15. Beth Lew-Williams, *Chinese Must Go: Violence, Exclusion, and the Making of the Alien in America* (Cambridge, MA: Harvard University Press, 2018).

16. James D. Phelan, "The Case Against the Chinaman," *Saturday Evening Post*, December 21, 1901.

17. Lon Kurashige, *Two Faces of Exclusion: The Untold History of Anti-Asian Racism in the United States* (Chapel Hill: University of North Carolina Press, 2016), 86–97.

18. Tasuki Harada, ed., *The Japanese Problem in California: Answers (By Representative Americans) to Questionnaire* (San Francisco: American Japanese Relations Committee of Tokyo, 1922), 14.

19. Harada, *Japanese Problem in California*, 17.

20. Campaign poster of Senator James Phelan of California, ca. 1921, Bancroft Library, University of California, Berkeley.

21. See, for instance, leading anti-Japanese publisher Valentine Stuart McClatchy's pamphlets: *The Germany of Asia: Japan's Policy in the Far East; Her "Peaceful Penetration" of the United States; How American Commercial and National Interests Are Affected* (Sacramento, California, April 1919); *Assimilation of Japanese: Can They Be Moulded into American Citizens?* (Sacramento, California, October 1921); and *Japanese Immigration and Colonization: Brief Prepared for Consideration of the State Department* (Sacramento, California, October 1921), all in Valentine Stuart McClatchy, ed., *Four Anti-Japanese Pamphlets* (New York: Arno Press, 1978).

22. Daniels, *Politics of Prejudice*, 91.

23. U.S. House of Representatives, *Statistics of the Congressional and Presidential Election of November 2, 1920* (Washington, DC: U.S. Government Printing Office, 1921).

24. Mae M. Ngai, "The Architecture of Race in American Immigration Law: A Reexamination of the Immigration Act of 1924," *Journal of American History* 86, no. 1 (June 1999): 70–71.

25. *Takao Ozawa v. United States*, 260 U.S. 178 (1922).

26. Daniels, *Politics of Prejudice*, 91–93.

27. *The Morning Daily Advance* (Hollister, California), May 19, 1920; *Nichibei Shimbun* (San Francisco), December 1, 1920.

28. "Lettuce Shipments End at Hollister," *Oakland Tribune*, November 22, 1925.

29. "Lettuce Price Is Off, Says Tashima," *Salinas Daily Index*, May 18, 1922; *Monrovia Daily News*, December 1925;

30. Fuyuko Kamisaka, *Mitsu no sokoku: Manshu ni totsuida nikkei amerikajin* (Tokyo: Chuo Koronsha, 1996), 34–37.

31. "Grapes, Lettuce Moving from Hollister Areas," *Salinas Index-Journal*, September 29, 1928; "Remorse Led to Suicide of 'Lettuce King,'" *Salinas Index-Journal*, September 20, 1933.

32. "Man Ends Own Life By Taking Poison," *Nichibei Shimbun* (San Francisco), September 20, 1933; "Obituary," *Nichibei Shimbun*, September 21, 1933.

33. "Miss Tashima to Sail for Tokyo, Japan," *Napa Valley Register*, October 26, 1933; Kamisaka, *Mitsu no sokoku*, 38.

Notes to Chapter 1

34. V. S. McClatchy, "Japanese or Americans: Which Shall Rule and Occupy the United States in Years to Come?" in McClatchy, *Four Anti-Japanese Pamphlets*, 44.

35. McClatchy, "Assimilation of Japanese: Can They Be Moulded into American Citizens; Remarks Before the Honolulu Rotary Club, October 27, 1921," in McClatchy, *Four Anti-Japanese Pamphlets*, 10–11.

36. Daniels, *Politics of Prejudice*, 91.

37. See Chapter 2 for McClatchy and other exclusionists' campaign to eliminate U.S.-born Japanese Americans' birthright citizenship and the movement's long-term transnational effect on Nisei migrants in the Japanese Empire.

38. Junichi Takeda, *Zaibei hiroshima kenjinshi* (Los Angeles: Zaibei Hiroshima Kenjinshi Hakkojo, 1929), 43.

39. Isamu Nodera, "A Survey of the Vocational Activities of the Japanese in the City of Los Angeles," Master's thesis, University of Southern California, 1936.

40. *Rafu Shimpo*, June 20, 1937.

41. K. Tateishi, "An Atypical Nisei," 203.

42. K. Tateishi, "An Atypical Nisei," 203.

43. K. Tateishi, "An Atypical Nisei," 201.

44. Yuji Ichioka, "Dai Nisei Mondai: Changing Japanese Immigrant Conceptions of the Second-Generation Problem, 1902–1941," in *Before Internment: Essays in Prewar Japanese American History*, ed. Gordon H. Chang and Eiichiro Azuma (Stanford, CA: Stanford University Press, 2006), 33.

45. This was not a practice unique to Japanese families in the United States, as first-generation Italian immigrants were also known to send their American-born children to Italy to live with relatives during this period. See Dino Cinel, *From Italy to San Francisco: The Immigrant Experience* (Stanford, CA: Stanford University Press, 1982), 127. Another study by Dino Cinel on Italian return migrants in the early 1900s suggests that a significant number of U.S.-born Italian Americans migrated to Italy with their return migrant parents. For instance, about 75% of the 25,000 foreigners admitted to four major Italian ports in 1906 were U.S. citizens by birth or naturalization. See Dino Cinel, *The National Integration of Italian Return Migration, 1870–1929* (Cambridge, UK: Cambridge University Press, 1991), 107.

46. Ichioka, "Dai Nisei Mondai," 33.

47. I use the history of the impact of Jim Crow laws on the great migration of African Americans to frame the system of racial oppression in the American West as a "sinister push" that compelled many Japanese Americans to migrate. See Douglas Flamming, *Bound for Freedom: Black Los Angeles in Jim Crow America* (Berkeley: University of California Press, 2005); Eric Arnesen, *Black Protest and the Great Migration: A Brief History with Documents* (Boston: Bedford/St.

Martin's, 2003); and Matthew Briones, *Jim and Jap Crow: A Cultural History of 1940s Interracial America* (Princeton, NJ: Princeton University Press, 2012).

48. Mikiso Hane, *Modern Japan: A Historical Survey* (Boulder, CO: Westview Press, 1986), 224; Yuji Ichioka, "Introduction," in Karl G. Yoneda, *Ganbatte: Sixty-Year Struggle of a Kibei Worker* (Los Angeles: Asian American Studies Center, University of California, Los Angeles, 1983), xi; Karl G. Yoneda, *Ganbatte: Sixty-Year Struggle of a Kibei Worker* (Los Angeles: Asian American Studies Center, University of California, Los Angeles, 1983), 6–9.

49. Pedro Iacobelli, Danton Leary, and Shinnosuke Takahashi, eds., *Transnational Japan as History: Empire, Migration, and Social Movements* (New York: Palgrave McMillian, 2016), 173–75.

50. Yoneda, *Ganbatte*, 8–9; John J. Stephan, "Hijacked by Utopia: American Nikkei in Manchuria," *Amerasia Journal* 23, no. 3 (1997): 7.

51. Takemaro, "Colonies and Countryside," 183–84. See also Hiroshima Kenmin no Chugoku Tohoku Chiku Kaitakushi Hensan Iinkai, *Hiroshimaken manshu kaitakushi* (Hiroshima: Hiroshima Kenmin no Chugoku Tohoku Chiku Kaitakushi Hensan Iinkai, 1989).

52. Ichioka, "Introduction," xi; Yoneda, *Ganbatte*, 17. See Chapters 3 and 4 for Yoneda's cooperation with U.S. authorities during World War II and his role as a leader of the anti-Axis activism within internment camps.

53. See the census reports, "Honpo ni kyoju suru beika shussei nikkeijinzucho," in the *Nikkei gaijin kankei zakken*, Showa Series, vol. 1–3, Diplomatic Archives of the Ministry of Foreign Affairs of Japan, Tokyo, Japan.

54. Soen Yamashita, *Nikkei shimin no nihon ryugaku jijo* (Tokyo: Bunseisha, 1935), 179–180; Soen Yamashita, *Nichibei wo tsunagu mono* (Tokyo: Bunseisha, 1938), 266.

55. Tsunegoro Hirohata, *Zaibei fukuoka kenjinshi* (Los Angeles: Zaibei Fukuoka Kenjinshi Hensan Jimusho, 1931).

56. Yamashita, *Nichibei wo tsunagu mono*, 266.

57. Kaigai Kyoiku Kyokai, *Kaigai kyoiku kyokai yoran* (Tokyo: Kaigai Kyoiku Kyokai, 1940).

58. Yamashita, *Nichibei wo tsunagu mono*, 156–57.

59. "Hawai homu yoran," August 1936, *Nikkei gaijin kankei zakken*, K.1.1.0.9.3, Diplomatic Archives of the Ministry of Foreign Affairs of Japan, Tokyo, Japan.

60. Eiichiro Azuma, "Nisei no nihon ryugaku no hikari to kage: Nikkei amerikajin no ekkyo kyoiku no rinen to mujun," in *Amerika nihonjin imin no ekkyo kyoikushi*, ed. Yoshida Akira (Tokyo: Nihon Tosho Center, 2005), 239–40.

61. Kamisaka, *Mitsu no sokoku*, 17–18.

62. Keisen Girls' School, *The Nisei*, vii; Azuma, "Nisei no nihon ryugaku," 234–38.

63. Kamisaka, *Mitsu no sokoku*, 51.
64. "The Forgotten Nisei."
65. Yamashita, *Nichibei wo tsunagu mono*, 156–57.
66. *Toa dobunkai kiji*, 1938–1940, Toa Dobunkai Collection, Tao Dobun Shoin Daigaku Kinen Center, Aichi University, Aichi, Japan.
67. Hattori Shingo, *Waga kuni ni okeru senzen no amerikan futtoboru katsudo no kiroku* (Tokyo, Japan American Football Association, 2004); "Fresno Has Fine Mayor! College Boy Returns to Raisin City and Greets Leymel," *Nichibei Times*, May 5, 1929.
68. "Shi-gun tatsu: Nihon saisho no beikokushiki shukyu," *Yomiuri Shimbun*, December 26, 1933.
69. *Asahi Shimbun*, March 24, 1935; Hattori, *Waga kuni ni okeru senzen no amerikan futtoboru katsudo no kiroku*.
70. "Japanese Dancer Scores Triumph on Coast State," *Nippu Jiji*, August 9, 1928.
71. "L.A. Dancer in Circuit," *Nichibei Shimbun*, September 15, 1929; George Yoshida, *Reminiscing in Swingtime: Japanese Americans in American Popular Music, 1925–1960* (San Francisco: National Japanese American Historical Society, 1997), 6. See also Norikoshi Takao, *Arisu: Burodouei wo miryo shita tensai dansa Kawahata Fumiko monogatari* (Tokyo: Kondansha, 1999).
72. *Kashu Mainichi*, June 16, 1935.
73. "Shiatoru shusshin no kashu Miyazawa keimai o-mote," *Taihoku Nippo*, May 25, 1935.
74. *Heishikan News*, August 10, 1940, Heishikan Collection, Japanese Overseas Migration Museum, Yokohama, Japan (hereafter cited as Heishikan Collection).
75. *Heishikan Newsletter*, June 2004, Heishikan Collection.
76. *Rafu Shimpo*, October 10, 1939; Consul General in Los Angeles to the Minister of Foreign Affairs, August 24, 1939, *Honsho shokuin yosei kankei zakken*, vol. 2, Diplomatic Archives of the Ministry of Foreign Affairs of Japan, Tokyo, Japan; K. Tateishi, "An Atypical Nisei," 202–3.
77. *Heishikan News*, August 10, 1940, Heishikan Collection.
78. "Heishikan no yurai oyobi genjo," *Heishikan News*, August 10, 1940, Heishikan Collection.
79. "Heishikan nikki," *Heishikan News*, August 10, 1940, Heishikan Collection.
80. "Hokkaido, karafuto kengaku ryoko," *Heishikan News*, September 16, 1940, Heishikan Collection.
81. "Hokkaido, karafuto kengaku ryoko," *Heishikan News*, September 16, 1940, Heishikan Collection.
82. "Heishikan kiroku," *Heishikan News*, June 5, 1942, Heishikan Collection; Kumei Teruko, "Nihon seifu to nisei ekkyo kyoiku: Heishikan wo jirei to shite,"

in *Amerika nihonjin imin no ekkyo kyoikushi*, ed. Yoshida Akira (Tokyo: Nihon Tosho Center, 2005); Kumei Teruko, "Yujo to yuko wo musunde: Heishikan kara rajio puresu-e," *Kaigai imin shiryokan kenkyu kiyo* 4 (2009): 1–10. See also Chapter 5.

Chapter 2

1. "In the Matter of Inaba, Toshiko and Inaba, Akira, Natives," U.S. Department of Labor Bureau of Immigration Board of Special Inquiry, September 12, 1928, RG 85, File 55642/657, National Archives and Records Administration (NARA), Washington, D.C.; Nichibei Shimbunsha, *Nichibei nenkan* (San Francisco: Nichibei Shimbunsha, 1911); Nichibei Shinbunsha, *Nichibei jushoroku* (San Francisco: Nichibei Shimbunsha, 1939).

2. Edward L. Haff, Acting Commissioner, U.S. Department of Labor Immigration Service, to M. E. Mitchell, Attorney at Law, September 17, 1928, RG 85, File 55642/657, NARA.

3. "In the Matter of Inaba"; "Honpo ni oite konin shitaru nikkei shimin no shiminken soshitsu ni yoru sokan ni kansuru ken," May 1, 1930, *Nikkei gaijin kankei zakken*, K.1.1.0.9.1, Diplomatic Archives of the Ministry of Foreign Affairs of Japan, Tokyo, Japan; *Toshiko Inaba v. John D. Nagle, Commissioner of Immigration* (N.D.Cal. 1929), petition for writ of habeas corpus, No. 19919 L.

4. *Toshiko Inaba v. John D. Nagle.*

5. "In the Matter of Inaba."

6. 59th United States Congress, "An Act Relating to Expatriation of Citizens and Their Protection Abroad; Citizenship or Women by Marriage; Citizenship of Children Born Abroad of Citizen Fathers" (34 Stat. 1228), March 2, 1907.

7. 67th United States Congress, "An Act Relative to the Naturalization and Citizenship of Married Women" (Pub. L. 67-346, 42 Stat. 1021b), September 22, 1922.

8. Haff to Mitchell, September 17, 1928.

9. 68th United States Congress, "An Act to Limit the Immigration of Aliens into the United States, and for Other Purposes (Pub. L. 68-139, 43 Stat. 153), May 26, 1924.

10. 68th United States Congress, "Act to Limit the Immigration of Aliens."

11. Michael Jin, "Americans in the Pacific: Rethinking Race, Gender, Citizenship, and Diaspora at the Crossroads of Asian and Asian American Studies," *Critical Ethnic Studies* 2, no. 1 (June 2016): 132–33.

12. Edward L. Haff, Acting Commissioner of Immigration, San Francisco, to Commissioner General of Immigration, Washington, D.C., January 3, 1930, RG 85, File 55642/657, NARA; U.S. Department of Labor Immigration Service, "Report of Execution of Department Decision No. 27184/23–10," January 17, 1930, RG 85, File 55642/657, NARA.

13. Mae M. Ngai, "The Architecture of Race in American Immigration Law: A Reexamination of the Immigration Act of 1924," *Journal of American History* 86, no. 1 (June 1999): 70–71.

14. V. S. McClatchy, "The Germany of Asia: Japan's Policy in the Far East; Her 'Peaceful Penetration' of the United States; How American Commercial and National Interests Are Affected" (April 1919), in V. S. McClatchy, ed., *Four Anti-Japanese Pamphlets* (New York: Arno Press, 1978), 36. See also Chapter 1.

15. U.S. Department of Commerce, Bureau of the Census, *Sixteenth Census of the United States: 1940* (Washington, DC: U.S. Government Printing Office, 1943).

16. McClatchy, "Germany of Asia," in McClatchy, *Four Anti-Japanese Pamphlets*, 36.

17. Leslie Bow, *Partly Colored: Asian Americans and Racial Anomaly in the Segregated South* (New York: NYU Press, 2010), 1–5.

18. Mae M. Ngai, "Birthright Citizenship and the Alien Citizen," *Fordham Law Review* 75, no. 5 (2007): 2522–23.

19. *The People of the State of California v. George W. Hall*, 4 Cal. 399 (1854).

20. Deenesh Sohoni, "Unsuitable Suitors: Anti-Miscegenation Laws, Naturalization Laws, and the Constructions of Asian Identities," *Law and Society Review* 41, no. 3 (September 2007): 587–618.

21. *Plessy v. Ferguson*, 163 U.S. 537 (1896).

22. *United States v. Wong Kim Ark*, 169 U.S. 649 (1898).

23. V. S. McClatchy, *America and Japan: Their Treatment of Foreigners and Resulting Conditions—Policies in Immigration, Exclusion Land Ownership and Lease, Citizenship, Dual Citizenship* (San Francisco: California Joint Immigration Committee, 1925), 14; Roger Daniels, *The Politics of Prejudice: The Anti-Japanese Movement in California and the Struggle for Japanese Exclusion* (Berkeley: University of California Press, 1962), 91; Yuji Ichioka, "'Dai Nisei Mondai': Changing Japanese Immigrant Conceptions of the Second-Generation Problem, 1902–1941," in *Before Internment: Essays in Prewar Japanese American History*, ed. Gordon H. Chang and Eiichiro Azuma (Stanford, CA: Stanford University Press, 2006), 18.

24. V. S. McClatchy, "Assimilation of Japanese: Can They Be Moulded into American Citizens?" (October 27, 1921), in McClatchy, *Four Anti-Japanese Pamphlets*, 13.

25. McClatchy, "Assimilation of Japanese," in McClatchy, *Four Anti-Japanese Pamphlets*, 17–19.

26. Martha Gardner, *The Qualities of a Citizen: Women, Immigration, and Citizenship, 1870–1965* (Princeton, NJ: Princeton University Press), 121–38.

27. *Toshiko Inaba v. John D. Nagle, Commissioner of Immigration* (N.D.Cal. 1929), petition for writ of habeas corpus, No. 19919 L.

28. Morikazu Ida, Consul General of Japan, to Edward L. Haff, Acting Commissioner of Immigration, October 27, 1928, RG 85, File 55642/657, NARA.
29. *Toshiko Inaba v. John D. Nagle*.
30. Ida to Haff, October 27, 1928.
31. "In the Matter of Inaba, Toshiko, Native," U.S. Department of Labor Bureau of Immigration Board of Special Inquiry, October 18, 1928, RG 85, File 55642/657, NARA; *Toshiko Inaba v. John D. Nagle*.
32. *Toshiko Inaba v. John D. Nagle*.
33. "News Happenings Around the Bay," *Sacramento Bee*, December 18, 1929; "Japanese Woman, Born Here, Refused Admittance to Country," *Sacramento Bee*, January 18, 1930.
34. "Custom Causes Jap Girl's Deportation," *El Paso Times*, December 18, 1929.
35. "U.S. Court of Appeals at S.F. Blocks Entry of Toshiko Inaba," *Nippu Jiji*, January 28, 1930.
36. "Nihonjin to konin ni yori soshitsu shitaru fujin beikoku shiminken no rikon go kaifuku shinsei ni taisuru kyoka hanketsu no ken," March 1927, *Nikkei gaijin kankei zakken*, K.1.1.0.9.1, Diplomatic Archives of the Ministry of Foreign Affairs of Japan.
37. "In the Matter of the Petition of Yoshiko Hoshino for Naturalization" (U.S. District Court for the Territory of Hawaii, 1927), No. 1466.
38. "In the Matter of the Petition of Yoshiko Hoshino."
39. "Nihon ni kikoku seru mono no beikoku shiminken ni kan suru ken," March 1927, *Nikkei gaijin kankei zakken*, K.1.1.0.9.1, Diplomatic Archives of the Ministry of Foreign Affairs of Japan.
40. Vice Consul of Japan in Los Angeles to Ray E. Nimmo, December 9, 1926, *Nikkei gaijin kankei zakken*, K.1.1.0.9.1, Diplomatic Archives of the Ministry of Foreign Affairs of Japan.
41. Ray E. Nimmo to Vice Consul of Japan in Los Angeles, December 30, 1926, *Nikkei gaijin kankei zakken*, K.1.1.0.9.1, Diplomatic Archives of the Ministry of Foreign Affairs of Japan.
42. Consul General of Japan in Los Angeles to the Minister of Foreign Affairs of Japan, February 15, 1927, *Nikkei gaijin kankei zakken*, K.1.1.0.9.1, Diplomatic Archives of the Ministry of Foreign Affairs of Japan.
43. Ichioka, "Dai Nisei Mondai," 19.
44. See the accounts of former Japanese American servicemen in the Japanese armed forces: Jim Yoshida, *The Two Worlds of Jim Yoshida* (New York: Morrow, 1972); M. Yoshida, "Sokoku to teikoku no aida," in *Chinkon senkan yamato* (Tokyo: Kodansha, 1974); Tachibana Yuzuru, *Teikoku kaigun shikan ni natta nikkei nisei* (Tokyo: Tsukiji Shokan, 1994); and Iwao Peter Sano, *One Thousand Days*

in Siberia: The Odyssey of a Japanese-American POW (Lincoln: University of Nebraska Press, 1997). See also Chapter 5.

45. "Nihonjin to konin ni yori soshitsu sitaru fujin beikoku shiminken."

46. Rinjiro Sodei, *Watashitachi wa teki datta noka* (Tokyo: Iwanami Shoten, 1995), 12.

47. "Honpo ni kyojuseru bei, ka shussei nikkeijin sucho no ken," 1932, *Nikkei gaijin kankei zakken*, K.1.1.0.9.1, Diplomatic Archives of the Ministry of Foreign Affairs of Japan.

48. Interim Consul General of Japan in San Francisco to Minister of Foreign Affairs, July 25, 1936, *Nikkei gaijin kankei zakken*, K.1.1.0.9.1, Diplomatic Archives of the Ministry of Foreign Affairs of Japan.

49. "Honpo ni oite."

50. "McClatchy Attacks 'Kibei' Citizens," *Nichibei Times*, June 10, 1936; "V. S. McClatchy Attacks Duel [*sic*] Citizenship and Kibei Shimin Organ," *Kashu Mainichi*, June 14, 1936.

51. V. S. McClatchy, "The Story of Japanese Immigration: Japan Demands What May Not Be Conceded," California Joint Immigration Committee Document 507, September 1937, William Randolph Hearst Papers, Box 5, Folder 19, BANC MSS 77/121C, Bancroft Library, University of California, Berkeley.

52. V. S. McClatchy to William Randolph Hearst, January 10, 1938, William Randolph Hearst Papers, Box 5, Folder 19, BANC MSS 77/121C, Bancroft Library, University of California, Berkeley.

53. "McClatchy," *Nichibei Shimbun*, May 20, 1937.

54. "Nikkei shimin kibei kinshi un-un no fusetsu ni kansuru ken," June 29, 1937, *Nikkei gaijin kankei zakken*, K.1.1.0.9.3, Diplomatic Archives of the Ministry of Foreign Affairs of Japan.

55. "The Cannon Bill," *Nichibei Shimbun*, May 8, 1937.

56. President of Hiroshima Overseas Association to Director, American Affairs Bureau, Ministry of Foreign Affairs, May 21, 1937, *Nikkei gaijin kankei zakken*, K.1.1.0.9.3, Diplomatic Archives of the Ministry of Foreign Affairs of Japan.

57. Governor of Wakayama Prefecture to Director, America Division, Ministry of Foreign Affairs, June 28, 1937, *Nikkei gaijin kankei zakken*, K.1.1.0.9.3, Diplomatic Archives of the Ministry of Foreign Affairs of Japan; "Dai nisei beikoku ni kiraharu," *Osaka Mainichi Shimbun* (Wakayama Edition), June 11, 1937.

58. "Keisho," May 1937, *Nikkei gaijin kankei zakken*, K.1.1.0.9.3, Diplomatic Archives of the Ministry of Foreign Affairs of Japan.

59. "Nikkei shimin kibei kinshi."

60. "Nichibei seinen renmei no koenkai kaisai ni kansuru ken," February 2, 1939, *Nikkei gaijin kankei zakken*, K.1.1.0.9.3, Diplomatic Archives of the Ministry of Foreign Affairs of Japan.

61. "Nichibei seinen renmei."

62. Karl G. Yoneda, *Ganbatte: Sixty-Year Struggle of a Kibei Worker* (Los Angeles: Asian American Studies Center, University of California, Los Angeles, 1983), 3–5.

63. Karl Akiya, in "Why They Volunteered," *Fighting Americans, Too!* 2nd ed, Volunteers for Victory, Topaz, Utah, April 1943, Edward N. Barnhart Papers, Box 49, Folder 6, Japanese American Research Project Collections, University of California, Los Angeles, Special Collections. See also Karl Akiya, *Jiyu-e no michi taiheiyo wo koete: Aru kibei nisei no jiden* (Kyoto: Korosha, 1996).

64. *Japan Times Weekly*, October 19, 1939.

65. Keisen Girls' School, *The Nisei: A Study of Their Life in Japan* (Tokyo: Keisen Girls' School), v, 16–28.

66. Zaibei Nihonjinkai, *Zaibei Nihonjinshi*, 1117–18; Ichioka, "Dai Nisei Mondai," 35.

67. Nagai Matsuzo, ed., *Nichibei bunka koshoshi* (Tokyo: Yoyosha, 1952).

Chapter 3

1. U.S. Department of War, *Final Report: Japanese Evacuation from the West Coast, 1942* (Washington, DC: U.S. Government Printing Office, 1943), 33–34.

2. U.S. Department of War, *Final Report*, 13–14.

3. For a detailed study on the multiple representations of the history of the Japanese American internment, see Alice Yang Murray, *Historical Memories of the Japanese American Internment and the Struggle for Redress* (Stanford, CA: Stanford University Press, 2008).

4. Commission on Wartime Relocation and Internment of Civilians (CWRIC), *Personal Justice Denied: Report of the Commission on Wartime Relocation and Internment of Civilians* (Washington, DC: U.S. Government Printing Office, 1982), 65.

5. CWRIC, *Personal Justice Denied*, 73.

6. CWRIC, *Personal Justice Denied*, 64–65.

7. CWRIC, *Personal Justice Denied*, 68–69, 73.

8. Lieutenant Commander Kenneth D. Ringle, U.S. Navy, to the Chief of Naval Operations, "Report on the Japanese Question," January 26, 1942, CWRIC Files, National Archives and Records Administration (NARA), Washington, D.C.

9. Munson was a Chicago businessman who gathered intelligence while acting as a special representative of the State Department.

10. Ringle, "Report on the Japanese Question."

11. Edward J. Ennis, Director, Alien Control Unit, "Memorandum for the Solicitor General, Re: Japanese Brief," April 30, 1943, CWRIC Files, NARA.

12. Ringle, "Report on the Japanese Question."

13. Ennis, "Memorandum for the Solicitor General."

14. Togo Tanaka, "History of JACL," Chapter 3, "Japanese American Evacuation and Resettlement Study," File T 6.25, Bancroft Library, University of California, Berkeley.

15. Michi Weglyn, *Years of Infamy: The Untold Story of America's Concentration Camps* (New York: Morrow, 1976), 44.

16. Bulletin, JACL Southern California Council, December 1941, JACL Anti-Axis Committee; Anti-Axis Committee Log, December 7, 1941, JACL Records, Box 301, Folder AAC, Japanese American Research Project (JARP) Collection, University of California, Los Angeles, Special Collections.

17. Minutes, Anti-Axis Committee, December 7, 1941, JACL Records, Box 301, Folder AAC, JARP Collection.

18. Minutes, Anti-Axis Committee, December 12, 1941, JACL Records, Box 301, Folder AAC, JARP Collection. See also Chapter 4 for Itami's prewar and wartime experiences.

19. Bulletin, Anti-Axis Committee, JACL Southern District Council; Bulletin, "Southern Federation Japanese American Citizens League Anti Axis Committee," Anti-Axis Committee, JACL Southern District Council (translated from Japanese), December 1941, JACL Box 301, Folder AAC, JARP Collection; Minutes, Anti-Axis Committee, December 12, 1941.

20. "Kibei Division Cabinet Disbands," *Kashu Mainichi*, December 22, 1941.

21. Peter Irons, *Justice at War* (Oxford, UK: Oxford University Press, 1983), 79–80.

22. Harry Y. Ueno, interviewed by Wendy Ng, Sunnyvale, California, January 23, 1997, in *REgenerations Oral History Project: Rebuilding Japanese American Families, Communities, and Rights in the Resettlement Era* (Los Angeles: Japanese American National Museum, 2000), 4: 484–85.

23. "Kibei Survey Launched: Giving Them Assistance, Chapter Aids," *Japanese American Courier*, February 20, 1942.

24. "Kibei Requested to Volunteer Information by National JACL," *Rocky Nippon*, February 20, 1942.

25. "Kibei Survey Launched."

26. Press Release 82 [February 1942] and JACL Bulletin 114 [February 1942], JACL Archives, San Francisco, California, quoted by Deborah Lim, *Research Report Prepared for the Presidential Select Committee on JACL Resolution #7 Submitted in 1990 by Deborah K. Lim* (a.k.a. "The Lim Report"), https://resisters.com/conscience-and-the-constituion/learn-more/jacl/the-lim-report/ (accessed June 17, 2013).

27. "Kibei Survey," published in the *Japanese American Courier*, February 20, 1942.

28. The WRA was subsequently transferred to the Department of the Interior in 1943.

29. CWRIC, *Personal Justice Denied*, 107, 154–55.

30. Dillon S. Myer, "The War Relocation Authority Is Firmly Committed to the Principle That American Children Should not Be Penalized for Accidents of Ancestry," March 14, 1944, in *Reinstitution of Selective Service: Summary of the Policies of the Selective Service System, War Department and W.R.A. Which Affect Nisei*, by the Citizens Committee of Topaz and the Community Council, Topaz, Utah, June, 1944, Edward N. Barnhart Papers, Box 49, Folder 6, JARP Collection.

31. "Community Analysis Section," in *The Pen*, published by *The Outpost* (Rohwer, Arkansas), November 6, 1943.

32. U.S. Department of the Interior, War Relocation Authority, *WRA: A Story of Human Conservation* (Washington, DC: U.S. Government Printing Office, 1946), 7; Dillon S. Myer, *Uprooted Americans: The Japanese Americans and the War Relocation Authority During World War II* (Tucson: University of Arizona Press, 1971).

33. Edward Spicer, Asael T. Hansen, Katherine Luomala, and Marvin Opler, *Impounded People: Japanese-Americans in the Relocation Centers* (Tucson: University of Arizona Press, 1969).

34. For Myer's role as the director of the War Relocation Authority and the commissioner of the Bureau of Indian Affairs, see Richard T. Drinnon, *Keeper of Concentration Camps: Dillon S. Myer and American Racism* (Berkeley: University of California Press, 1987).

35. Mike M. Masaoka, in "Appended Section," U.S. House of Representatives, 83rd Congress, 2nd Session, Committee on the Judiciary, Subcommittee No. 5, Hearings on H.R. 7435, to Amend the Japanese-American Evacuation Claims Act of 1948 (Washington, DC: U.S. Government Printing Office, 1954).

36. Mike M. Masaoka, memorandum to "national board members, national council members, active and associated members, sponsors, friends, and supports of the national JACL," April 22, 1944, JACL Records, Box 301, Folder Mike M. Masaoka, JARP Collection.

37. Weglyn, *Years of Infamy*, 119.

38. Paul R. Spickard, "The Nisei Assume Power: The Japanese Citizens League, 1941–1942," *Pacific Historical Review* 52, no. 2 (May 1983): 147–48.

39. Dillon S. Myer to WRA Project Directors, February 8, 1944, William C. Carr Papers, Box 55, Folder 1, JARP Collection.

40. Myer, "War Relocation Authority Is Firmly Committed."

41. "Separation of Kibei from Nisei," Lieutenant General John L. DeWitt to the Chief of Staff, U.S. Army, War Department, August 23, 1942, attached to DeWitt's letter to the Chief of Staff, U.S. Army, Washington, D.C., October 5, 1942, CWRIC Files, NARA.

42. Memorandum, Western Defense Command, August 1942, CWRIC Files, NARA.

43. Fred Tayama, "Brief Report of the Kibei Meeting Held at Mess Hall 15, Manzanar Relocation Center, August 8, 1942," attached to Tayama's letter to Major Richard E. Rudisill, August 9, 1942, CWRIC Files, NARA.

44. Karl Yoneda, "Notes and Observations of 'Kibei Meeting' held August 8th, 1942 at Kitchen 15," CWRIC Files, NARA; Karl Yoneda, *Manzanar kyosei shuyojo nikki* (Tokyo: PMC Shuppan, 1988), 163–64.

45. James Oda, *Heroic Struggles of Japanese Americans: Partisan Fighters from America's Concentration Camps* (North Hollywood, CA: James Oda, 1981), 50–51.

46. Assistant Secretary of War John J. McCloy to Dillon S. Myer, October 30, 1942, CWRIC Files, NARA.

47. U.S. Department of the Interior, War Relocation Authority, *WRA*, 45–46. It should also be noted that Myer at this point was reluctant to undertake a segregation project, which would have been a logistical nightmare to the new director.

48. Spicer et al., *Impounded People*.

49. War Relocation Authority, "Administrative Instruction No. 100," Washington, D.C., July 15, 1943; War Relocation Authority, "The Segregation Program: A Statement for Appointed Personnel in W.R.A. Centers" [July 1943], War Relocation Authority (WRA) Records Collection, RG 210, NARA.

50. John F. Embree, "Dealing with Japanese Americans," Community Analysis Report No. 1, October 1942, WRA Documents Section, C-1258 of 7-BU-COS-WP, pp. 6–7, William C. Carr Papers, Box 55, Folder 1, JARP Collection.

51. Dillon S. Myer to WRA Staff Members [1942], C-1258-C-NOBU, William C. Carr Papers, Box 55, Folder 1, JARP Collection.

52. WRA Community Analysis Section, "Community Analysis Report No. 6," July 21, 1943, WRA Documents Section, William C. Carr Papers, Box 55, Folder 1, JARP Collection.

53. "English Classes for Issei, Kibei, and Nisei Planned," *Press Bulletin*, Poston War Relocation Center, October 22, 1942.

54. "English Classes for Kibei," *Daily Tulean Dispatch*, Tule Lake War Relocation Center, September 2, 1942.

55. WRA Community Analysis Section, "Project Analysis Series No. 8," July 1943, p. 3, Carey McWilliams Papers, Box 2, Folder 2, WRA Records Collection, H1944.1, Claremont Colleges Special Collections.

56. WRA Community Analysis Section, "Project Analysis Series No. 8."

57. *Heart Mountain Sentinel*, September 4, 1943.

58. WRA Community Analysis Section, "Community Analysis Report No. 7," October 16, 1943, p. 4, William C. Carr Papers, Box 55, Folder 1, JARP Collection.

59. Myer, *Uprooted Americans*, 72.

60. *Daily Tulean Dispatch*, February 8, 1942.

61. Question 27 of the infamous loyalty questionnaire read, "Are you willing to serve in the armed forces of the United States on combat duty, wherever ordered?" Question 28 was arguably even more controversial: "Will you swear unqualified allegiance to the United States of America and faithfully defend the United States from any or all attack by foreign or domestic forces, and forswear any form of allegiance or obedience to the Japanese emperor, or any other foreign government, power, or organization?" See War Relocation Authority, "Application for Leave Clearance," July 1943, William C. Carr Papers, Box 55, Folder 1, JARP Collection.

62. John F. Embree, "Registration at Central Utah," WRA Community Analysis Series No. 1, February 23, 1942, Carey McWilliams Papers, Box 2, Folder 2, WRA Records Collection, H1944.1, Claremont Colleges Special Collections.

63. Embree, "Registration at Central Utah."

64. Embree, "Registration at Central Utah."

65. Federal Bureau of Investigation, "Memorandum for the Director," Washington, D.C., March 23, 1942, p. 3, CWRIC Files, NARA.

66. Roger Daniels, *Concentration Camps: North America—Japanese in the United States and Canada During World War II*, rev. ed. (Malabar, FL: Robert E. Krieger, 1981), 107.

67. Eric L. Muller, *Free to Die for Their Country: The Story of the Japanese American Draft Resisters in World War II* (Chicago: University of Chicago Press, 2001), 186.

68. Myer's reference to a WRA registration report, in Myer to WRA Project Directors, February 8, 1944.

69. "Segregation to Start September 1, Declares Myer," *Topaz Times* (Topaz, Utah), special ed., July 14, 1943, p. 1, Edward N. Barnhart Papers, Box 49, Folder 6, JARP Collection.

70. Mike M. Masaoka, *They Call Me Moses Masaoka: An American Saga* (New York: Morrow, 1987), 131.

71. Masaoka, *They Call Me Moses Masaoka*, 131.

72. WRA Community Analysis Section, "Community Analysis Report No. 7," 5.

73. War Relocation Authority, "Administrative Instruction No. 100," 2–3.

74. War Relocation Authority, "Administrative Instruction No. 100," 3.

75. War Relocation Authority, *Segregation of Persons of Japanese Ancestry in Relocation Centers* (Washington, DC: War Relocation Authority, 1943).

76. Embree, "Registration at Central Utah," 6.

77. Karl Akiya, in "Why They Volunteered," in *Fighting Americans, Too!* 2nd ed., Volunteers for Victory, Topaz, Utah, April 1943, Edward N. Barnhart Papers, Box 49, Folder 6, JARP Collection.

78. Ernest S. Iiyama, in "Why They Volunteered."

79. "Army Intelligence Calls Nisei, Kibei," *Minidoka Irrigator*, October 31, 1942.

80. *Minidoka Irrigator*, November 11, 1942.

81. See Chapter 4 for the role of Kibei linguists in the Pacific.

82. Hiroshi Mayeda, interviewed by Alice Murata, Schaumberg, Illinois, October 5, 1997, in *REgenerations Oral History Project*, 1: 451–52.

83. Hiroshi "Harry" Kobashigawa, interviewed by author, Los Angeles, California, September 8, 2005.

84. John Weckerling, "Nisei Language Experts: Japanese Americans Play Vital Role in U.S. Intelligence Service in World War II," in *John Aiso and the M.I.S.: Japanese-American Soldiers in the Military Intelligence Service, World War II*, ed. Tad Ichinokuchi (Los Angeles: The M.I.S. Club of Southern California, 1988), 196.

85. James C. McNaughton, *Nisei Linguists: Japanese Americans in the Military Intelligence Service During World War II* (Washington, DC: U.S. Department of the Army, 2006), 27–28; Masaharu Ano, "Loyal Linguists: Nisei of World War II Learned Japanese in Minnesota," *Minnesota History* 45, no. 7 (Fall 1977): 273–87.

86. WRA Community Analysis Section, "Japanese Americans Educated in Japan," January 28, 1944, p. 1, William C. Carr Papers, Box 55, Folder 1, JARP.

87. WRA Community Analysis Section, "Japanese Americans Educated in Japan," 7.

88. WRA Community Analysis Section, "Japanese Americans Educated in Japan," 7–8.

89. Marvin Opler, "Cultural Dilemma of a Kibei Youth," in *Clinical Studies in Culture Conflict*, ed. Georgene Seward (New York: Ronald Press, 1958), 297–99.

90. Opler, "Cultural Dilemma of a Kibei Youth," 302–16.

91. WRA Community Analysis Section, "Japanese Americans Educated in Japan," 8.

92. WRA Community Analysis Section, "Japanese Americans Educated in Japan," 9.

93. WRA Community Analysis Section, "Japanese Americans Educated in Japan," 9–10.

94. WRA Community Analysis Section, "Japanese Americans Educated in Japan," 13.

95. WRA Community Analysis Section, "Japanese Americans Educated in Japan," 12.

96. *Pacific Citizen*, September 9, 1944.

97. Japanese American Citizens League, "PFC Thomas Higa Speech Tour, September 15–December 10, 1944," Thomas Higa Papers, Box 153, Folder 8, JARP Collection.

98. Japanese American Citizens League, "PFC Thomas Higa Speech Tour."

99. "Japanese-American, Wounded in Italy, Says Unit Was Treated Like Other G.I.'s," *New York Times*, November 19, 1944.

100. *Pacific Citizen*, September 9, 1944; Thomas D. Murphy, *Ambassadors in Arms* (Honolulu: University of Hawaii Press, 1954), 274–79.

101. Ayako Ellen Nakamura (Bridgeton, New Jersey) to Mike M. Masaoka, November 21, 1944, Thomas Higa Papers, Box 153, Folder 8, JARP Collection.

102. Donna C. Gabaccia, "Is Everywhere Nowhere? Nomads, Nations, and the Immigrant Paradigm of United States History," *Journal of American History* 86, no. 3 (December 1999): 1115.

103. Lon Kurashige, *Japanese American Celebration and Conflict: A History of Ethnic Identity and Festival, 1934–1990* (Berkeley: University of California Press, 2002), 6, 9, 91.

104. Embree, "Registration at Central Utah," 5.

105. Alice Kessler-Harris, "In the Nation's Image: The Gendered Limits of Social Citizenship in the Depression Era," *Journal of American History* 86, no. 3 (December 1999): 1251.

106. Leslie Hatamiya, *Righting a Wrong: Japanese Americans and the Passage of the Civil Liberties Act of 1988* (Stanford, CA: Stanford University Press, 1993), 58.

107. Yuji Ichioka, "Introduction," in Karl G. Yoneda, *Ganbatte: Sixty-Year Struggle of a Kibei Worker* (Los Angeles: Asian American Studies Center, University of California, Los Angeles, 1983), xi–xii. See also Chapters 1 and 4 for how Yoneda's prewar experiences in the Japanese Empire influenced his wartime patriotism.

Chapter 4

1. Kimiko Tamura, "Otto, Itami Akira" [My Husband Itami Akira], *Ryumon* (September 1987), 55.

2. "Minami kyushu, kaze to hai ni oowaru," *Jiji Shimpo*, January 14, 1914; "Kagoshima kaigan kara nozomu sakurajima no funka," *Jiji Shimpo*, January 17, 1914.

3. David Akira Itami, "Itami Akira no jihitsu no hennenshiki kubun ichidaiki" [The Chronicle of Akira Itami's Life as Written by Himself], *Ryumon* (September 1987): 42.

4. Itami, "Itami Akira no jihitsu," 42. See Chapters 1 and 2. See also Yuji Ichioka, "Introduction," in Karl G. Yoneda, *Ganbatte: Sixty-Year Struggle of a Kibei Worker* (Los Angeles: Asian American Studies Center, University of California, Los Angeles, 1983), xii. In 1940 it was reported that 10,000 Nisei returned to the United States from Japan; see Zaibei Nihonjinkai, *Zaibei nihonjinshi* (San Francisco: Zaibei Nihonjinkai, 1940), 1117–18. Brian Hayashi notes that figures

suggested by contemporary estimates are probably too low; see Brian Masaru Hayashi, *Democratizing the Enemy: The Japanese American Internment* (Princeton, NJ: Princeton University Press, 2004), 44–45, 238n11.

5. "Shasetsu" [Opinion], *Kashu Mainichi*, March 21, 1942; "Notice," *Kashu Mainichi* (English section), March 21, 1942; Itami, "Itami Akira no jihitsu."

6. Index record for Akira Itami, U.S. Department of War, World War II Army Enlistment Records, RG 64, Box 1235, National Archives and Record Administration (NARA), Washington, D.C.

7. War Department General Order No. 82, Washington, D.C., August 1, 1946, Records of the Adjutant General's Office, 1917–, RG 407, NARA, Washington, D.C.

8. Kinashi Kozo, *Dave Itami Akira no shogai* (Tokyo: Paru Shuppan, 1985); Itami, "Itami Akira no jihitsu"; Certificate of Death, Akira Itami, December 26, 1950, *Ryumon* (September 1987): 41.

9. Nippon Hoso Kyokai (NHK), *NHK taiga dorama taizen: 50 sakuin tettei gaido* (Tokyo: NHK Shuppan, 2011), 128–29.

10. Yamasaki Toyoko, *Futatsu no Sokoku* (Tokyo: Shinchosha, 1983); *Sanga Moyu*, dir. Murakami Yuji et al., 1984, Nippon Hoso Kyokai, Tokyo.

11. Andrew Gordon, *A Modern History of Japan: From Tokugawa Times to the Present*, 3rd ed. (New York: Oxford University Press, 2014), 84.

12. Yamasaki, *Futatsu no Sokoku*, 588; *Sanga Moyu*, "Aratanaru tabidachi," Episode 52, December 23, 1984.

13. "Futatsu no Sokoku no hazama de Itami Akira," Worksheet 19-1, Kajiki Folklore Museum [ca. 1995]; Michael Jin, "Itami Memorial," 2014, JPEG file.

14. Kajiki Kyodokan, *Futatsu no Sokoku, Itami ten* [Brochure] (Kajiki, Japan: Kajiki Folklore Museum, 2004).

15. See Shimamura Kyo, *Sanga Moyu: Jitsuroku* (Tokyo: Yumanite Shuppan, 1983); Miyazaki Masahiro, *Futatsu no sanga Nikkei amerikajin kaku tatakaeri* (Tokyo: Dainamikku Serazu, 1984); Asahi Ado Honsha, *"Sanga Moyu" shujinko moderu no shogai: Ketteiban korega shinsoda* (Kagoshima, Japan: Asahi Ado, 1984); Kinashi, *Dave Itami Akira no shogai*; Michi Itami, "Chichi Akira Itami no rekuiemu," *Daito Forum* 13 (Spring 2000): 9–15; Shimada Masakazu, with Kondo Masaomi and Watanabe Tomie, "Busu no naka no Itami Akira: Tokyo saiban tsuyakusha Shimada Masakazu shi ni kiku," *Daito Forum* 13 (Spring 2000): 16–35; Kinashi Kozo, "Hakuun raikyo," *Daito Forum* 13 (Spring 2000): 37–49; Hotta Akira, "Shonen jidai no Itami Akira," *Daito Forum* 13 (Spring 2000): 81–89; and Steve Sameshima, *Tenno o sukutta otoko: amerika rikigun johobu, nikkei kibei Nisei akira itami* (Kagoshima, Japan: Nanpo Shinsha, 2013).

16. See Introduction and Chapter 1.

17. Itami, "Itami Akira no jihatsu." See also Chapter 1.

18. Kinashi, "Hakuun raikyo."
19. Suiryu Seiki, "Itami Akira no omoide," *Ryumon* (September 1987): 45.
20. Horita Satoru, "Shonen jidai no Itami Akira," *Daito Forum* 13 (Spring 2000): 82.
21. Sameshima, *Tenno o sukutta otoko*, 17–18.
22. Kinashi, "Hakuun raikyo," 37.
23. Sameshima, *Tenno o sukutta otoko*, 19.
24. Kayoko Takeda, *Interpreting the Tokyo War Crimes Tribunal: A Sociopolitical Analysis* (Ottawa, Canada: University of Ottawa Press, 2010), 28.
25. Atsushi Hagihara, *Kiichiro Hiranuma to kindai nihon: Kanryo no kokkashugi to taiheiyo senso-e no michi* (Kyoto: Kyoto University Press, 2016).
26. Murata Katsumi, "Itami Akira no hito to shiso," *Daito Forum* 13 (Spring 2000): 50.
27. Goto Tokuji, "Senso wa izu no seishu," *Daito Forum* 13 (Spring 2000): 22–23.
28. Ono Koji, "Itami Akira-shi no kokoro: Kajiki to okurando to no aida ni," *Daito Forum* 13 (Spring 2000): 90; "Nichibei ryokoku no kakehashi," *Daito Bunka*, October 15, 1999.
29. "Nisei's Suicide Peace Lesson," *Valley Morning Star*, April 11, 1965; "Erroneous Information Calls for a Correction," *Honolulu Star Bulletin*, May 2, 1965.
30. William Wetherall, "Japan's Pop 'Roots' Fails to Cast New Light on Minority Problems," *Far Eastern Economic Review* 122, no. 41 (1983): 62–63; Yuji Ichioka, "A Nisei Critique of *Futatsu no Sokoku*," *Rafu Shimpo*, March 19–29, 1984.
31. Kono Rikako, "Kibei nisei no aidentiti" [Kibei Nisei's Identity], *Daito Forum* 13 (Spring 2000): 96–97.
32. Kumatani Minako, "Nikkei amerikajin no unmei" [The Fate of Japanese Americans], *Daito Forum* 13 (Spring 2000): 94–96.
33. M. Itami, "Chichi Akira Itami no rekuiemu"; "Erroneous Information Calls for a Correction."
34. Itami, "Itami Akira no jihitsu."
35. Ken C. Kawashima, *The Proletarian Gamble: Korean Workers in Interwar Japan* (Durham, NC: Duke University Press, 2009); Mikiso Hane, *Modern Japan: A Historical Survey* (Boulder, CO: Westview Press, 1986), 224.
36. Sameshima, *Tenno o sukutta otoko*, 12; Kinashi, *Dave Itami Akira no shogai*.
37. Itami wrote poems about his factory life in Alaska for the San Francisco–based Japanese-language newspaper *Nichibei Shimbun*: Akira Itami, "Arasuka yori" [From Alaska], *Nichibei Shimbun*, June 21, 1932; Akira Itami, "Dock," *Nichibei Shimbun*, July 26, 1932.
38. Itami, "Itami Akira no jihitsu"; Sameshima, *Tenno o sukutta otoko*, 42. Itami wrote a short story based on his experience as a cannery worker in Alaska:

Akira Itami, "Roppu" [The Rope], *Shukaku: Nikkei amerika bungaku zasshi shuhei* 1 (Tokyo: Fuji Shuppan, 1997), 25–27.

39. "Hokubei shijin kyokai rafude soshiki," *Shinsekai Asahi*, October 26, 1936.

40. Bunichi Kagawa, "Sokan no kotoba," *Shukaku* 1 (November 1936): 1; Zaibei Nihonjinkai, *Zaibei nihonjinshi*, 701; Mizuno Mariko, "Kagawa bunichi no bungeikan to kyosei shuyojo taiken: iminchi bungei kara kibei nisei bungaku no hatten ni oite," *Shakai Shisutemu Kenkyu*, 11 (February, 2008): 173–74.

41. See *Shukaku*, vols. 5 and 6.

42. Sei Fujii, "Itami kisha to wagasha," *Kashu Mainichi*, June 19, 1941.

43. See Itami's "Air Mail" columns in *Kashu Mainichi* in December 1939 and January 1940.

44. "Air Mail," *Kashu Mainichi*, January 13, 1940.

45. "Air Mail," *Kashu Mainichi*, January 9, 1940.

46. *Kashu Mainichi* (English section), April 25, 1939.

47. "Join the J.A.C.L.," *Doho*, February 1, 1940.

48. "Conscription Discussed; Girls Scant at Meet," *Kashu Mainichi*, October 16, 1940; "Shikyo kibeibu no ikan-na sakumei ketsui," *Doho*, December 1, 1940.

49. Masao Yamashiro, *Toi taigan: Aru kibei nisei no kaiso* (Tokyo: Gurobyusha, 1984), 176–77.

50. Bulletin, Anti-Axis Committee, JACL Southern District Council, December 1941, JACL, Box 301, Folder AAC, Japanese American Research Project (JARP) Collection; "Southern Federation Japanese American Citizens League Anti Axis Committee," Bulletin, Anti-Axis Committee, JACL Southern District Council (translated from Japanese), December 1941, JACL, Box 301, Folder AAC, Japanese American Research Project (JARP) Collection.

51. Anti-Axis Committee log, December 8, 1941, JACL, Box 301, Folder AAC, JARP Collection.

52. Minutes, Anti-Axis Committee, December 12, 1941, JACL, Box 301, Folder AAC, JARP Collection.

53. FBI File No. 100-10834, March 27, 1942, Yuji Ichioka Papers, Box 38, Folder 1, JARP Collection.

54. Akira Itami in "Letters," *Time*, March 16, 1942.

55. "Notice," *Kashu Mainichi*, March 21, 1942; "Shasetsu" [Opinion], *Kashu Mainichi*, March 21, 1942.

56. "Voluntary Evacuees Given Instructions," *Kashu Mainichi*, March 20, 1942.

57. "'Manzanar Will Be Extremely Successful,' Nisei Writes *Doho*," *Doho*, April 10, 1942.

58. Akira Itami, in "Letters," *Time*, May 4, 1942.

59. James Oda, *Heroic Struggles of Japanese Americans: Partisan Fighters from America's Concentration Camps* (North Hollywood, CA: James Oda, 1981), 119–20.

60. Karl G. Yoneda, *Ganbatte: Sixty-Year Struggle of a Kibei Worker* (Los Angeles: Asian American Studies Center, University of California, Los Angeles, 1983), 135–37; Oda, *Heroic Struggles of Japanese Americans*, 46–48.

61. See Karl Yoneda's "Notes and Observations of 'Kibei Meeting' Held August 8th, 1942 at Kitchen 15," Commission on Wartime Relocation and Internment of Civilians Files, NARA; Oda, *Heroic Struggles of Japanese Americans*, 53.

62. Yoneda, *Ganbatte*, 116, 118–19, 136.

63. M. Yamashiro, *Toi taigan*, 182–84.

64. Oda, *Heroic Struggles of Japanese Americans*, 119–22.

65. Shimamura, *Sanga Moyu*; Kinashi, *Dave Itami Akira no shogai*.

66. Kinashi, "Hakuun raikyo," 42.

67. Shimamura, *Sanga Moyu*.

68. James C. McNaughton, *Nisei Linguists: Japanese Americans in the Military Intelligence Service During World War II* (Washington, DC: U.S. Department of the Army, 2006), 349–50.

69. "Nisei Who Regained U.S. Citizenship Is War Hero," *Pacific Citizen*, April 28, 1945.

70. "Nisei Tells Japs in Iwo Caves: Come Out—Or Stay Forever," *Seattle Times*, April 23, 1945.

71. McNaughton, *Nisei Linguists*, 263.

72. See Chapter 3 for the discussion of Private First Class Thomas Higa's national speaking tour in 1944.

73. Thomas Taro Higa, *Aru nisei no wadachi, 1915–1985* (Kaneohe, Hawaii: Higa Publications, 1988); McNaughton, *Nisei Linguists*, 366.

74. Examples of MIS veterans' accounts include the Military Intelligence Service of Northern California Biographies, National Japanese American Historical Society, San Francisco; Tad Ichinokuchi, ed., *John Aiso and the M.I.S.: Japanese-American Soldiers in the Military Intelligence Service, World War II* (Los Angeles: Military Intelligence Service Club of Southern California, 1988); Higa, *Aru nisei no wadachi*; James Oguro, ed., *Sempai Gumi* (Honolulu: MIS Veterans of Hawaii, 1981); Joseph D. Harrington, *Yangkee Samurai: The Secret Role of Nisei in America's Pacific Victory* (Detroit: Pettigrew Enterprises, 1979); Clifford Uyeda and Barry Saiki, eds., *The Pacific War and Peace: Americans of Japanese Ancestry in Military Intelligence Service, 1941 to 1952* (San Francisco: Military Intelligence Service Association of Northern California and National Japanese American Historical Society, 1991); Military Intelligence Service Veterans Club of Hawaii, *Secret Valor: M.I.S. Personnel, World War II Pacific Theater, Pre-Pearl Harbor to Sept. 8, 1951* (Honolulu: Military Intelligence Service Veterans Club of Hawaii, 1993); Military Intelligence Service Northwest Association, *Unsung Heroes: The Military Intelligence Service, Past-Present-Future* (Seattle: MIS Northwest Association, 1996); Stanley Falk and Warren M. Tsuneishi, eds., *MIS in the War Against*

Japan (Washington, DC: Japanese American Veterans Association, 1995); Richard M. Sakakida and Wayne S. Kiyosaki, *A Spy in Their Midst: The World War II Struggle of a Japanese-American Hero* (Lanham, MD: Madison Books, 1995); and Hawaii Nikkei History Editorial Board, *Japanese Eyes, American Heart: Personal Reflections of Hawaii's World War II Nisei Soldiers* (Honolulu: Tendai Educational Foundation, 1998).

75. "Frank Hachiya: He Was American at Birth, and at Death," *The Oregonian*, May 20, 1945.

76. "Snubbed Japanese Dies a Pacific Hero," *New York Times*, February 16, 1945; "Private Hachiya, American," *New York Times*, February 17, 1945; "Hachiya Gave His Life for Our Country," *Hood River News*, February 23, 1945.

77. U.S. Selective Service System, *Special Groups* (Washington, DC: Selective Service System, 1953), 141.

78. "Private Hachiya, American," *New York Times*, February 17, 1945.

79. "Jap-American Bravery Hailed by Cameraman: Loyalty Proved in Battle, He Says," *Chicago Tribune*, April 1945.

80. Richard L. Neuberger, "The Nisei Come Back to Hood River," *Saturday Review of Literature*, August 10, 1946.

81. "Nisei Gets Medal," *Pittsburgh Press*, August 15, 1946; War Department General Orders No. 82, Washington, D.C., August 1, 1946.

82. "Nisei Wins Fight to 'Prove Self': Downs FBI Distrust, Gets Merit Award," *Minneapolis Morning Tribune*, September 16, 1946.

83. Falk and Tsuneishi, *MIS in the War Against Japan*, 97–98.

84. Harry K. Fukuhara, "Military Occupation of Japan," *Discover Nikkei: Japanese Migrants and Their Descendants*, May 2, 2005, http://www.discovernikkei.org/en/journal/2005/5/2/military-occupation/ (accessed December 21, 2005). This essay was originally presented by the National Japanese American Veterans Council as one of its essay contest winners in 2004.

85. Fukuhara, "Military Occupation of Japan."

86. Yamasaki lists Fukuhara in the "People Who Contributed to the Research" section. See Yamasaki, *Futatsu no Sokoku*, 595.

87. See the Chapter "Brothers" in Yamasaki, *Futatsu no Sokoku*, 105–233.

88. Yamasaki, *Futatsu no Sokoku*, 177–81.

89. Yamasaki, *Futatsu no Sokoku*, 196–200.

90. Yamasaki, *Futatsu no Sokoku*, 208–12.

91. Yamasaki, *Futatsu no Sokoku*, 587–89.

92. "Hard Soap: A TV Series Reopens Old Wounds," *Time*, April 23, 1984, p. 55; Clifford Uyeda, "Futatsu no Sokoku: Synopsis and Comments," *Pacific Citizen*, December 23–30, 1983.

93. Commission on Wartime Relocation and Internment of Civilians, *Personal Justice Denied: Report of the Commission on Wartime Relocation and Internment of*

Civilians (Seattle: University of Washington Press; and Washington DC: Civil Liberties Public Education Fund, 1997), 459.

94. "Hard Soap," 55.

95. Yamasaki, *Futatsu no Sokoku*, 590–92; "Hard Soap," 55.

Chapter 5

1. Tamotsu Murayama, "Dai nisei to nichibei senso," *Kaigai no Nippon* 16, no. 7 (August 1942): 10.

2. Tamotsu Murayama, "Dai nisei no shinkyo," *Kaigai no Nippon* 16, no. 6 (July 1942), 7. For the origins of the early-twentieth-century Japanese intellectual debates about the role of Japanese emigrants in developing Japan's expanding settler colonial empire, see Eiichiro Azuma, *Between Two Empires: Race, History, and Transnationalism in Japanese America* (Oxford, UK: Oxford University Press, 2005).

3. Ikeda Norizane, *Hinomaru awa: Taibei boryaku hoso monogatari* (Tokyo: Chuo Koronsha, 1979), 13.

4. "Pair Stresses Japanese Fealty," *Arizona Republic*, March 6, 1935.

5. "Tamotsu Murayama Elected President of Local J.A.C.L.," *Shinsekai Asahi*, January 30, 1937.

6. "Murayama Quits from Presidency of Frisco J.A.C.L.," *Shinsekai Asahi*, February 6, 1937.

7. Quoted in John J. Stephan, *Hawaii Under the Rising Sun: Japan's Plans for Conquest After Pearl Harbor* (Honolulu: University of Hawaii Press, 1984), 162.

8. Stephan, *Hawaii Under the Rising Sun*, 163.

9. Quoted in Stephan, *Hawaii Under the Rising Sun*, 163.

10. Quoted in Stephan, *Hawaii Under the Rising Sun*, 164.

11. Quoted in Komaki Saneshige, *Dai toa chiseigaku shinron* (Tokyo: Hoshino Shoten, 1943), 208.

12. Stephan, *Hawaii Under the Rising Sun*, 165.

13. Murayama, "Dai nisei to nichibei senso," 10.

14. See Chapter 3 for examples of Nisei loyalty to the U.S. government during World War II.

15. Tamotsu Murayama, *Amerika nisei: Sono kunan no rekishi* (Tokyo: Jiji Press, 1964), 217–18.

16. Mike M. Masaoka, memorandum to "national board members, national council members, active and associated members, sponsors, friends, and supports of the national JACL," April 22, 1944, JACL Records, Box 301, Folder Mike M. Masaoka, Japanese American Research Project, University of California, Los Angeles.

17. N. Ikeda, *Hinomaru awa*, 13.

18. N. Ikeda, *Hinomaru Awa*; Kumei Teruko, "Nihon seifu to nisei ekkyo kyoiku: Heishikan wo jirei to shite," in *Amerika nihonjin imin no ekkyo kyoikushi*,

ed. Yoshida Akira (Tokyo: Nihon Tosho Center, 2005); Kumei Teruko, "Yujo to yuko wo musunde: Heishikan kara rajio puresu-e," *Kaigai imin shiryokan kenkyu kiyo* 4 (2009): 1–10.

19. Kumei, "Yujo to yuko wo musunde," 5; N. Ikeda, *Hinomaru awa*, 10–11.

20. N. Ikeda, *Hinomaru awa*, 11–13.

21. N. Ikeda, *Hinomaru awa*, 13.

22. N. Ikeda, *Hinomaru awa*, 10–11.

23. The Japanese government and the governments of the British Dominions, including Australia, agreed to exchange all members of diplomatic missions in the autumn of 1942. Yuriko Nagata, *Unwanted Aliens: Japanese Internment in Australia* (St. Lucia, Australia: University of Queensland Press, 1996), 96.

24. N. Ikeda, *Hinomaru awa*, 10–11.

25. Masao Ekimoto, telephone interview with author, August 23, 2011.

26. *Heishikan Newsletter*, November 2006, Heishikan Collection, Japanese Overseas Migration Museum, Yokohama, Japan.

27. *Heishikan News*, June 1942–1944, Heishikan Collection; Masao Ekimoto, telephone interview with author, August 23, 2011; *Heishikan Newsletter*, November 2006.

28. *Heishikan News*, August 10, 1941; Masao Ekimoto, telephone interview with author, August 23, 2011.

29. Masao Ekimoto, telephone interview with author, August 13, 2011.

30. Shigetoshi Kizu, *Nihon yusen senpaku 100-nenshi* (Tokyo: Kaijinsha, 1984).

31. Kizu, *Nihon yusen senpaku 100-nenshi*; Masao Ekimoto, telephone interview with author, August 13, 2011.

32. Masao Ekimoto, telephone interview with author, August 13, 2011.

33. Masao Ekimoto, telephone interview with author, August 13, 2011.

34. "Gaimusho no nisei yosei kikan 'heishikan,'" *Hokubei Mainichi*, 1999.

35. Hiroda Ikuro, "Tatakau 'nisei gakko' monogatari," *Bungei Shunshu*, April 1956. According to Kumei Teruko, the closest match to Hiroda's self-described identity is former Heishikan student and Canadian Nisei Kazumaro Uyeno; see Kumei Teruko, "Nihon seifu to nisei ekkyo kyoiku: Heishikan wo jirei to shite," in *Amerika nihonjin imin no ekkyo kyoikushi*, ed. Yoshida Akira (Tokyo: Nihon Tosho Center, 2005), 274n25.

36. Shimojima Tetsuro, "Gaimusho no hanzai: Moteasobareta nikkei joho soshiki 'heishikan' no higeki," *Gendai* (April 1997): 276–96.

37. *Heishikan Newsletter*, November 2006; Kumei, "Nihon seifu to nisei ekkyo kyoiku"; Kumei, "Yujo to yoko wo musunde."

38. *Heishikan Folio*, November 1960, p. 6, Heishikan Collection.

39. *Heishikan Newsletter*, November 2006, Heishikan Collection.

40. *Heishikan Newsletter*, November 2006, Heishikan Collection.

41. Naoko Shibusawa, "Femininity, Race, and Treachery: How 'Tokyo Rose' Became a Traitor to the United States After the Second World War," *Gender and History* 22, no. 1 (April 2010): 169–88; Judith Keene, *Treason on the Airwaves: Three Allied Broadcasters on Axis Radio During World War II* (Westport, CT: Praeger, 2009); Russell Warren Howe, *The Hunt for "Tokyo Rose"* (New York: Madison Books, 1990); Masayo Duus, *Tokyo Rose: Orphan of the Pacific* (New York: Kodansha International, 1979); Jane Robbins, *Tokyo Calling: Japanese Overseas Radio Broadcasting, 1937–1945* (Florence, Italy: European Press Academic, 2001); Ryo Namikawa, "Japanese Overseas Broadcasting: A Personal View," in *Film and Radio Propaganda in World War II*, ed. K. R. M. Short (London: Croom Helm, 1983); Lester Strong, "When 'Tokyo Rose' Came to Albuquerque," *New Mexico Historical Review* 66, no. 1 (January 1991): 73–92.

42. On March 22, 1976, the *Chicago Tribune* published the first report by its Tokyo correspondent Ronald Yates, who discovered that the FBI had forced the key witnesses to fabricate their testimonies alleging Toguri's propaganda work for the Japanese government during World War II. See *Chicago Tribune*, March 22, 1976; and Howe, *Hunt for "Tokyo Rose,"* 304–6.

43. N. Ikeda, *Hinomaru awa*; Keene, *Treason on the Airwaves*; Howe, *Hunt for "Tokyo Rose"*; Duus, *Tokyo Rose*; Robbins, *Tokyo Calling*; Namikawa, "Japanese Overseas Broadcasting."

44. Office of the U.S. Political Advisor, Kobe, Japan, "Forwarding Information Regarding Heishikan, Former Japanese Ministry of Foreign Affairs Institute," June 16, 1949, State Department Records, RG 59, Central Decimal Files, 894.42/67–1949, National Archives and Records Administration, Washington, D.C.

45. 76th Congress, H.R. 9980; Pub. L. 76–853 Stat. 1137, Washington, D.C., October 14, 1940.

46. Kumei, "Nihon seifu to nisei ekkyo kyoiku," 264.

47. "Heishikan wa supai gakkoka" [Was Heishikan a Spy School?], *Hokubei Mainichi*, 1999.

48. 76th Congress, H.R. 9980.

49. Although Kadoike Hiroshi has speculated that between 20,000 and 30,000 Nisei served on various battlefronts in Asia-Pacific from 1942 to 1945, this figure is not based on any military or government record. See Kadoike Hiroshi, *Nihongun heishi ni natta amerikajin tachi: Bokoku to tatakatta nikkei nisei* (Tokyo: Genshu Shuppansha, 2010), 34–35; and Kadoike Hiroshi, interviewed by author, Osaka, Japan, August 10, 2010.

50. See, for example, Jim Yoshida, *The Two Worlds of Jim Yoshida* (New York: Morrow, 1972); Yoshida Mitsuru, "Sokoku to teikoku no aida," in *Chinkon senkan yamato* (Tokyo: Kodansha, 1974); Roy Ito and S-20 and Nisei Veterans

Association, *Stories of My People: A Japanese Canadian Journal* (Hamilton, Canada: S-20 and Nisei Veterans Association, 1994); Tachibana Yuzuru, *Teikoku kaigun shikan ni natta nikkei nisei* (Tokyo: Tsukiji Shokan, 1994); and Iwao Peter Sano, *One Thousand Days in Siberia: The Odyssey of a Japanese-American POW* (Lincoln: University of Nebraska Press, 1997).

51. "Pride, Pain Linger for Japanese-Americans Caught on Wrong Side of War," *Los Angeles Times*, September 9, 1990.

52. Masao Ekimoto, telephone interview with author, August 23, 2011.

53. Shigeo Yamada, "An Idaho Potato Goes to Japan" (unpublished transcript) [1990]; John Ellis, *World War II: A Statistical Survey—The Essential Facts and Figures for All the Combatants* (New York: Facts on File, 1993); John W. Dower, *War Without Mercy: Race and Power in the Pacific War* (New York: Pantheon Books, 1986), 297.

54. Yamada, "An Idaho Potato Goes to Japan."

55. Tachibana, *Teikoku kaigun shikan ni natta nikkei nisei*, 128–29, 142–43, 154–55; Yamada, "An Idaho Potato Goes to Japan"; Ikeda Takekuni, "Imperial Navy's Final Sortie," *Naval History* 21, no. 5 (October 2007): 34–43.

56. Yamada, "An Idaho Potato Goes to Japan"; T. Ikeda, "Imperial Navy's Final Sortie."

57. Yamada, "An Idaho Potato Goes to Japan"; T. Ikeda, "Imperial Navy's Final Sortie."

58. Iwao Peter Sano, interviewed by author, Palo Alto, California, March 12, 2007; Sano, *One Thousand Days in Siberia*, 14–24.

59. Sano, *One Thousand Days in Siberia*, 31–38; Iwao Peter Sano, interviewed by author, Palo Alto, California, March 12, 2007.

60. Sano, *One Thousand Days in Siberia*, 31–38; Iwao Peter Sano, interviewed by author, Palo Alto, California, March 12, 2007.

61. William Nimmo, *Behind a Curtain of Silence: Japanese in Soviet Custody, 1945–1956* (Westport, CT: Greenwood Press, 1988); Kurahira Toshio, *Shiberia yokuryu: Mikan no higeki* (Tokyo: Iwanami Shinsho, 2009); John W. Dower, *Embracing Defeat: Japan in the Wake of World War II* (New York: Norton, 1999), 51–52.

62. Sano, *One Thousand Days in Siberia*, 197; Supreme Commander for the Allied Powers, *Reports of General MacArthur* (Washington, DC: Center for Military History, 1994), 150.

63. Yamada, "Idaho Potato Goes to Japan"; Supreme Commander for the Allied Powers, *Reports of General MacArthur*, 233, 254–58.

64. Sano, *One Thousand Days in Siberia*, 201–2.

65. J. Yoshida, *Two Worlds*, 32–52.

66. Egawa Hidefumi, Yamada Ryoichi, and Hayata Yoshiro, *Kokusekiho* (Tokyo: Yuhikaku, 1997), 252–53; J. Yoshida, *Two Worlds*, 58–59.

67. J. Yoshida, *Two Worlds*.
68. J. Yoshida, *Two Worlds*.
69. "Pride, Pain Linger for Japanese-Americans Caught on Wrong Side of War," *Los Angeles Times*, September 9, 1990.
70. Sano, *One Thousand Days in Siberia*, 203–4, 208–9; Peter Sano, interviewed by author, July 12, 2007, Palo Alto, California; Peter Sano, Guest Lecture, World War II Memories in the United States and Japan from the University of California, Santa Cruz, Santa Cruz, California, February 15, 2013.
71. William Hillcourt, "Scouting in Japan," *Boy's Life*, November 1969. After the war Murayama also contributed to the California-based *Pacific Citizen*, for example, a 1955 article on Japanese "war brides"; see Tamotsu Murayama, "20,000 War Brides in America," *Pacific Citizen*, February 12, 1955.
72. Fuji Scouts Club of Japan, *Murayama tamotsu to boi sukauto: Murayama Tamotsu "tanjo 100 shunen" kinen* [pamphlet], Saitama, Japan, February 22, 2006.
73. Bill Hosokawa, *Nisei: The Quiet Americans—The Story of a People* (New York: Morrow, 1969). See also Chapter 3.
74. Bill Hosokawa, *Colorado's Japanese Americans: From 1886 to the Present* (Boulder: University of Colorado Press, 2005), 171–73.

Chapter 6

1. Kaz Suyeishi, "Nikushimi o idaku de naku" [Not Holding onto Resentment], Hibaku Kaikenki (Atomic Bomb Memoir) Collection, Hiroshima National Peace Memorial Hall for the Atomic Bomb Victims, Hiroshima, Japan.
2. By 1936 almost 50,000 Japanese emigrants from Hiroshima had settled on the U.S. West Coast and in Hawaii. See President of Hiroshima Overseas Association to Director, America Division, Ministry of Foreign Affairs, July 25, 1937, *Nikkei Gaijin Kankei Zakken*, K.1.1.0.9.3, Diplomatic Archives of the Ministry of Foreign Affairs of Japan, Tokyo, Japan.
3. Kaz Suyeishi, interviewed by author, Torrance, California, December 31, 2015; "Zero Hour: Forty-Three Seconds over Hiroshima," *Newsweek*, July 29, 1985.
4. Suyeishi, "Nikushimi o idaku de naku"; Hiroshima Prefecture, "Kokumin giyutai no soshiki unyo ni kan suru ken imei tsucho," May 7, 1945, Kokumin giyutai ikken toji, Hiroshima Municipal Archives, Hiroshima, Japan.
5. According to a Mitsubishi Heavy Industries August 1945 internal corporate memo disclosed by Takahashi Makoto, the chair of the Coalition for Legal Support of the Wartime Korean Women's Labor Corps at Mitsubishi in Nagoya, there were 12,913 conscripted laborers from Korea working for Mitsubishi by the end of World War II. The Mitsubishi shipping plant in Hiroshima was among the largest employees of these workers. See "Ilbon joenbeom giop gangjae jingyong sashil ipjung junggeo jaryo gongae 'nungil,'" *Hankyorae Shinmun*, September 23, 2019.

6. Kaz Suyeishi, interviewed by author, Torrance, California, December 31, 2015.

7. "Zero Hour"; Suyeishi, "Nikushimi o idaku de naku"; John W. Dower, "Foreword," in Rinjiro Sodei, *Were We the Enemy? American Survivors of Hiroshima* (Boulder, CO: Westview Press, 1998), xii.

8. "Zero Hour."

9. See Naoko Wake, "Surviving the Bomb in America: Silent Memories and the Rise of Cross-National Identity," *Pacific Historical Review* 86, no. 3 (2017): 472–509.

10. Dean Toji, "Hibakusha: Japanese American Atomic Bomb Survivors," *East Wind: Politics and Culture of Asians in the U.S.* 1, no. 2 (Fall/Winter 1982): 3; "Americans Recall Seeing the Horrors of Hiroshima," *Albuquerque Journal*, July 30, 1995.

11. "Hiroshima's Americans: The Forgotten Victims," *Austin American-Statesman*, April 9, 1972; "In The Shadow of Hiroshima," *San Francisco Examiner*, August 13, 1978.

12. Rinjiro Sodei, *Were We the Enemy? American Survivors of Hiroshima* (Boulder, CO: Westview Press, 1998), 82.

13. Although it is difficult to ascertain the exact number of atomic bomb casualties, the earliest postwar study conducted by the U.S. military's Manhattan Project in 1946 estimated that the number of immediate deaths was 6,600 in Hiroshima and 3,900 in Nagasaki. These figures do not include post-attack casualties from radiation related illnesses or other injuries. See U.S. Army Corps of Engineers, Manhattan District, *The Atomic Bombing of Hiroshima and Nagasaki: Report on the Effects of the Atomic Bombs Which Were Dropped on the Japanese Cities of Hiroshima and Nagasaki* (Dinslaken, Germany: Pergamonmedia, 2019). See also Vincent C. Jones, *Manhattan: The Army and the Atomic Bomb—United States Army in World War II* (Washington, DC: Center of Military History, United States Army, 1988), 545–48.

14. "The Secret Sufferers," *Newsweek*, April 10, 1972; "The Forgotten Victims: Americans at Hiroshima," *San Francisco Examiner*, April 11, 1972; Sodei, *Were We the Enemy*, 80–82.

15. See Wake, "Surviving the Bomb in America"; and Satoshi Ikeno and Nakao Kayoko, "Zaibei hibakusha kyokai bunretsu no yoin bunseki to kongo no engo kadai," *Jinbun fukushigaku kenkyu* 6, no. 1 (November 2013): 47–68.

16. "U.S. Victims of Hiroshima Bombing Plead for Aid," *Boston Globe*, April 10, 1972; Sodei, *Were We the Enemy*, 82–86.

17. "U.S. Victims of Hiroshima."

18. Sodei, *Were We the Enemy*, 85; "The Secret Sufferers."

19. "U.S. Victims of Hiroshima"; Frank W. Putnam, "Atomic Bomb Casualty Commission in Retrospect," *Proceedings of the National Academy of Sciences*

of the United States of America 95, no. 10 (May 1998): 5426–31; Itsuzo Shigematsu, "Greetings: 50 Years of Atomic Bomb Casualty Commission—Radiation Effects Research Foundation Studies," *Proceedings of the National Academy of Sciences of the United States of America* 95, no. 10 (May 1998): 5424–25.

20. "85 A-Bomb Survivors in Los Angeles Seek Aid," *Los Angeles Times*, November 7, 1971; "Americans Who Became Hiroshima Bomb Victims," *Deseret News*, April 17, 1972.

21. Wake, "Surviving the Bomb in America," 491.

22. See Ikeno and Nakao, "Zaibei hibakusha"; and Wake, "Surviving the Bomb in America."

23. "Americans in Hiroshima Become Forgotten Victims," *Pottstown Mercury*, April 19, 1972.

24. United States Congress, "Proceedings and Debates of the 93rd Congress, First Session, January 3, 1973," *Congressional Record*, vol. 119, pt. 1 (Washington, DC: U.S. Government Printing Office, 1973), 65; United States Congress, "Proceedings and Debates of the 93rd Congress, First Session, January 24, 1973," *Congressional Record*, vol. 119, pt. 2 (Washington, DC: U.S. Government Printing Office, 1973), 2150.

25. "Survivors Suffer," *Scranton Tribune*, August 14, 1975.

26. "Survivors Suffer."

27. United States Congress, "Proceedings and Debates of the 97th Congress, January 6, 1981," *Congressional Record*, vol. 127, pt. 1 (Washington, DC: U.S. Government Printing Office, 1981), 221.

28. United States Congress, "Proceedings and Debates of the 97th Congress, January 22, 1981," *Congressional Record*, vol. 127, pt. 1 (Washington, DC: U.S. Government Printing Office, 1973), 722.

29. "Fight a Private War," *Charlotte Observer*, August 6, 1985.

30. See John W. Dower, "Triumphal and Tragic Narratives of the War in Asia," *Journal of American History* 82, no. 3 (December 1995): 1124–35; and Yui Daizaburo, "Between Pearl Harbor and Hiroshima/Nagasaki: Nationalism and Memory in Japan and the United States," in *Living with the Bomb: American and Japanese Cultural Conflicts in the Nuclear Age*, ed. Laura Hein and Mark Selden (New York: M.E. Sharpe, 1997), 52–72.

31. Dower, "Foreword," xi.

32. See Toyonaga Keisaburo, "Colonialism and Atom Bomb: About Survivors of Hiroshima Living in Korea," in *Perilous Memories: The Asia-Pacific War(s)*, ed. Takashi Fujitani, Geoffrey M. White, and Lisa Yoneyama (Durham, NC: Duke University Press, 2001), 378–94; and Lisa Yoneyama, *Hiroshima Traces: Time, Space and the Dialectics of Memory* (Berkeley: University of California Press, 1999).

33. Lisa Yoneyama, *Cold War Ruins: Transpacific Critique of American Justice and Japanese War Crimes* (Durham, NC: Duke University Press, 2016), viii–ix.

34. Section (b) of Article 14 of the Treaty of San Francisco stipulates that "except as otherwise provided in the present Treaty, the Allied Powers waive all reparations claims of the Allied Powers, other claims of the Allied Powers and their nationals arising out of any actions taken by Japan and its nationals in the course of the prosecution of the war, and claims of the Allied Powers for direct military costs of occupation." See The Treaty of Peace with Japan, signed in San Francisco, September 8, 1951, *United Nations Treaty Series*, 1952.

35. House of Representatives, Japan, *Genshi bakudan hibakusha no iryosaku ni kansuru horitsu* [Law Concerning Medical Care for the Victims of the Atomic Bombing], Horitsu dai 41 go (March 31, 1957).

36. Kazue Suyeishi, "Nihon seifu ni shien o motometa" [We Sought Aid from the Japanese Government], an interview with Nippon Hoso Kyokai (NHK), August 4, 2008, Senso Shogen Collection, Nippon Hoso Kyokai Archives, Tokyo, Japan; Kaz Suyeishi, interviewed by author, Torrance, California, December 31, 2015.

37. Kaz Suyeishi, interviewed by author, Torrance, California, December 31, 2015.

38. U.S. Department of Justice, Immigration and Naturalization Service, "Passenger and Crew Lists of Vessels Arriving at New York, NY," vol. 18353, November 23, 1953, Roll 8393, Records of the Immigration and Naturalization Service, RG 85, National Archives and Records Administration (NARA), Washington, D.C.

39. Yoshiko [Sogawa] Suzuki, "Genbaku, zenshin ni abita garasu" [Atomic Bombing: Glass Pieces That Pierced My Body], an interview with Nippon Hoso Kyokai (NHK), August 13, 2008, Senso Shogen Collection, Nippon Hoso Kyokai Archives, Tokyo, Japan.

40. U.S. Department of Commerce, Bureau of the Census, *Fourteenth Census of the United States Taken in the Year 1920* (Washington, DC: U.S. Government Printing Office, 1922).

41. Suzuki, "Genbaku."

42. Suzuki, "Genbaku"; U.S. Department of Labor, Immigration and Naturalization Service, "List of Manifest of Alien Passengers for the United States," July 13, 1938, Registers of Japanese, Filipinos, and Hawaiians Held for Boards of Special Inquiry at San Francisco, California, Records of the Immigration and Naturalization Service, RG 85, NARA, Washington, D.C.

43. Internee Data File, 1942–1946, War Relocation Authority (WRA) Records Collection, RG 210, NARA, College Park, Maryland; Suzuki, "Genbaku."

44. Wartime Civil Control Administration, Western Defense Command and Fourth Army, "Notice and General Instructions to Japanese Seeking Repatriation," 1987.3020.03, National Museum of American History, Washington, D.C.; Bruce Elleman, *Japanese-American Civilian Prisoner Exchanges and Detention Camps, 1941–1945* (London: Routledge, 2006), 18–19.

45. The 1,513 repatriates included 627 Japanese nationals, 737 Japanese Latin Americans, and 149 Japanese American citizens. William R. Langdon, Departmental Representative on Board the M.S. *Gripsholm*, to the Secretary of State, "General Report of Second American-Japanese Repatriation Operation: Section Two," in *Foreign Relations of the United States: Diplomatic Papers, 1943*, Vol. III, *The British Commonwealth, Eastern Europe, the Far East*, ed. William M. Franklin and E. R. Perkins (Washington, DC: U.S. Government Printing Office, 1963), doc. 800.

46. Scott P. Corbett, *Quiet Passages: The Exchange of Civilians Between the United States and Japan During the Second World War* (Kent, OH: Kent State University Press, 1987), 93.

47. Langdon to the Secretary of State, "General Report"; Corbett, *Quiet Passages*, 93.

48. Suzuki, "Genbaku."

49. Public Law 100-383, Title I, August 10, 1988, 102 Stat. 904.

50. Alice Yang Murray, *Historical Memories of the Japanese American Internment and the Struggle for Redress* (Stanford, CA: Stanford University Press, 2008), 334–35.

51. A. Naomi Paik, *Rightlessness: Testimony and Redress in U.S. Prison Camps Since World War II* (Chapel Hill: University of North Carolina Press, 2016), 52.

52. Murray, *Historical Memories*, 334.

53. Sodei, *Were We the Enemy*, 151–52.

54. Leif-Eric Easley, "Obama's Nuclear Legacy: Reconciliation and Nonproliferation in Asia after Hiroshima," *Asian Institute for Policy Studies Issue Brief* 5, no. 14 (October 2016): 1–30.

55. Michelle Malkin, Twitter post, May 10, 2016, 8:38 a.m., https://twitter.com/michellemalkin (accessed May 10, 2016); Mike Gallagher, Twitter post, May 10, 2016, 8:52 a.m., https://twitter.com/radiotalkermike (accessed May 12, 2016). See also "Obama's Trip to Hiroshima, and the Looming 'Apology Tour' Narrative," *Washington Post*, May 10, 2016; "Should Obama Apologize in Hiroshima? The Purpose of Presidential Apologies," *National Interest*, May 15, 2016; "Hiroshima and the Politics of Apologizing," *Atlantic*, May 26, 2016; and "Atomic Bomb Survivors: Obama Apology Nice, but Priority Is Disarmament," *Reuters*, May 19, 2016, https://www.reuters.com/article/us-japan-obama-hiroshima-survivors-idUSKCN0YA0MJ (accessed May 25, 2016).

56. "Obama to Be First Sitting President to Visit Hiroshima," *New York Times*, May 10, 2016; "Atomic Bomb Survivors: Obama Apology Nice."

57. As a participant in the 1982 rally for nuclear disarmament (the "Nuclear Freeze" movement) in New York before the second United Nations Session on Disarmament, a young Barack Obama wrote an article in the Columbia University magazine *Sundial* in which he passionately advocated for a "nuclear free

world"; see Barack Obama, "Breaking the War Mentality," *Sundial*, March 10, 1983; and "Obama's Youth Shaped His Nuclear-Free Vision," *New York Times*, July 4, 2009.

58. Office of the Press Secretary, The White House, "Remarks by President Barack Obama in Prague as Delivered," April 5, 2016, https://obamawhitehouse.archives.gov/the-press-office/remarks-president-barack-obama-prague-delivered (accessed May 1, 2016).

59. The Norwegian Nobel Institute, "The Nobel Peace Prize for 2009," July 19, 2009, https://www.nobelprize.org/prizes/peace/2009/press-release (accessed May 20, 2016).

60. Preparatory Commission for the Comprehensive Nuclear-Test-Ban Treaty Organization, *Annual Report 2017: United for the Cause* (Vienna: Preparatory Commission for the Comprehensive Nuclear-Test-Ban Treaty Organization, 2018), 77–82.

61. Office of the Press Secretary, The White House, "Remarks by President Obama and Prime Minister Abe of Japan at Hiroshima Peace Memorial," May 27, 2016, https://obamawhitehouse.archives.gov/the-press-office/2016/05/27/remarks-president-obama-and-prime-minister-abe-japan-hiroshima-peace (accessed June 1, 2016).

62. In conceptualizing the invisibility, statelessness, and rightlessness of Nisei victims of the U.S. atomic bombing, I have benefited from engaging A. Naomi Paik's work on U.S. prison camps since World War II. Paik argues that rightlessness has been rendered "exceptional" and "external" to the dominant narrative of the United States as a champion of rights at home and abroad. However, Paik also demonstrates that rightless people have found ways to expose this contradiction inherent in the national narrative by asserting their voices in alternative creative spaces that complicate the meaning of rights and the power of the state. See Paik, *Rightlessness*.

63. Dower, "Foreword," ix–xii.

Epilogue

1. "Trump Interview," dir. Matthew O'Neill and Perri Peltz, *Axios*, Episode 1.1, November 4, 2018, Home Box Office (HBO).

2. Executive Office of the President, "Protecting the Nation from Foreign Terrorist Entry into the United States," Executive Order 13769, February 1, 2017, *Federal Register* 82 FR 8977; Executive Office of the President, "Resuming the United States Refugee Admissions Program with Enhanced Vetting Capabilities," Executive Order 13815, October 24, 2017, *Federal Register* 82 FR 58701.

3. See reactions, pro and con, to Trump's interview in opinion pieces such as "Trump's Proposal to End Birthright Citizenship Is Unconstitutional," *Washington*

Post, October 30, 2018; "Citizenship Shouldn't Be a Birthright," *Washington Post*, July 18, 2018; "Donald Trump's Unconstitutional Dreams," *New York Times*, October 31, 2018; "Birthright Citizenship Isn't Just the Law, It's Crucial to Assimilation in the U.S.," *Los Angeles Times*, November 1, 2018; and "Trump's Attack on Birthright Citizenship Betrays His Ignorance—and His Weakness," *Guardian*, November 3, 2018.

4. See, for example, V. S. McClatchy's writings from the early decades of the twentieth century: V. S. McClatchy, *America and Japan: Their Treatment of Foreigners and Resulting Conditions—Policies in Immigration, Exclusion Land Ownership and Lease, Citizenship, Dual Citizenship* (San Francisco: California Joint Immigration Committee, 1925); and McClatchy's pamphlets "The Germany of Asia: Japan's Policy in the Far East; Her 'Peaceful Penetration' of the United States; How American Commercial and National Interests Are Affected" (April 1919) and "Assimilation of Japanese: Can They Be Moulded into American Citizens?" (October 27, 1921), both in V. S. McClatchy, ed., *Four Anti-Japanese Pamphlets* (New York: Arno Press, 1978). See also Chapters 1 and 2.

5. Mae M. Ngai, "Birthright Citizenship and the Alien Citizen," *Fordham Law Review* 75, no. 5 (2007): 2527.

6. Eiichiro Azuma, "Yuji Ichioka and New Paradigm in Japanese American History," in Yuji Ichioka, *Before Internment: Essays in Prewar Japanese American History*, ed. Gordon H. Chang and Eiichiro Azuma (Stanford, CA: Stanford University Press, 2006), xvi.

7. Masao Ekimoto, "Live the Moment" (unpublished transcript), May 20, 2004.

8. Kanda Minoru, interviewed by author, May 4, 2008, Osaka, Japan.

9. Kanda Minoru, interviewed by author.

10. Kanda Minoru, "Toranku no naka ni irete motte kaetta mono wa nani ka: Hawai dekasegi imin issei Kato Risaku to sono matsuei," paper presented at the Migration Studies Society Meeting, Osaka, Japan, May 8, 2010.

11. Kanda Minoru, interviewed by author; Kanda, "Toranku no naka."

12. Arif Dirlik, "Asians on the Rim: Transnational Capital and Local Community in the Making of Contemporary Asian America," *Amerasia Journal* 22, no. 3 (1996): 13.

Selected Bibliography

Archives
Bancroft Library, University of California, Berkeley
    William Randolph Hearst Papers
    Japanese American Evacuation and Resettlement Records
Claremont Colleges, Special Collections, Claremont, California
    Carey McWilliams Papers, War Relocation Authority Records Collection
Diplomatic Archives of the Ministry of Foreign Affairs of Japan, Tokyo, Japan
    Honsho Shokuin Yosei Kankei Zakken
    Nikkei Gaijin Kankei Zakken, Showa Series
Hiroshima National Peace Memorial Hall for the Atomic Bomb Victims, Hiroshima, Japan
    Hibaku Taikenki (Atomic Bomb Memoir) Collection
Japanese American Research Project (Yuji Ichioka; JARP) Collection, University of California, Los Angeles, Special Collections
    Verne Austin Papers
    Edward N. Barnhart Papers
    William C. Carr Papers
    Thomas Higa Papers
    Japanese American Citizens League (JACL) Records
Japanese Overseas Migration Museum, Yokohama, Japan
    Heishikan Collection
Kajiki Folklore Museum, Kajiki, Kagoshima, Japan
    Itami Akira Collection
National Archives and Records Administration (NARA), Washington, D.C.; College Park, Maryland; and San Bruno, California

Commission on Wartime Relocation and Internment of Civilians Records
Department of State Records
Records of the Adjutant Generals Office, U.S. Department of War
Records of the Immigration and Naturalization Service
Nippon Hoso Kyokai Archives, Tokyo, Japan
　　Senso Shogen Collection
Tao Dobun Shoin Daigaku Kinen Center, Aichi University, Aichi, Japan
　　Toa Dobunkai Collection, *Toa dobunkai kiji*, 1938–1940

Newspapers and Periodicals
Albuquerque Journal
Arizona Republic (Phoenix, AZ)
Asahi Shimbun (Tokyo)
Atlantic
Austin American-Statesman
Boston Globe
Boy's Life (Irving, TX)
Bungei Shunshu (Tokyo)
Canberra Times
Chicago Daily News
Chicago Daily Tribune
Christian Science Monitor
Daito Bunka (Tokyo)
Daito Forum (Tokyo)
Doho (Los Angeles)
El Paso Times
Evening Daily Advance (Hollister, California)
Far Eastern Economic Review
Fortune
Gendai (Tokyo)
Granada Pioneer
Hankyorae Shinmun (Seoul)
Harper's Weekly
Heart Mountain Sentinel
Hokubei Mainichi (San Francisco)
Honolulu Star Bulletin
Hood River News (Oregon)
Japan Times Weekly (Tokyo)
Japanese American Courier (Seattle)

Jiji Shimpo (Kagoshima)
Kaigai no Nippon (Tokyo)
Kashu Mainichi (Los Angeles)
Klamath Falls Herald and News
Los Angeles Evening Herald Express
Los Angeles Times
Minidoka Irrigator
Minneapolis Morning Tribune
Monrovia Daily News
Morning Daily Advance (Hollister, California)
Napa Valley Register
National Interest (Washington, D.C.)
New York Times
Newsweek
Nichibei Shimbun (San Francisco)
Nippu Jiji (Honolulu)
Oakland Tribune
Oregon Journal
Oregonian
Osaka Mainichi Shumbun
Outpost (Rohwer, Arkansas)
Pacific Citizen (Los Angeles)
Pittsburgh Press
Portland Oregonian
Poston Press Bulletin
Rafu Shimpo (Los Angeles)
Reuters
Rocky Nippon (Denver)
Ryumon (Kagoshima)
Sacramento Bee
Salinas Daily Index
Salinas Index-Journal
San Francisco Chronicle
San Francisco Examiner
Saturday Evening Post (Indianapolis)
Saturday Review of Literature
Seattle Times
Shinsekai Asahi Shimbun (San Francisco)
Taihoku Nippo (Seattle)

Time
Times, The (London)
Topaz Times
Tulean Dispatch
Washington Post
Yomiuri Shimbun (Tokyo)

Sources

Agnew, Vijay. *Diaspora, Memory, and Identity: A Search for Home*. Toronto: University of Toronto Press, 2005.

Akiya, Karl. *Jiyu-e no michi taiheiyo wo koete: Aru kibei nisei no jiden*. Kyoto: Korosha, 1996.

Anderson, Ronald S. *Education in Japan: A Century of Modern Development*. Washington, DC: U.S. Government Printing Office, 1974.

Ano, Masaharu. "Loyal Linguists: Nisei of World II Learned Japanese in Minnesota." *Minnesota History* 45, no. 7 (Fall 1977): 273–87.

Arnesen, Eric. *Black Protest and the Great Migration: A Brief History with Documents*. Boston: Bedford/St. Martin's, 2003.

Asahi Ado Honsha. *"Sanga Moyu" shujinko moderu no shogai: Ketteiban, korega shinsoda*. Kagoshima, Japan: Asahi Ado, 1984.

Asato, Norkio. "Mandating Americanization: Japanese Language Schools and the Federal Survey of Education in Hawai'i, 1916–1920." *History of Education Quarterly* 43, no. 1 (Spring 2003): 10–38.

Atkins, E. Taylor. *Blue Nippon: Authenticating Jazz in Japan*. Durham, NC: Duke University Press, 2001.

Azuma, Eiichiro. *Between Two Empires: Race, History, and Transnationalism in Japanese America*. Oxford, UK: Oxford University Press, 2005.

———. "Brokering Race, Culture, and Citizenship: Japanese Americans in Occupied Japan and Postwar National Inclusion." *Journal of American–East Asian Relations* 16, no. 3 (Fall 2009): 183–211.

———. *In Search of Our Frontier: Japanese America and Settler Colonialism in the Construction of Japan's Borderless Empire*. Berkeley: University of California Press, 2019.

———. "Nisei no nihon ryugaku no hikari to kage: Nikkei amerikajin no ekkyo kyoiku no rinen to mujun." In *Amerika nihonjin imin no ekkyo kyoikushi*, ed. Yoshida Akira. Tokyo: Nihon Tosho Center, 2005.

———. "'The Pacific Era Has Arrived': Transnational Education Among Japanese Americans, 1932–1941." *History of Education Quarterly* 43, no. 1 (Spring 2003): 39–73.

———. "Yuji Ichioka and New Paradigm in Japanese American History." In *Yuji Ichioka, Before Internment: Essays in Prewar Japanese American History*, ed. Gordon H. Chang and Eiichiro Azuma, xvi–xxviii. Stanford, CA: Stanford University Press, 2006.

Bow, Leslie. *Partly Colored: Asian Americans and Racial Anomaly in the Segregated South*. New York: NYU Press, 2010.

Brettell, Caroline B. *Migration Theory: Talking Across Disciplines*. New York: Routledge, 2008.

Briones, Matthew. *Jim and Jap Crow: A Cultural History of 1940s Interracial America*. Princeton, NJ: Princeton University Press, 2012.

Brooks, Charlotte. *American Exodus: Second-Generation Chinese Americans in China, 1901–1949*. Berkeley: University of California Press, 2019.

Brubaker, Rogers. "The 'Diaspora' Diaspora." *Ethnic and Racial Studies* 28, no. 1 (January 2005): 1–19.

Chan, Shelly. *Diaspora's Homeland: Modern China in the Age of Global Migration*. Durham, NC: Duke University Press, 2018.

Chung, Su (Lucille Davis). *Court Dishes of China: The Cuisine of the Ch'ing Dynasty*. Rutland, VT: Charles E. Tuttle, 1966.

Cinel, Dino. *From Italy to San Francisco: The Immigrant Experience*. Stanford, CA: Stanford University Press, 1982.

———. *The National Integration of Italian Return Migration, 1870–1929*. Cambridge, UK: Cambridge University Press, 1991.

Collins, Donald E. *Native American Aliens: Disloyalty and the Renunciation of Citizenship by Japanese Americans During World War II*. Westport, CT: Greenwood Press, 1985.

Commission on Wartime Relocation and Internment of Civilians. *Personal Justice Denied: Report of the Commission on Wartime Relocation and Internment of Civilians*. Washington, DC: U.S. Government Printing Office, 1982.

Corbett, Scott P. *Quiet Passages: The Exchange of Civilians Between the United States and Japan During the Second World War*. Kent, OH: Kent State University Press, 1987.

Daniels, Roger. *Concentration Camps: North America—Japanese in the United States and Canada During World War II*, rev. ed. Malabar, FL: Robert E. Krieger, 1981.

———. *The Politics of Prejudice: The Anti-Japanese Movement in California and the Struggle for Japanese Exclusion*. Berkeley: University of California Press, 1962.

Dirlik, Arif. "Asians on the Rim: Transnational Capital and Local Community in the Making of Contemporary Asian America." *Amerasia Journal* 22, no. 3 (1996): 1–24.

Doto: Nikkei amerika bungaku zasshi shusei 3. Tokyo: Fuji Shuppan, 1997.
Dower, John W. *Embracing Defeat: Japan in the Wake of World War II*. New York: Norton, 1999.
———. "Triumphal and Tragic Narratives of the War in Asia." *Journal of American History* 82, no. 3 (December 1995): 1124–35.
———. *War Without Mercy: Race and Power in the Pacific War*. New York: Pantheon Books, 1986.
Drinnon, Richard. *Keeper of Concentration Camps: Dillon S. Myer and American Racism*. Berkeley: University of California Press, 1987.
Duus, Masayo. *Tokyo Rose: Orphan of the Pacific*. New York: Kodansha International, 1979.
Easley, Leif-Eric. "Obama's Nuclear Legacy: Reconciliation and Nonproliferation in Asia After Hiroshima." *Asian Institute for Policy Studies Issue Brief* 5, no. 14 (October 2016): 1–30.
Egawa, Hidefumi, Yamada Ryoichi, and Hayata Yoshiro. *Kokusekiho* [Nationality Law]. Tokyo: Yuhikaku, 1997.
Elleman, Bruce. *Japanese-American Civilian Prisoner Exchanges and Detention Camps, 1941–1945*. London: Routledge, 2006.
Ellis, John. *World War II: A Statistical Survey—The Essential Facts and Figures for All the Combatants*. New York: Facts on File, 1993.
Falk, Stanley, and Warren M. Tsuneishi, eds. *MIS in the War Against Japan*. Washington, DC: Japanese American Veterans Association, 1995.
Flamming, Douglas. *Bound for Freedom: Black Los Angeles in Jim Crow America*. Berkeley: University of California Press, 2005.
Franklin, William M., and E. R. Perkins, eds. *Foreign Relations of the United States: Diplomatic Papers, 1943*, Vol. III, *The British Commonwealth, Eastern Europe, the Far East*. Washington, DC: U.S. Government Printing Office, 1963.
Fuji Scouts Club of Japan, *Murayama tamotsu to boi sukauto: Murayama Tamotsu "tanjo 100 shunen" kinen* [pamphlet]. Saitama, Japan, February 22, 2006.
Fujitani, Takashi. *Race for Empire: Koreans as Japanese and Japanese as Americans During World War II*. Berkeley: University of California Press, 2011.
Fujitani, Takashi, Geoffrey M. White, and Lisa Yoneyama, eds. *Perilous Memories: The Asia-Pacific War(s)*. Durham, NC: Duke University Press, 2001.
Fujiura, Koh. *Natsumero no hitobito*. Tokyo: Yomiuri Shimbunsha, 1971.
Gabaccia, Donna R. "Is Everywhere Nowhere? Nomads, Nations, and the Immigrant Paradigm of United States History." *Journal of American History* 86, no. 3 (December 1999): 1115–34.
Gardner, Martha. *The Qualities of a Citizen: Women, Immigration, and Citizenship, 1870–1965*. Princeton, NJ: Princeton University Press, 2005.

Geiger, Andrea. *Subverting Exclusion: Transpacific Encounters with Race, Caste, and Borders, 1885–1928*. New Haven, CT: Yale University Press, 2011.

Gilroy, Paul. *The Black Atlantic: Modernity and Double Consciousness*. Cambridge, MA: Harvard University Press, 1993.

Gordon, Andrew. *A Modern History of Japan: From Tokugawa Times to the Present*, 3rd ed. New York: Oxford University Press, 2014.

Grodzins, Morton. *The Loyal and the Disloyal: Social Boundaries of Patriotism and Treason*. Chicago: University of Chicago Press, 1956.

Hagihara, Atsushi. *Hiranuma Kiichiro to kindai nihon: Kanryo no kokkashugi to taiheiyo senso-e no michi*. Kyoto: Kyoto University Press, 2016.

Hall, Stuart. "Cultural Identity and Diaspora." In *Identity: Community, Culture, Difference*, ed. Jonathan Rutherford, 222–37. London: Lawrence & Wishart, 1990.

Hane, Mikiso. *Modern Japan: A Historical Survey*. Boulder, CO: Westview Press, 1986.

Hansen, Arthur A. "James Matsumoto Omura: An Interview." *Amerasia Journal* 13, no. 2 (Fall 1986): 99–113.

Hansen, Arthur A., and David A. Hacker. "The Manzanar Riot: An Ethnic Perspective." *Amerasia Journal* 2, no. 2 (1974): 112–57.

Hansen, Arthur A., and Betty E. Mitson, eds. *Voices Long Silent: An Oral Inquiry into the Japanese American Education*. Fullerton: California State University Oral History Program, 1974.

Harada, Tasuki, ed. *The Japanese Problem in California: Answers (by Representative Americans) to Questionnaire*. San Francisco: American Japanese Relations Committee of Tokyo, 1922.

Harrington, Joseph D. *Yankee Samurai: The Secret Role of Nisei in America's Pacific Victory*. Detroit: Pettigrew Enterprises, 1979.

Hatamiya, Leslie. *Righting a Wrong: Japanese Americans and the Passage of the Civil Liberties Act of 1988*. Stanford, CA: Stanford University Press, 1993.

Hattori, Shingo. *Waga kuni ni okeru senzen no amerikan futtoboru katsudo no kiroku*. Tokyo: Japan American Football Association, Japan, 2004.

Hawaii Nikkei History Editorial Board. *Japanese Eyes, American Heart: Personal Reflections of Hawaii's World War II Nisei Soldiers*. Honolulu: Tendai Educational Foundation, 1998.

Hayashi, Brian Masaru. *Democratizing the Enemy: The Japanese American Internment*. Princeton, NJ: Princeton University Press, 2004.

Higa, Thomas Taro. *Aru nisei no wadachi, 1915–1985*. Kaneohe, HI: Higa Publications, 1988.

Hirabayashi, Lane Ryo. *The Politics of Fieldwork: Research in an American Concentration Camp*. Tucson: University of Arizona Press, 1999.

Hirabayashi, Lane Ryo, Akemi Kikumura-Yano, and James H. Hirabayashi, eds. *New World, New Lives: Globalization and People of Japanese Descent in the Americas and from Latin America in Japan.* Stanford, CA: Stanford University Press, 2002.

Hirahata, Frank. "Fifty Years After the Pacific War: 'Molded to Conform, But . . .'" *Amerasia Journal* 23, no. 3 (1997): 145–63.

Hirohata, Tsunegoro. *Zaibei fukuoka kenjinshi.* Los Angeles: Zeibei Fukuoka Kenjinshi Hensan Jimusho, 1931.

Hiroshima Kenmin no Chugoku Tohoku Chiku Kaitakushi Hensan Iinkai. *Hiroshimaken manshu kaitakushi.* Hiroshima: Hiroshima Kenmin no Chugoku Tohoku Chiku Kaitakushi Hensan Iinkai, 1989.

Hosokawa, Bill. *Colorado's Japanese Americans: From 1886 to the Present.* Boulder: University of Colorado Press, 2005.

———. *JACL in Quest of Justice.* New York: Morrow, 1982.

———. *Nisei: The Quiet Americans—The Story of a People.* New York: Morrow, 1969.

Howe, Russell Warren. *The Hunt for "Tokyo Rose."* New York: Madison Books, 1990.

Hsu, Madeline Y. *Dreaming of Gold, Dreaming of Home: Transnationalism and Migration Between the United States and South China, 1882–1943.* Stanford, CA: Stanford University Press, 2000.

Iacobelli, Pedro, Danton Leary, and Shinnosuke Takahashi, eds. *Transnational Japan as History: Empire, Migration, and Social Movements.* New York: Palgrave Macmillan, 2016.

Ichinokuchi, Tad, ed. *John Aiso and the M.I.S.: Japanese-American Soldiers in the Military Intelligence Service, World War II.* Los Angeles: M.I.S. Club of Southern California, 1988.

Ichioka, Yuji. *Before Internment: Essays in Prewar Japanese American History*, ed. Gordon H. Chang and Eiichiro Azuma. Stanford, CA: Stanford University Press, 2005.

———. "Beyond National Boundaries: The Complexity of Japanese-American History." *Amerasia Journal* 23, no. 3 (Winter 1997–1998): vii–xi.

———. "Dai Nisei Mondai: Changing Japanese Immigrant Conceptions of the Second-Generation Problem, 1902–1941." In *Before Internment: Essays in Prewar Japanese American History*, ed. Gordon H. Chang and Eiichiro Azuma. Stanford, CA: Stanford University Press, 2006.

———. "Introduction." In *Ganbatte: Sixty-Year Struggle of a Kibei Worker*, by Karl G. Yoneda, xi–xvii. Los Angeles: Asian American Studies Center, University of California, Los Angeles, 1983.

———. "Japanese Immigrant Nationalism: The Issei and the Sino-Japanese War, 1937–1941." *California History* 69, no. 3 (1990): 260–75.

———. "Japanese Immigrant Response to the 1920 Alien Land Law." *Agricultural History* 58 (1984): 157–78.

———. "The Meaning of Loyalty: The Case of Kazumaro Buddy Uno." *Amerasia Journal* 23, no. 3 (Winter 1997–1998): 45–71.

———, ed. *Views from Within: The Japanese American Education and Resettlement Study*. Los Angeles: University of California, Los Angeles Asian American Studies Center, 1989.

Igarashi, Yoshikuni. *Bodies of Memory: Narratives of War in Postwar Japanese Culture, 1945–1970*. Princeton, NJ: Princeton University Press, 2000.

Ikeda, Norizane. *Hinomaru awa: Taibei boryaku hoso monogatari*. Tokyo: Chuo Koronsha, 1979.

Ikeda, Takekuni. "The Imperial Navy's Final Sortie." *Naval History* 21, no. 5 (October 2007): 34–43.

Ikeno, Satoshi, and Kayoko Nakao. "Zaibei hibakusha kyokai bunretsu no yoin bunseki to kongo no engo kadai." *Jinbun fukushigaku kenkyu* 6, no. 1 (November 2013): 47–68.

Iriye, Akira. *Global and Transnational History: The Past, Present, and Future*. New York: Palgrave Macmillan, 2013.

Irons, Peter. *Justice at War*. Oxford, UK: Oxford University Press, 1983.

Ito, Roy, and S-20 and Nisei Veterans Association. *Stories of My People: A Japanese Canadian Journal*. Hamilton, Canada: S-20 and Nisei Veterans Association, 1994.

Jin, Michael. "Americans in the Pacific: Rethinking Race, Gender, Citizenship, and Diaspora at the Crossroads of Asian and Asian American Studies." *Critical Ethnic Studies* 2, no. 1 (Spring 2016): 128–47.

———. "The Japanese American Transnational Generation: Rethinking the Spatial and Conceptual Boundaries of Asian America." In *The Routledge Handbook of Asian American Studies*, ed. Cindy I-Fen Cheng, 246–59. New York: Routledge, 2017.

Jones, Vincent C. *Manhattan: The Army and the Atomic Bomb—United States Army in World War II*. Washington, DC: Center of Military History, United States Army, 1988.

Jung, Moon-Ho. "Seditious Subjects: Race, State Violence, and the U.S. Empire." *Journal of Asian American Studies* 14, no. 2 (June 2011): 221–47.

Kadoike, Hiroshi. *Nihongun heishi ni natta amerikajin tachi: Bokoku to tatakatta nikkei nisei*. Tokyo: Genshu Shuppansha, 2010.

Kaigai Hyakunen Kinen Bunka Jigyokai. *Nichibei bunka koshoshi*. Tokyo: Yoyosha, 1954–1956.

Kaigai Kyoiku Kyokai. *Kaigai kyoiku kyokai yoran*. Tokyo: Kaigai Kyoiku Kyokai, 1940.

———. *Zaidan hojin kaigai kyoiku kyokai yoran*. Kawasaki: Kaigai Kyoiku Kyokai, 1938.

Kajiki Kyodokan. *Futatsu no Sokoku, Itami ten* [*Futatsu no Sokoku*: Itami Exhibit]. Kajiki, Japan: Kajiki Folklore Museum, 2004.

Kamisaka, Fuyuko. *Mitsu no sokoku: Manshu ni totsuida nikkei amerikajin*. Tokyo: Chuo Koronsha, 1996.

Kaplan, Caren. *Questions of Travel: Postmodern Discourses of Displacement*. Durham, NC: Duke University Press, 1996.

Karuka, Manu. *Empire's Tracks: Indigenous Nations, Chinese Workers, and the Transcontinental Railroad*. Berkeley: University of California Press, 2019.

Kato, Masuo, ed. *Teikoku amerika*. Tokyo: Domei Press, 1942.

Kawashima, Ken C. *The Proletarian Gamble: Korean Workers in Interwar Japan*. Durham, NC: Duke University Press, 2009.

Kawashima, Yasuhide. *The Tokyo Rose Case: Treason on Trial*. Lawrence: University Press of Kansas, 2013.

Keene, Judith. *Treason on the Airwaves: Three Allied Broadcasters on Axis Radio During World War II*. Westport, CT: Praeger, 2009.

Keisen Girls' School. *The Nisei: A Study of Their Life in Japan*. Tokyo: Keisen Girls' School, 1939.

Kessler-Harris, Alice. "In the Nation's Image: The Gendered Limits of Social Citizenship in the Depression Era." *Journal of American History* 86, no. 3 (December 1999): 1251–79.

Kinashi, Kozo. *Dave Itami Akira no shogai: Kyokuto kokusai gunji saiban hishi*. Tokyo: Paru Shuppan, 1985.

Kiyota, Minoru. *Beyond Loyalty: The Story of a Kibei*, trans. Linda Klepinger Keenan. Honolulu: University of Hawaii Press, 1997.

Kizu, Shigetoshi. *Nihon yusen senpaku 100-nenshi*. Tokyo: Kaijinsha, 1984.

Komaki, Saneshige, ed. *Dai toa chiseigaku shinron*. Tokyo: Hoshino Shoten, 1943.

Konvits, Milton R. *The Alien and the Asiatic in American Law*. Ithaca, NY: Cornell University Press, 1946.

Kosaka, Eliko. "Caught in Between Okinawa and Hawai'i: 'Kibei' Diaspora in Masao Yamashiro's *The Kibei Nisei*." *Amerasia Journal* 41, no. 1 (2015): 23–36.

Kramer, Paul A. "A Complex of Seas: Passages Between Pacific Histories." *Amerasia Journal* 42, no. 3 (2016): 32–41.

Kumei, Teruko. "1930 nendai no kibei undo: Amerika kokusekiho to no kanren ni oite." *Imin kenkyu* 30 (1993): 149–62.

———. "Nihon seifu to nisei ekkyo kyoiku: Heishikan wo jirei to shite." In *Amerika nihonjin imin no ekkyo kyoikushi*, ed. Yoshida Akira, 251–75. Tokyo: Nihon Tosho Center, 2005.

———. "Yujo to yuko wo musunde: Heishikan kara rajio puresu-e." *Kaigai imin shiryokan kenkyu kiyo* 4 (2009): 1–10.

Kurahira, Toshio. *Shiberia yokuryu: Mikan no higeki*. Tokyo: Iwanami Shinsho, 2009.

Kurashige, Lon. *Japanese American Celebration and Conflict: A History of Ethnic Identity and Festival, 1934–1990*. Berkeley: University of California Press, 2002.

———. *Two Faces of Exclusion: The Untold History of Anti-Asian Racism in the United States*. Chapel Hill: University of North Carolina Press, 2016.

Lee, Erika. *America for Americans: A History of Xenophobia in the United States*. New York: Basic Books, 2019.

———. *At America's Gates: Chinese Immigration During the Exclusion Era, 1882–1943*. Chapel Hill: University of North Carolina Press, 2003.

Levitt, Peggy, and Mary C. Waters, eds. *The Changing Face of Home: The Transnational Lives of the Second Generation*. New York: Russell Sage Foundation, 2002.

Lew-Williams, Beth. *Chinese Must Go: Violence, Exclusion, and the Making of the Alien in America*. Cambridge, MA: Harvard University Press, 2018.

Lifton, Robert Jay, and Greg Mitchell. *Hiroshima in America: Fifty Years of Denial*. New York: Putnam's Sons, 1995.

Lowe, Lisa. *Immigrant Acts: On Asian American Cultural Politics*. Durham, NC: Duke University Press, 1996.

Maehara, Kinuko. "To Okinawa and Back Again: Hawai no okinawaken kibei nisei no raifu stori." *Imin kenkyu* 2 (2006): 23–42.

Masaoka, Mike M. *They Call Me Moses Masaoka: An American Saga*. New York: Morrow, 1987.

McClatchy, Valentine Stuart. *America and Japan: Their Treatment of Foreigners and Resulting Conditions—Policies in Immigration, Exclusion Land Ownership and Lease, Citizenship, Dual Citizenship*. San Francisco: California Joint Immigration Committee, 1925.

———, ed. *Four Anti-Japanese Pamphlets*. New York: Arno Press, 1978.

McNaughton, James C. *Nisei Linguists: Japanese Americans in the Military Intelligence Service During World War II*. Washington, DC: U.S. Department of the Army, 2006.

McWilliams, Carey. *Prejudice: Japanese-Americans—Symbol of Racial Intolerance*. Hamden, CT: Shoe String Press, 1971.

———. *What About Our Japanese Americans?* New York: Public Affairs Committee, 1944.

Miike, Noboru, and Takahara Shiro. *Watakushi no umareta hawai*. Tokyo: Seitoku Shoin, 1942.

Military Intelligence Service Northwest Association. *Unsung Heroes: The Military Intelligence Service—Past-Present-Future.* Seattle: MIS Northwest Association, 1996.

Military Intelligence Service Veterans Club of Hawaii. *Secret Valor: M.I.S. Personnel, World War II Pacific Theater, Pre-Pearl Harbor to Sept. 8, 1951.* Honolulu: Military Intelligence Service Veterans Club of Hawaii, 1993.

Minamikawa, Fuminori. *"Nikkei amerikajin" no rekishi shakaigaku: Esunishiti, jinshu, nashonarizumu.* Tokyo: Sairyusha, 2007.

Ministry of Foreign Affairs of Japan. "Waga kuni to kakukoku to no aida no shomondai." *Waga gaiko no kinkyo,* no. 7 (November 1963).

Miyazaki, Masahiro. *Futatsu no sanga: Nikkei amerikajin kaku tatakaeri.* Kagoshima, Japan: Asahi Ado, 1984.

Mizuno, Mariko. "Kagawa bunichi no bungeikan to kyosei shuyojo taiken: Iminchi bungei kara kibei nisei bungaku no hatten ni oite." *Shakai shisutemu kenkyu* 11 (February 2008): 169–82.

Modell, John. *The Economics and Politics of Racial Accommodation: The Japanese of Los Angeles, 1900–1942.* Urbana: University of Illinois Press, 1977.

Morishige, Toshio. *Hiroshima-ken taizai beifu shusshosha meibo.* Hiroshima: Hiroshima-ken Kaigai Kyokai, 1932.

Morley, David, and Kuan-Hsing Chen, eds. *Stuart Hall: Critical Dialogues in Cultural Studies.* London: Routledge, 1996.

Muller, Eric L. *Free to Die for Their Country: The Story of the Japanese American Draft Resisters in World War II.* Chicago: University of Chicago Press, 2001.

Murakawa, Yoko. *Kyokaisenjo no shiminken: Nichibei senso to nikkei amerikajin.* Tokyo: Ochanomizu Shobo, 2007.

Murayama, Tamotsu. *Amerika nisei: Sono kunan no rekishi.* Tokyo: Jiji Tsushinsha, 1964.

———. *Hawai nisei: Kutsujoku kara eiko-e.* Tokyo: Jiji Tsushinsha, 1966.

Murphy, Thomas D. *Ambassadors in Arms.* Honolulu: University of Hawaii Press, 1954.

Murray, Alice Yang. *Historical Memories of the Japanese American Internment and the Struggle for Redress.* Stanford, CA: Stanford University Press, 2008.

———. "Oral History Research, Theory, and Asian American Studies." *Amerasia Journal* 26, no. 1 (2000): 105–18.

Myer, Dillon S. *Uprooted Americans: The Japanese Americans and the War Relocation Authority During World War II.* Tucson: University of Arizona Press, 1971.

Nagai, Matsuzo, ed. *Nichibei bunka koshoshi.* Tokyo: Yoyosha, 1952.

Nagata, Yuriko. *Unwanted Aliens: Japanese Internment in Australia.* St. Lucia, Australia: University of Queensland Press, 1996.

Namikawa, Ryo. "Japanese Overseas Broadcasting: A Personal View." In *Film and Radio Propaganda in World War II*, ed. K. R. M. Short. London: Croom Helm, 1983.

Ngai, Mae M. "The Architecture of Race in American Immigration Law: A Reexamination of the Immigration Act of 1924." *Journal of American History* 86, no. 1 (June 1999): 67–92.

———. "Birthright Citizenship and the Alien Citizen." *Fordham Law Review* 75, no. 5 (2007): 2521–30.

———. *Impossible Subjects: Illegal Aliens and the Making of Modern America*. Princeton, NJ: Princeton University Press, 2005.

Nichibei Shimbunsha. *Nichibei jushoroku*. San Francisco: Nichibei Shimbunsha, 1939.

———. *Nichibei nenkan*. San Francisco: Nichibei Shimbunsha, 1911.

Nihon Beifu Kyokai. *Dai nisei no mansen kengakuki*. Tokyo: Runbini Shuppansha, 1939.

———. *Dai nisei no nihon ryugaku ni tsuite*. Tokyo: Runbini Shuppansha, 1934.

———. *Dai nisei to kokuseki mondai*. Tokyo: Runbini Shuppansha, 1938.

———. *Dai nisei to nihon no gakko*. Tokyo: Runbini Shuppansha, 1938.

Nimmo, William. *Behind a Curtain of Silence: Japanese in Soviet Custody, 1945–1956*. Westport, CT: Greenwood Press, 1988.

Nippon Hoso Kyokai (NHK). *NHK Taiga dorama sutori: Sanga Moyu—Yamasaki Toyoko saku "Futatsu no Sokoku" yori*. Tokyo: Nippon Hoso Shuppan Kyokai, 1984.

———. *NHK taiga dorama taizen: 50 sakuin tettei gaido*. Tokyo: NHK Shuppan, 2011.

Nishiyama, Sen. "Unexpected Encounters." *Amerasia Journal* 23, no. 3 (1997): 125–42.

Nodera, Isamu. "A Survey of the Vocational Activities of the Japanese in the City of Los Angeles." Master's thesis, University of Southern California, 1936.

Norikoshi, Takao. *Arisu: burodouei wo miryo shita tensai dansa Kawahata Fumiko monogatari*. Tokyo: Kondansha, 1999.

Oda, James. *Heroic Struggles of Japanese Americans: Partisan Fighters from America's Concentration Camps*. North Hollywood, CA: James Oda, 1981.

Oguro, James, ed. *Sempai Gumi*. Honolulu: MIS Veterans of Hawaii, 1981.

Okihiro, Gary Y. "Resistance in America's Concentration Camps: A Re-Evaluation." *Amerasia Journal* 2 (Fall 1973): 20–34.

———. "Tule Lake Under Martial Law: A Study of Japanese Resistance." *Journal of Ethnic Studies* 5, no. 3 (Fall 1977): 71–85.

Opler, Marvin. "Cultural Dilemma of a Kibei Youth." In *Clinical Studies in Culture Conflict*, ed. Georgene Seward, 297–316. New York: Ronald Press, 1958.

Paik, A. Naomi. *Rightlessness: Testimony and Redress in U.S. Prison Camps Since World War II.* Chapel Hill: University of North Carolina Press, 2016.

Parrenas, Rhacel Salazar, and Lok C. D. Siu, eds. *Asian Diasporas: New Formations, New Conceptions.* Stanford, CA: Stanford University Press, 2007.

Preparatory Commission for the Comprehensive Nuclear-Test-Ban Treaty Organization. *Annual Report 2017: United for the Cause.* Vienna, Austria: Preparatory Commission for the Comprehensive Nuclear-Test-Ban Treaty Organization, 2018.

Putnam, Frank W. "The Atomic Bomb Casualty Commission in Retrospect." *Proceedings of the National Academy of Sciences of the United States of America* 95, no. 10 (May 1998): 5426–31.

REgenerations Oral History Project: Rebuilding Japanese American Families, Communities, and Rights in the Resettlement Era. Los Angeles: Japanese American National Museum, 2000.

Robbins, Jane. *Tokyo Calling: Japanese Overseas Radio Broadcasting, 1937–1945.* Florence, Italy: European Press Academic, 2001.

Robinson, Greg. *After Camp: Portraits in Midcentury Japanese American Life and Politics.* Berkeley: University of California Press, 2012.

Ross, Robert Howard. "Social Distance as It Exists Between the First and Second Generation Japanese in the City of Los Angeles and Vicinity." Master's thesis, University of Southern California, 1939.

Rutherford, Jonathan, ed. *Identity: Community, Culture, Difference.* London: Lawrence & Wishart, 1990.

Sakaguchi, Mitsuhiro. "Kibei nisei o meguru dansho: Seattle kibei nikkei shimin kyokai no soshiki to katsudo o chushin ni." *Imin kenkyu nenpo* 7 (March 2001): 23–38.

———. *Nihonjin amerika iminshi.* Tokyo: Fuji Shuppan, 2001.

Sakakida, Richard M., and Wayne S. Kiyosaki. *A Spy in Their Midst: The World War II Struggle of a Japanese-American Hero.* Lanham, MD: Madison Books, 1995.

Sakamoto, Pamela Rotner. *Midnight in Broad Daylight: A Japanese American Family Caught Between Two Worlds.* New York: Harper Perennial, 2016.

Sameshima, Steve. *Tenno o sukutta otoko: Amerika rikigun johobu, nikkei kibei nisei Akira Itami.* Kagoshima: Nanpo Shinsha, 2013.

Sano, Iwao Peter. *One Thousand Days in Siberia: The Odyssey of a Japanese-American POW.* Lincoln: University of Nebraska Press, 1997.

Sawada, Mitziko. *Tokyo Life, New York Dreams: Urban Japanese Visions of America, 1890–1924.* Berkeley: University of California Press, 1996.

Senate of California. *Chinese Immigration: The Social, Moral, and Political Effect of Chinese Immigration—Policy and Means of Exclusion.* Memorial of the Senate of California to the Congress of the United States. Sacramento: California State Printing Office, 1877.

Shibusawa, Naoko. "The Artist Belongs to the People: The Odyssey of Taro Yashima." *Journal of Asian American Studies* 8, no. 3 (October 2005): 257–75.

———. "Femininity, Race, and Treachery: How 'Tokyo Rose' Became a Traitor to the United States After the Second World War." *Gender and History* 22, no. 1 (April 2010): 169–88.

Shigematsu, Itsuzo. "Greetings: 50 Years of Atomic Bomb Casualty Commission—Radiation Effects Research Foundation Studies." *Proceedings of the National Academy of Sciences of the United States of America* 95, no. 10 (May 1998): 5424–25.

Shimamura, Kyo. *Sanga Moyu: Jitsuroku*. Tokyo: Dainamikku Serazu, 1984.

Shukaku: Nikkei amerika bungaku zasshi shusei 1. Tokyo: Fuji Shuppan, 1997.

Simpson, Caroline Chung. *An Absent Presence: Japanese Americans in Postwar American Culture, 1945–1960*. Durham, NC: Duke University Press, 2001.

Smith, Bradford. *Americans from Japan*. Philadelphia: Lippincott, 1948.

Sodei, Rinjiro. *Watashitachi wa teki datta noka* [Were We the Enemy?]. Tokyo: Iwanami Shoten, 1995.

———. *Were We the Enemy? American Survivors of Hiroshima*. Boulder, CO: Westview Press, 1998.

Sohoni, Deenesh. "Unsuitable Suitors: Anti-Miscegenation Laws, Naturalization Laws, and the Constructions of Asian Identities." *Law and Society Review* 41, no. 3 (September 2007): 587–618.

Spicer, Edward, Asael T. Hanse, Katherine Luomala, and Marvin Opler. *Impounded People: Japanese-Americans in the Relocation Centers*. Tucson: University of Arizona Press, 1969.

Spickard, Paul R. *Japanese Americans: The Formation and Transformations of an Ethnic Group*, rev. ed. New Brunswick, NJ: Rutgers University Press, 2009.

———. "The Nisei Assume Power: The Japanese Citizens League, 1941–1942." *Pacific Historical Review* 52, no. 2 (May 1983): 147–74.

Stephan, John J. *Hawaii Under the Rising Sun: Japan's Plans for Conquest After Pearl Harbor*. Honolulu: University of Hawaii Press, 1984.

———. "Hijacked by Utopia: American Nikkei in Manchuria." *Amerasia Journal* 23, no. 3 (1997): 1–42.

Strong, Lester. "When 'Tokyo Rose' Came to Albuquerque." *New Mexico Historical Review* 66, no. 1 (January 1991): 73–92.

Supreme Commander for the Allied Powers. *Reports of General MacArthur*. Washington, DC: Center for Military History, 1994.

Suzuki, Yukio. *Keibatsu: Kekkon de katamerareru nihon no shihaisha shudan*. Tokyo: Kobunsha, 1965.

Tachibana, Yuzuru. *Teikoku kaigun shikan ni natta nikkei nisei*. Tokyo: Tsukiji Shokan, 1994.
Takahashi, Jere. *Nisei/Sansei: Shifting Japanese Identities and Politics*. Philadelphia: Temple University Press, 1997.
Takeda, Junichi. *Zaibei hiroshima kenjinshi* [History of the Development of the People from Hiroshima Prefecture]. Los Angeles: Zaibei Hiroshima Kenjinshi Hakkojo, 1929.
Takeda, Kayoko. *Interpreting the Tokyo War Crimes Tribunal: A Sociopolitical Analysis*. Ottawa, Canada: University of Ottawa Press, 2010.
Takeda, Shinpei, and Naoko Wake. *Umi o koeta hiroshima/nagasaki*. Nagasaki: Yururi Shobo, 2014.
Takemaro, Mori. "Colonies and Countryside in Wartime Japan." In *Farmers and Village Life in Twentieth-Century Japan*, ed. Ann Waswo and Nishida Yoshiaki, 175–98. New York: Routledge Curzon, 2003.
Takezawa, Yasuko, and Gary Y. Okihiro, eds. *Trans-Pacific Japanese American Studies: Conversations on Race and Racializations*. Honolulu: University of Hawaii Press, 2016.
Tateishi, John. *And Justice for All: An Oral History of the Japanese American Detention Camps*. New York: Random House, 1984.
Tateishi, Kay. "An Atypical Nisei." *Amerasia Journal* 23, no. 3 (1997): 199–216.
Tessaku: Nikkei amerika bungaku zasshi shusei, 5–6. Tokyo: Fuji Shuppan, 1997.
Thelen, David. "The National and Beyond: Transnational Perspectives on United States History." *Journal of American History* 86, no. 3 (December 1999): 965–75.
Thomas, Dorothy Swaine, and Richard S. Nishimoto. *The Salvage*. Berkeley: University of California Press, 1952.
———. *The Spoilage*. Berkeley: University of California Press, 1946.
Toji, Dean. "Hibakusha: Japanese American Atomic Bomb Survivors." *East Wind: Politics and Culture of Asians in the U.S.* 1, no. 2 (Fall/Winter 1982): 3–5.
Tomita, Mary Kimoto. "Coming of Age in Japan." *Amerasia Journal* 23, no. 3 (1997): 165–80.
———. *Dear Miye: Letters from Japan, 1939–1946*, ed. Robert Lee. Stanford, CA: Stanford University Press, 1995.
Toyonaga Keisaburo. "Colonialism and Atom Bomb: About Survivors of Hiroshima Living in Korea." In *Perilous Memories: The Asia-Pacific War(s)*, ed. Takashi Fujitani, Geoffrey M. White, and Lisa Yoneyama, 378–94. Durham, NC: Duke University Press, 2001.
Tsuda, Takeyuki, ed. *Diasporic Homecomings: Ethnic Return Migration in Comparative Perspective*. Stanford, CA: Stanford University Press, 2009.
———. *Japanese American Ethnicity: In Search of Heritage and Homeland Across Generations*. New York: NYU Press, 2016.

U.S. Army Corps of Engineers, Manhattan District. *The Atomic Bombing of Hiroshima and Nagasaki: Report on the Effects of the Atomic Bombs Which Were Dropped on the Japanese Cities of Hiroshima and Nagasaki.* Dinslaken, Germany: Pergamonmedia, 2019.

U.S. Department of Commerce, Bureau of the Census. *Fifteenth Census of the United States: 1930.* Washington, DC: U.S. Government Printing Office, 1932.

———. *Fourteenth Census of the United States Taken in the Year 1920.* Washington, DC: U.S. Government Printing Office, 1922.

———. *Sixteenth Census of the United States: 1940.* Washington, DC: U.S. Government Printing Office, 1943.

U.S. Department of State. *Report of the Honorable Roland S. Morris on Japanese Immigration and Alleged Discriminatory Legislation Against Japanese Residents in the United States.* Washington, DC: U.S. Government Printing Office, 1921.

U.S. Department of the Interior, War Relocation Authority. *WRA: A Story of Human Conservation.* Washington, DC: U.S. Government Printing Office, 1946.

U.S. Department of War. *Final Report: Japanese Evacuation from the West Coast, 1942.* Washington, DC: U.S. Government Printing Office, 1943.

U.S. House of Representatives. *Statistics of the Congressional and Presidential Election of November 2, 1920.* Washington, DC: U.S. Government Printing Office, 1921.

U.S. Selective Service System. *Special Groups.* Special Monograph 10. Washington, DC: U.S. Selective Service System, 1953.

U.S. Social Security Administration. *Death Master File* [database]. Alexandra, VA: National Technical Information Service.

Uyeda, Clifford, and Barry Saiki, eds. *The Pacific War and Peace: Americans of Japanese Ancestry in Military Intelligence Service, 1941 to 1952.* San Francisco: Military Intelligence Service Association of Northern California and National Japanese American Historical Society, 1991.

Wake, Naoko. "Surviving the Bomb in America: Silent Memories and the Rise of Cross-National Identity." *Pacific Historical Review* 86, no. 3 (2017): 472–506.

War Relocation Authority. *Myths and Facts About the Japanese Americans: Answering Common Misconceptions Regarding Americans of Japanese Ancestry.* Washington, DC: Department of the Interior, April 1945.

———. *Segregation of Persons of Japanese Ancestry in Relocation.* Denver: A. B. Hirschfield Press, 1943.

Waswo, Ann, and Nishida Yosiaki, eds. *Farmers and Village Life in Twentieth-Century Japan.* New York: Routledge Curzon, 2003.

Wax, Rosalie H. *Doing Fieldwork: Warnings and Advice.* Chicago: University of Chicago Press, 1971.

Weckerling, John. "Nisei Language Experts: Japanese Americans Play Vital Role in U.S. Intelligence Service in World War II." In *John Aiso and the M.I.S.: Japanese-American Soldiers in the Military Intelligence Service, World War II*, ed. Tad Ichinokuchi. Los Angeles: M.I.S. Club of Southern California, 1988.

Weglyn, Michi. *Years of Infamy: The Untold Story of America's Concentration Camps*. New York: Morrow, 1976.

Wetherall, William. "Japan's Pop 'Roots' Fails to Cast New Light on Minority Problems." *Far Eastern Economic Review* 122, no. 41 (1983): 62–63.

Wilson, Rob. *Reimagining the American Pacific: From* South Pacific *to* Bamboo Ridge *and Beyond*. Durham, NC: Duke University Press, 2000.

Wong, Sau-ling C. "Denationalization Reconsidered: Asian American Cultural Criticism at a Theoretical Crossroads." *Amerasia Journal* 21, nos. 1–2 (1995): 1–28.

Yamamoto, Eriko. "Miya Sannomiya Kikuchi: A Pioneer Nisei Woman's Life and Identity." *Amerasia Journal* 23, no. 3 (1997): 73–101.

Yamane, Nobuyo. "A Nisei Woman in Rural Japan." *Amerasia Journal* 23, no. 3 (1997): 183–96.

Yamasaki, Toyoko. *Futatsu no Sokoku* [Two Homelands]. Tokyo: Shinchosha, 1983.

Yamashiro, Jane H. *Redefining Japaneseness: Japanese Americans in the Ancestral Homeland*. New Brunswick, NJ: Rutgers University Press, 2017.

Yamashiro, Masao. *Kibei nisei: Kaitai shite iku "nihonjin."* Tokyo: Gogatsu Shobo, 1995.

———. *Toi taigan: Aru kibei nisei no kaiso*. Tokyo: Gurobyusha, 1984.

Yamashita, Soen. *Nichibei o tsunagu mono*. Tokyo: Bunseisha, 1938.

———. *Nikkei shimin no nihon ryugaku jijo*. Tokyo: Bunseisha, 1938.

Yenne, Bill. *Rising Sons: The Japanese American GIs Who Fought for the United States in World War II*. New York: Macmillan, 2007.

Yoneda, Karl G. *Ganbatte: Sixty-Year Struggle of a Kibei Worker*. Los Angeles: Asian American Studies Center, University of California, Los Angeles, 1983.

———. *Manzanar kyosei shuyojo nikki*. Tokyo: PMC Shuppan, 1988.

Yoneyama, Lisa. *Cold War Ruins: Transpacific Critique of American Justice and Japanese War Crimes*. Durham, NC: Duke University Press, 2016.

———. *Hiroshima Traces: Time, Space, and the Dialectics of Memory*. Berkeley: University of California Press, 1999.

Yoo, David. *Growing up Nisei: Race, Generation, and Culture Among Japanese Americans of California, 1924–49*. Urbana: University of Illinois Press, 2000.

Yoshida, Akira, ed. *Amerika nihonjin imin no ekkyo kyoikushi*. Tokyo: Nihon Tosho Center, 2005.

Yoshida, George. *Reminiscing in Swingtime: Japanese Americans in American Popular Music, 1925–1960*. San Francisco: National Japanese American Historical Society, 1997.
Yoshida, Jim. *The Two Worlds of Jim Yoshida*. New York: Morrow, 1972.
Yoshida, Mitsuru. *Chinkon senkan yamato*. Tokyo: Kodansha, 1974.
Yui Daizaburo. "Between Pearl Harbor and Hiroshima/Nagasaki: Nationalism and Memory in Japan and the United States." In *Living with the Bomb: American and Japanese Cultural Conflicts in the Nuclear Age*, ed. Laura Hein and Mark Selden. New York: M.E. Sharpe, 1997, 52–72.
Zaibei Nihonjinkai. *Zaibei nihonjinshi* [History of Japanese in America]. San Francisco: Zeibei Nihonjinkai, 1940.

Index

Note: Unless otherwise noted [viz. "(Japan)"], government organizations and laws are American. Page numbers in italic type indicate figures or tables.

African Americans, 42–43
Ainu people, 35–36
Akiya, Karl Ichiro, 54
Akutagawa Ryunosuke, 93
Alien Land Law (California), 14–15, 145
alien land laws, 7, 14–15, 19–21, 145
Alliance News Agency, 116
American Legion, 19
American Legion of Hood River, 105
Angel Island, 38–40, 45, 54
anti-Asian sentiment and legislation, 3, 17–18, 39–43. *See also* anti-Japanese sentiment in United States; Chinese immigrants
anti-Japanese sentiment in United States: anti-Semitism compared to, 18; early examples of, 161n7; fear of Japan underlying, 18, 94–95; incarceration policy based on, 11, 59–60; in interwar period, 2–3, 7, 15; legal means of, 7, 15, 19; military veterans as subject of, 105; Nisei migrants as contributing to, 50–51; precursor of, 18; promulgators of, 19; socioeconomic impact of, 19–20, 22, 87–88, 121, 145; U.S.-Japan relations influenced by, 95. *See also* exclusion movement
Aoyama School, 27
Asahi Shimbun (newspaper), 1, *3*
Asama Maru (ship), 93, 122
Asian Americans. *See* Asians in the United States
Asians in the United States: portrayed as unassimilable, 7, 40; racialization of, 7, 17, 40–44, 46–47. *See also* anti-Asian sentiment and legislation
Asiatic Exclusion League, 15
assimilation: Asians' purported incapacity for, 7, 40; of Japanese Americans after the war, 66–68, 71–73, 80–81; Japanese Americans' purported incapacity for, 18, 19, 21, 41, 56, 153; of Kibei, 70–82
Associated Press, 116
athletics. *See* intercollegiate athletics
Atomic Bomb Casualty Commission (ABCC), 139
atomic bomb survivors, 12, 136–51; absence of, from U.S. narrative about the war, 136–37, 141, 147, 150–51; ignored by Japanese American community,

215

atomic bomb survivors (*continued*) 148; illnesses suffered by, 137–39; Japanese legislation on, 142; medical treatment of, in U.S. vs. Japan, 138–44; redress and reparations for, 136–44, 147–51; return of, to United States, 136–51; transpacific identities and experiences of, 144–45, *146*, 147, 151
Axios (documentary), 152
Azuma, Eiichiro, 12, 16, 153

Ban, George, 96–97
Batterton, Dick, 133
Biddle, Francis, 59
birthright citizenship, 21, 39–45, 152–53
Bow, Leslie, 42
Boy Scouts Federation of Japan, 132–33
Brinkley-Rogers, Paul, 139

Cable Act, 39, 44, 46–47, 52–53
CABS. *See* Committee of Atomic Bomb Survivors
California: anti-Japanese sentiment and legislation in, 14–15, 19–21, 42, 44, 50; Chinese exclusion movement in, 17–18; state role in Japanese incarceration, 59–60; Supreme Court of, 42
California Farm Bureau Federation, 19, 60
California State Federation of Labor, 19
California State Federation of Women's Clubs, 19
California State Grange, 19
Camp Savage, Minnesota, 76, 101–2
Cannon, Raymond, 51–52
Carter, John Franklin, 60
CAS. *See* War Relocation Authority (WRA): Community Analysis Section
Central California Japanese Agricultural Association, 14–15
Chiba, Toyoji, 14–15
Chiba Koh, 14
Chinese Exclusion Act, 17–18, 43
Chinese immigrants, exclusion movement targeting, 7, 17–18, 42
citizenship: of African Americans, 42–43; of Asians and Asian Americans, 42–44; birthright as basis of, 21, 39–45, 152–53; exclusion movement and, 9, 38–44; influence of marriage on, 9, 39, 44–47; Issei and, 72; Japanese ineligibility for, 19, 38–39, 41, 47; Kibei and, 68, 72, 78; as legal difficulty for incarceration policy, 57; Nisei and, 5–6, 8–9, 11, 48–53, 152–53; Nisei migrants and, 115; regaining of, 131–32; stripping of, from Nisei, 9, 12, 21–22, 38–42, 45–47, 124–28, 131
Civil Liberties Act, 147
class, and Japanese American assimilation, 82
Clinton, Bill, 149
cold war, 141–42
Columbia Records Japan, 33
Commission on Wartime Relocation and Internment of Civilians (CWRIC), 112
Committee of Atomic Bomb Survivors (CABS), 139–40, 148
Communist Party, 96, 101
Comprehensive Test-Ban Treaty (CTBT), 149–50
Cousens, Charles, 124

Daito Bunka Gakuin, Tokyo, 84, 89–90, 93
Dajo Primary School, Kajiki, 88, 93
dance, 31, 33
Danielson, George, 140–41, 148
Davis, Kenneth F., 2
DeWitt, John L., 11, 56–57, 59, 61, 68, 76
diaspora: of Asian peoples, 5–6; concept of, 5, 162n13; marginalized people as, 4; Nisei as, 4–8, *10*, 11–13, 16–17, 154–55
Dirlik, Arlif, 155
Doho (newspaper), 96–97, 99–100
Doi, Terry Takeshi, 104
Doiguchi, Yuichi, 35
Domei News Agency, 34, 36, 50–51, 116, 126
Dred Scott v. Sandford, 42

education: of cultural brokers, 34–36; internationalism/transnationalism in, 27–29, 82; of Japanese Americans in Japan, 26–31, 34–36, 49–50, 120–25,

128, 131; of Kibei in Japan, 11, 51, 54, 62, 64, 71, 88–90, 106–7; of Kibei in United States, 94;
Eisenhower, Milton, 66
Ekimoto, Masao, 120–21, 123, 127, 153–54
El Paso Times (newspaper), 46
Embree, John F., 71, 73, 75, 82
Ennis, Edward J., 60–61
Eroshenko, Vasili Yakovlevich, 24–25
Espionage Act, 73
exclusion movement: Chinese as target of, 7, 17–18, 42; citizenship as concern of, 9, 38–44; geopolitics in relation to, 3, 6; history of, 7, 17; individual responses to, 14; in interwar period, 15, 18–24, 153; socioeconomic impact of, on Japanese Americans, 19–20, 22. *See also* anti-Japanese sentiment in United States
Executive Order 9066, 64, 99, 145
Executive Order 9102, 66
Expatriation Act, 39

Family Registry Law (Japan), 45–46
fascism, 54, 76, 82, 96–97, 99
Federal Bureau of Investigation (FBI), 62–64, 69, 98
The Final Report: Japanese Evacuation from the West Coast, 56–57, 68
football, 29–31
442nd Regimental Combat Team, 82, 104
Fourteenth Amendment, 42, 43–44, 152
Fox News Channel, 149
Fujii, Sei, 34, 94–96, 98–99, 121
Fukuhara, Harry, 107–8
Fuller, Melville, 43–44
Furuya, Kaoru, 36
Futatsu no Sokoku. See Yamasaki Toyoko

Gabaccia, Donna R., 81
Gallagher, Mike, 149
Gendai (magazine), 123
gender, and Japanese American loyalty, 81–82
Gentleman's Agreement, 161n7
Gila River War Relocation Center, 144–45, 147
Goto Tokuji, 90

Great Depression, 2, 7, 20, 88, 89
Greater East Asia Co-Prosperity Sphere, 34, 90, 96
Gripsholm (ship), 147

Hachiya, Frank, 104–5
Haff, Edward, 45–46
Hall, Stuart, 6
Harlan, John Marshall, 43–44
Hawaii Home Planning Committee, 27
Hearst, William Randolph, 19, 22, 50, 94
Heart Mountain War Relocation Center, 72
Heishikan, 34–36, 120–26
Heishikan News (newspaper), 35
Hibakusha (film), *143*
Hide, Norio, 122, 124
Higa, Thomas Taro, 80–81, 104
Hirai, Raymond, 69
Hirano, Robert, 99
Hiranuma Kiichiro, 90
Hirata, Minako, 130
Hirohata, Tsunegoro "Paul," 26
Hirohito, Emperor, 108
Hiroshima: atomic bomb dropped on, 12, 107–8, 110, 136–38, 147, 150, 188n13; atomic bomb survivors from, 12, 136–51; emigration from, 8, 20, 25; return migrants to, 24, 26, 135–36, 145, 147
Hiroshima First Girls' Prefectural High School, 135
Hiroshima Jogakuin, 137
Hiroshima Overseas Association, 51
Hirsch, Michael, 131
Hoga Rokuro, 86
Hokkaido, 35–36
Hokubei Shijin Kyokai (Association of Poets in North America), 94
Home Ministry (Japan), 26, 49
Hood, Richard, 63
Hoover, J. Edgar, 59
Hoshino, Yoshiko, 47
Hosokawa, Bill, 133–34

Ikeda Norizane, 120
Immigration Act, 7, 9, 19, 38–39, 44, 47–48, 50

218   *Index*

Inaba, Akira, 38
Inaba, Toshiko, 38–40, 45–47, 49
Inada, Betty, 33
incarceration of Japanese Americans: anti-Japanese sentiment underlying, 11, 59–60; assimilation projects during, 66–68, 71–72; California's role in, 59–60; citizenship as legal difficulty for policy of, 57; Issei experiences of, 70–72; Itami and, 98–101; Japanese American cooperation in, 58, 59, 98–100; Japanese references to, 117, 118; Kibei experiences of, 57–59, 69–71, 73–77, 83; Kibei role in policy of, 11, 56–57, 61; policy debates over, 11–12, 56–57, 59–61, 64; redress and reparations for, 82, 111–13, 148; scholarship on, 5, 58; segregation of Kibei in, 68–70, 74–76, 78, 174n47; unrest and dissatisfaction in camps, 69, 73–74
intercollegiate athletics, 29–31
internment. *See* incarceration of Japanese Americans
Ishibashi Tanzan, 16
Ishibashi Utako, 16
Ishikawa, Bill, 36
Issei (first-generation Japanese Americans): alien status of, 57; citizenship not available to, 72; in internment camps, 70–72; JACL and, 61–62, 68, 97–98; loyalty of, 60; sending of children to Japan by, 23; and U.S. military service, 80–81
Itami, David Akira, 84–111; birth of, 87; displays of loyalty and patriotism by, 98–102; education of, 84, 88–90; employment of, as laborer, 84, 93–94; family of, 87, 102, *106*; and internment camps, 98–101; and JACL, 62–63, 96–101; Japanese upbringing of, 84, 87–90, 93, 111; as journalist, 84–85, 94–96, 98–100; memorial to, *91*; novel based on life of, 85–89, 91–92, 107–13; overview of life of, 84–85; poems and stories by, 179n37, 179n38; return of, to United States, 84–85, 93–111; service with U. S. Military Intelligence, 85, 101–6, *106*;

suicide of, 85, 92, 107; and U.S.-Japan relations, 94–98
Itami, Jojiro, 87–88
Itami, Kimiko, 105–6
Itami, Michi, 92

JACL. *See* Japanese American Citizens League
Japan: colonialism/imperialism of, 7–9, 15, 16, 25, 33–36, 54, 90, 93, 96–97, 141; militarism of, 1, 25, 28, 89–90, 94–95, 141; nationalism and national identity in, 89, 91–92, 111, 114; Nisei experiences in, 8–9, 12, 24–37, 52; occupation forces in, 108, 129–32, 138, 141; social discrimination practiced in, 9
Japan American Football Association, 31
Japanese American Citizens League (JACL): Anti-Axis Committee, 62–63, 80, 97–98; contest sponsored by, 34; cooperation of, with government, 58, 61–70, 79–83, 97–98; in internment camps, 100–101; and Issei, 61–62, 68, 97–98; Itami and, 62–63, 96–101; and Kibei, 50, 57–59, 61–70, 73–74, 80–83, 96–98, 104; leftists in, 96–97, 100–101; Los Angeles Chapter Kibei Division, 62–63, 96–100; loyalty emphasized by, 51, 58–59, 66–68, 73, 80–83, 97–98, 104, 112, 118, 133; Murayama and, 115, 117; redress campaign of, 112, 148; as representative of Japanese American community, 50, 57, 96
Japanese American Courier (newspaper), 63
Japanese Americans: assimilation of, following the war, 66–68, 71–73, 80–81; incarceration of, 5, 11, 56–58; loyalty of, 11, 72–73, 80–81, 99; as model minority, 67, 148; population of, *21*; portrayed as unassimilable, 18, 19, 21, 41, 56, 153; racialization of, 8–9, 11, 15, 18, 21–22, 56, 60; as transpacific diaspora, 6; and U.S. military service, 73, 75–76. *See also* anti-Japanese sentiment in United States; exclusion movement; Kibei; Nisei in America; Nisei migrants

Japanese Association of America, 95
Japanese Association of North America, 55
Japanese Exclusion League of California, 19, 44
Japanese Socialist Party, 25
Japan Times (newspaper), 34, 132
Japan Times Weekly (newspaper), 53, 54–55
jazz, 33
Jim Crow laws, 42–43
Johnson-Reed Act. *See* Immigration Act
Joint Intelligence Center, Pacific Ocean Area (JICPOA), 103–4

Kabayama Sukehide, 119
Kagoshima Prefecture, 84, 86, 88–90, 93, 103, 110
Kaigai Kyoiku Kyokai (Institute of International Education), 27
Kaigai no Nippon (magazine), 114, 118
Kajiki, Kagoshima Prefecture, 84, 86, 88
Kajiki Prefectural Middle School, 88–89
Kanda Minoru, 154–55
Kanda Yoshi, 117
Kashu Mainichi (newspaper), 34, 62, 84–85, 94–96, 98–99, 121
Kato, Jiro, 154
Kato, Kimie, 154
Kawabata, Alice Fumiko, 31, *32*, 33
Kawai, Haruko, 28–29
Kawai Michiko, 28–29
Kawai Tatsuo, 34, 120, 122
Kawamura Masahei, 117
Keio University, 31, 127
Keisen Jogakuen (Keisen Girls' School), 1, 28–29, 54–55
Kibei (Japanese American returnees from Japan), 11–12; American distrust of, 11, 50–52, 56–57, 61, 73–74, 79–80, 105–6; American education of, 94; assimilation and rehabilitation of, 70–82; "bachelors" among, 70–71, 75–76; citizenship of, 68, 72, 78; cooperation of, with government and JACL, 59; Fukuhara's story, 107–8; Higa's story, 80–81; influence of, on U.S. policy toward Japanese Americans, 11, 56–57; influence of marriage on, 61; in internment camps, 57–59, 69–71, 73–77, 83; Itami's story, 62–63, 84–111; JACL and, 62–64, *65*, 96–98; Japanese American suspicions of, 11–12, 57–58, 61–66, 68, 73–74, 79; Japanese education of, 11, 51, 54, 62, 64, 71, 88–90, 106–7; and Japanese military service, 76–77; loyalty of, 61–66, 73–77, 83, 98–102, 106–11; motivations of, 54; as "new immigrants," 77–82; Nisei relations with, 11–12, 61–66, 68–69, 73–75, 78–79; ostracization of, 11, 58, 61–72; as "problem," 58–59, 67–68, 71–72, 77, 79–81; pro-Japan sentiments of, 11, 56–57, 61, 69–71, 76–77, 79, 98–101, 107; return of, before Pacific War, 9; scholarship on, 58; transnational/dual identity of, 77–97, 109–11, 113; and U.S. military service, 73, 75–77, 90, 101–7, 175n61; WRA and, 67–77
Kirshbaum, Jack D., 139
Kishi, Ben, 69, 101
Kishi Nobusuke, 14
Kishino Yoshi, 90
Kono Rikako, 92
Korea: atomic bomb survivors from, 141, 144; conscription of workers from, 136, 187n5; Japanese settlers in, 25
Korean War, 131
Kumatani Minako, 92
Kuramoto, Kanji, 136, 139–40, 148
Kuramoto, Shigeaki, 127
Kurashige, Tetsuichi, 53
Kyotow, George, 35–36

Law Concerning Medical Care for the Victims of the Atomic Bombing (Japan), 142
League of Young Japanese Americans, 52–53
linguists, in military service, 76–77, 102–7
Los Angeles City College, 94
Loyal Order of Moose, 19
loyalty, to U.S. government: of Issei, 60; of Japanese Americans, 11, 72–73, 80–81, 99; of Kibei, 61–66, 73–77, 83,

220   *Index*

loyalty, to U.S. government (*continued*) 98–102, 106–11; of Nisei, 5, 11, 58–60, 62, 66–68, 70, 76, 81–83, 112–15, 118–19, 148; WRA questionnaire to assess, 64, 72–73, 175n61

Maki Hideji, 103
Malkin, Michelle, 149
Manchuria, 1–2, 14, 15, 25
Manchurian Railroads, 34
Manzanar Black Dragon Association, 101–2
Manzanar Citizens Federation, 101
Manzanar War Relocation Center, 63, 69, 85, 99–102
marriage, and citizenship, 9, 39, 44–47
Married Women's Independent National Act. *See* Cable Act
Marshall, George, 31, 68
Marxism, 96
Masaoka, Joe, 101
Masaoka, Mike M., 58, 63–64, 66–68, 74, 101, 112, 118–19, 133, 148
Masuda, Sam, 34–35, 121
Matsumoto, Ken, 58, 61, 98
Matsumoto Koshiro, 86
Matsumoto Takizo "Frank," 29, 31
McClatchy, V. S., 21, 22, 41–42, 44, 50–51, 94
McCloy, John J., 70, 76
Medicare, 144
Meiji University, 29–31, 127
Miike, Noboru "Fred," 117
Military Intelligence Service (MIS), 76–77, 85, 102–7
Military Intelligence Service Language School (MISLS), 76, 101–2, 107
military service: Japanese, 49, 76–77, 116, 122, 126–31; U.S., 73, 75–77, 80–82, 90, 101–7, 117, 175n61
Millis, Harry A., 18
Ministry of Foreign Affairs (Japan), 27, 34, 48–53, 103; Broadcasting Section of Intelligence Bureau, 119–20, 122–26; European and American Affairs Bureau, 14, 16, 51
Mitsubishi Heavy Industries, 135, 187n5

Miyagawa, Mine, 33
Miyagawa, Rickey, 33
Mizuho Gakuen, 27
monitors. *See* radio monitors
Muller, Eric L., 74
Munson, Curtis B., 60, 171n9
Murakami Tsugio, 118
Murayama, Tamotsu, 114–20, 132–34, *133*
Murray, Alice Yang, 147
music, 33
Myer, Dillon S., 57, 66–68, 70–71, 73–77, 81, 83, 119, 174n47

Nagatsuka Takashi, 24
Nakase Setsuo, 117
Nakata, Kokuro, 36
National Academy of Sciences, 139
Nationality Act, 12, 125, 126
Nationality Law (Japan), 53, 130
national narratives: atomic bomb survivors' absence from, 136–37, 141, 147, 150–51; contradictions/hypocrisy of, 4–5, 23, 48, 150, 161n25; exclusion of peoples and perspectives from, 161n25, 192n62; Kibei role in, 58, 87; Nisei migrants' role in, 4–5, 13, 24, 153. *See also* white nationalism
Native Americans, 67
Native Sons and Daughters of California, 19
Native Sons and Daughters of the Golden West, 60
Natsume Soseki, 93
Newsweek (magazine), 139
New York Times (newspaper), 105
Ngai, Mae M., 42, 153
NHK. *See* Nippon Hoso Kyokai
Nichibei Gakuin, 127
Nichibei Home, 122
Nichibei Shimbun (newspaper), 51
Nichigo Bunka School, 27
Nimmo, Ray E., 48–49
Nineteenth Amendment, 44
Nippon Hoso Kyokai (NHK), 85, 92, 111–12, 116–17
Nisei (second-generation Japanese Americans) in America: citizenship of, 5–6,

8–9, 11, 12, 21–22, 38–44, 48–53, 152–53; cooperation of, with government, 62–69, 98; emigration of, 2–8, 12, 16; exchanged for prisoners during war, 144, 145; Kibei relations with, 11–12, 61–66, 68–69, 73–75, 78–79; as linguists in war, 102–7; loyalty of, 5, 11, 58–60, 62, 66–68, 70, 76, 81–83, 112–15, 118–19, 148; scholarship on, 58; socioeconomic impact of anti-Japanese sentiment on, 22–24, 121, 145; and U.S. military service, 73, 75, 101–6, 117, 175n61. *See also* anti-Japanese sentiment in United States; exclusion movement

Nisei (second-generation Japanese Americans) migrants: American cultural capital of, 28–33, 37; atomic bomb survivors among, 12, 136–51; Chiba's story, 14–16; citizenship issues for, 41, 115; complexity of experiences of, 2, 5–7, 17, 24, 29, 153; conventional view of, 160n20; as cultural brokers, 24, 34–36; cultural duality and loyalty dilemmas of, 114–26, 129–34, 154; educational experiences of, 26–31, 34–36, 49–50, 120–25, 128, 131; experiences of, in Japan, 8–9, 12, 24–37, 52; Inaba's story, 38–40, 45–47, 49; intellectual exchange fostered by, 24–25; Japanese colonialism as avenue for, 7–8, 15, 16, 33–36; Japanese distrust of, 117–18, 134; and Japanese military service, 49, 116, 122, 126–31; Murayama's story, 114–20, 132–34; numbers of, 26, 49, 158n5; as occupation force employees, 129–32, 138; places of settlement for, 26; postwar decisions of, 132; pro-Japan sentiments of, 117, 133; role of, in national narratives, 4–5, 13, 24, 153; scholarship on, 3–5, 11–12; sent as children to Japan by their parents, 23, 88, 127–28; socioeconomic opportunities for, in Japan, 23, 29, 31–33, 37, 54–55, 116–17, 121; Sogawa's story, 144–48; Suyeishi's story, 135–36, 139–40, 143, 148, 151; Tashima's story, 1–3, 6, 7, 8, 20–21,

27–29; Tateishi's story, 22–23, 34–36; as transpacific diaspora, 4–8, *10*, 11–13, 16–17, 154–55; and U.S. military service, 80–82; vulnerability of, to U.S. anti-Japanese sentiment/laws, 21–22, 40–41, 44, 48–51; Yoneda's story, 24–26, 53–54

The Nisei: A Survey of Their Educational, Vocational, and Social Problems (Keisen Jogakuen), 54–55
Nodera, Isamu, 22
Noguchi, Thomas, 139–40
nuclear weapons, 149–50

Obama, Barack, 149–50
occupation, of Japan, 108, 129–32, 138, 141
Oda, James, 69, 96–97, 100–102
Office of Naval Intelligence, 62
Ogishima, George, 123
Okamoto, Ted, 97
100th Infantry Battalion, 104, 117
Ono Koji, 90
Opler, Marvin, 77–78, 83
Ota, Jiro "Jimmy," 31
Owens Valley Reception Center, 99–100
Ozawa v. United States, 19, 47

Pacific War: Japanese American loyalty during, 56–83; Japanese military service in, 49, 76–77, 116, 122, 126–31; Kibei during, 56–85, 87, 97–113; Nisei migrants' loyalty during, 114–31; U.S. military service in, 73, 75–77, 80–82, 90, 101–7, 117, 175n61
Paik, A. Naomi, 6, 148, 161n25, 192n62
pan-Asianism, 90, 114
Park, Robert E., 18
Pasadena High School, California, 94
Pearl Harbor attack, 11, 55, 58, 61–62, 70, 84, 101, 120, 122, 130
Phelan, James, 18–19
Plessy v. Ferguson, 43
pop culture, 33
Poston War Relocation Center, 72
prisoners of war, Japanese, 128–29

racialization: of Asian peoples, 7, 17, 40–44, 46–47; in Japan, 9; of Japanese Americans, 8–9, 11, 15, 18, 21–22, 56, 60
radio monitors, in Japanese intelligence units, 119–26
Rafu Shimpo (newspaper), 22
Reagan, Ronald, 147
redress and reparations: for atomic bomb survivors, 136–44, 147–51; for incarceration, 82, 111–13, 147–48; postwar policies on, 141–42
Rikkyo University, 31
Ringle, Kenneth D., 60–61
Rinjiro, Sodei, 148
Rocky Nippon (newspaper), 63
Roosevelt, Franklin, 60, 64, 85, 99, 101
Roosevelt, Theodore, 161n7
Rosenthal, Joe, 105
Roybal, Edward, 140–41, 148
Rudisill, Richard E., 69
Rudkin, Franklin H., 46
Rusch, Paul, 31
Russo-Japanese War, 18, 36

Sacramento Bee (newspaper), 42, 46, 50
Saiki, Susumu, 122, 126
Saint John's University, Shanghai, 27
Sakhalin (Karafuto Prefecture), 36
samurai, 86, 88–90, 93
San Francisco Chronicle (newspaper), 114
San Francisco Examiner (newspaper), 50
San Francisco Peace Treaty, 142
Sanga Moyu (television series), 85–89, 92, 111–12
Sano, Iwao Peter, 127–32
Sano, Patrick, 128
Sansei (third-generation Japanese Americans), 155
Santa Ana Junior College, 34
Sato Hachiro, 90
Seiunsha, 88
Shimojima Tetsuro, 123
Shimomura, Floyd, 112
Shinsekai Asahi (newspaper), 114
Shukaku (magazine), 94
Shunyo Maru (ship), 53

Sigma Nu Kappa, 29, *30*, 31
Sino-Japanese War, 121
Sogawa, Yoshiko, 144–45, *146*, 147–48
Sogi Takateru, 103, 110
Spicer, Edward, 67
sports. *See* intercollegiate athletics
Stillwell, Joseph W., 59–60
Stimson, Henry, 64
Suiryu Seiko, 89
Supreme Commander for the Allied Powers (SCAP), 129–30
Suyeishi, Kaz Tanaka, 135–36, 139–40, 143–44, 148, 151

Tabata, Fumiko, 120
Taihoku Nippo (newspaper), 33
Taisho era, 93, 96
Taiyo Maru (ship), 38
Takao Ozawa v. United States, 19, 47
Takeda, Junichi, 22
Takeno, Roy, 99
Tanaka, Togo, 51, 101
Tashima, Takayuki, 20
Tashima, Yukiko, 1–2, *3*, 7, 20–21, 27–29
Tashima, Yutaka, 28
Tateishi, Kay, 22–23, 34–36, 121, 126
Tatsuma Maru (ship), 121–22
Tayama, Fred, 58, 62–63, 66, 69, 101
Teia Maru (ship), 147
Terada, Kazuo, 99
Teruko, Kumei, 123
33rd Infantry Division, 107–8
Time (magazine), 100
Toa Dobun Shoin, Shanghai, 29
Toguri, Iva (Tokyo Rose), 124–25, 185n42
Tojo Hideki, 85
Tokyo, return migrants in, 26–27
Tokyo Imperial University, 15
Tokyo Rose. *See* Toguri, Iva
Tokyo War Crimes Tribunal, 85, 90, 105
Tomomatsu Toshio, 117
Topaz War Relocation Center, 73, 75, 82, 83
Truman, Harry, 67
Trump, Donald, 152
Tsurumi, K., 48
Tsutsumida, Tamaye, 36

Tule Lake War Relocation Center, 71–75, 78, 174n47

Ueno, Harry, 63
United States v. Wong Kim Ark, 43–44
University of Southern California, 31
U.S. Army Western Defense Command, 11, 56, 59–60, 66
U.S. Bureau of Immigration, 38–40, 45–47
U.S. Bureau of Indian Affairs, 67
U.S. Congress: anti-Asian legislation in, 7, 9, 17–19, 39; legislation on redress and reparations for incarceration, 82, 112, 147; and treatment of atomic bomb survivors, 140–41, 148
U.S. Defense Department, 140
U.S. Health and Human Services Department, 140
U.S. Justice Department, 62, 68, 98, 144
U.S. Public Health Service, 139
U.S. Refugee Admissions Program, 152
U.S. State Department, 95, 125, 140, 145
U.S. War Department, 11, 70, 76, 103
Uyeda, Clifford, 112
Uyeno, Kazumaro, 36

Wakabayashi, Ron, 112
War Relocation Authority (WRA), 57–59, 64, 66–77, 79–83, 100, 104, 119, 144, 172n28; Community Analysis Section (CAS), 67, 70–72, 77–79, 81–83
Warren, Earl, 60
Wartime Civilian Control Administration, 66, 99–100
Waseda International Institute, 27
Waseda University, 31, 122

Webb-Haney Act, 14
Weckerling, John, 76
Weglyn, Michi, 62
white nationalism, 7, 11, 15, 18–19, 40
women's rights, 44
Women's Volunteer Citizens Corps (Japan), 135–36
Wong Kim Ark, 43–44
World War II. *See* Pacific War
WRA. *See* War Relocation Authority

Yahagi (ship), 127
Yamada, Shigeo, 127, 129, 131
Yamamoto Torao, 39, 45–46
Yamasaki Toyoko, *Futatsu no Sokoku* (Two Homelands), 85–89, 91–92, 107–13
Yamashiro, Masao, 102
Yamashita, Soen, 26
Yamato (ship), 127
Yano, Mary, 137–39
Yano, Toshiko, 138–39
yellow peril rhetoric, 7, 18–19, 22
YMCA, 27
Yomiuri Shimbun (newspaper), 31
Yoneda, Karl Goso, 24–26, 53–54, 69, 79, 82–83, 101–2
Yoneyama, Lisa, 142
Yonsei (fourth-generation Japanese Americans), 155
Yoshida, Jim, 130–31
Young Buddhist Association, 23
Young Democrats (Nisei group), 73

Zero Hour (radio show), 124
Zheng Xaoxu, 1
Zheng Zihan, 1–2, 3, 27–28

The authorized representative in the EU for product safety and compliance is:
Mare Nostrum Group
B.V Doelen 72
4831 GR Breda
The Netherlands

www.ingramcontent.com/pod-product-compliance
Lightning Source LLC
Chambersburg PA
CBHW022006220426
43663CB00007B/981